A Comprehensive Study of Tang Poetry II

Tang poetry is one of the most valuable cultural inheritances of Chinese history. Its distinctive aesthetics, delicate language and diverse styles constitute great Literature in itself, as well as a rich topic for literary study. This two-volume set constitutes a classic analysis of Tang poetry in the "Golden Age" of Chinese poetry (618–907 CE).

This volume focuses on the prominent Tang poets and poems. Beginning with an introduction to the "four greatest poets"—Li Bai, Du Fu, Wang Wei, and Bai Juyi—the author discusses their subjects, language, influence, and key works. The volume also includes essays on a dozen of masterpieces of Tang poetry, categorized by topics such as love and friendship, aspirations and seclusion, as well as travelling and nostalgia. As the author stresses, Tang poetry is worth rereading because it makes us invigorate our mental wellbeing, leaving it powerful and full of vitality.

This book will appeal to researchers and students of Chinese literature, especially of classical Chinese poetry. People interested in Chinese culture will also benefit from the book.

Lin Geng was a literary historian, a scholar in ancient Chinese literature, and a modern poet. He was a professor and doctoral supervisor of Peking University. His poetic and rational qualities interact in his writing and research, forming a distinct characteristic rarely seen in the literary world.

China Perspectives

The *China Perspectives* series focuses on translating and publishing works by leading Chinese scholars, writing about both global topics and China-related themes. It covers Humanities & Social Sciences, Education, Media and Psychology, as well as many interdisciplinary themes.

This is the first time any of these books have been published in English for international readers. The series aims to put forward a Chinese perspective, give insights into cutting-edge academic thinking in China, and inspire researchers globally.

To submit proposals, please contact the Taylor & Francis Publisher for China Publishing Programme, Lian Sun (Lian.Sun@informa.com)

Titles in literature currently include:

Seven Lectures on Wang Guowei's Renjian Cihua
Florence Chia-Ying Yeh

A Companion to Shen Congwen
Sihe Chen, Gang Zhou, Jeffrey Kinkley

Keywords in Western Literary Criticism and Contemporary China
Volume 1
Hu Yamin

Keywords in Western Literary Criticism and Contemporary China
Volume 2
Hu Yamin

A Comprehensive Study of Tang Poetry I
Lin Geng

A Comprehensive Study of Tang Poetry II
Lin Geng

For more information, please visit https://www.routledge.com/China-Perspectives/book-series/CPH

A Comprehensive Study of Tang Poetry II

Lin Geng

Routledge
Taylor & Francis Group

LONDON AND NEW YORK

This book is published with financial support from the Chinese Fund for the Humanities and Social Sciences.

First edition published 2021
by Routledge
2 Park Square, Milton Park, Abingdon, Oxon, OX14 4RN

and by Routledge
52 Vanderbilt Avenue, New York, NY 10017

Routledge is an imprint of the Taylor & Francis Group, an informa business

© 2021 Lin Geng

Translated by Wang Feng (Yangtze University)

The right of Lin Geng to be identified as author of this work has been asserted by him in accordance with sections 77 and 78 of the Copyright, Designs and Patents Act 1988.

All rights reserved. No part of this book may be reprinted or reproduced or utilised in any form or by any electronic, mechanical, or other means, now known or hereafter invented, including photocopying and recording, or in any information storage or retrieval system, without permission in writing from the publishers.

Trademark notice: Product or corporate names may be trademarks or registered trademarks, and are used only for identification and explanation without intent to infringe.

English Version by permission of The Commercial Press.

British Library Cataloguing-in-Publication Data
A catalogue record for this book is available from the British Library

Library of Congress Cataloging-in-Publication Data
A catalog record has been requested for this book

ISBN: 978-0-367-64518-2 (hbk)
ISBN: 978-0-367-64603-5 (pbk)
ISBN: 978-1-003-12491-7 (ebk)

Typeset in Times New Roman
by codeMantra

Contents

Preface to the Chinese edition vii
Foreword to the Chinese edition: Lin Geng's Poetic Thoughts and Academic Contributions ix
ZHONG YUANKAI

Translator's notes xxix

1　The four great Tang poets　1

2　The poet Li Bai　43

3　On exaggeration in Li Bai's poetry　105

4　Starting with the characteristics of the Tang poetry　107

5　A note on the Tang poetry　110

6　A note on frontier fortress poetry　113

7　Wang Zhihuan's "Song of Liangzhou"　118

8　On Liangzhou　123

9　"Ancient Style: compassion for peasants": an integration of realism and romanticism　126

10　Spring is late, the green wild graceful　128

11　On a poem by Xie Tiao　130

12　On Yu Xin's poem about Zhaojun　132

13 On Wang Changling's "Out of the Fortress"	134
14 On Meng Haoran's innocent enjoyment	136
15 On Wang Wei's "Song of Weicheng"	140
16 On Wang Wei's "Farewell in the Mountain"	142
Postscript to the Chinese edition	144
Appendix: Mr Lin Geng's academic chronology	145
Index	155

Preface to the Chinese edition

Why do I particularly love the Tang poetry?

When I was in primary school, all the texts I read were in classical Chinese. So I read and recited some classical Chinese poems—among them there was Li Shen's "Pity for Peasants": "Hoeing in the Sun at midday, / They drop their sweat on the clay. / Who knows each grain on the plate / Is out of work hard and great?" Sometimes when I or other children drop rice on the table, we were often told how we should cherish the rice and how hard peasants' farming is. I understood these facts; however, I always felt this poem was more impressive. At that time, I did not know what the Tang poetry is, but now I know its excellence. It is easy to understand and impressive. To be easy is not difficult; however, it's difficult to make it impressive. What is admirable is that I still feel renewed in reading the poems again long after I had memorised them by heart when I was small. It is not the long-known facts that are fresh, but the indescribable feeling. It seems that I am refreshing my understanding of the world in re-reading this poem. This is due to the difference between the artistic language and concepts. Such a fresh sense of understanding lies not only in the works with strong ideas, but in ordinary good poems. For example, Meng Haoran's "Spring Dawn" reads: "Spring sleep is woken at dawn hours / When birds are chirping there and here. / The night wind and rain in my ear, / Fallen are how many flowers?" What an invigorating experience of seeing the blue sky after the rain, and how pure it is when the subtle melancholy of the fallen flowers is washed away. Flowers always fall in the end, and fallen flowers are always pitiable. This is how spring comes and goes in blooming and fallen flowers. How to understand such a world? It seems like a new enlightenment. The most valuable part of the Tang poetry lies in its enlightenment of people in every aspect of life with the most novel experience. Its energetic spirit, and simple but profound language make it the perfect achievement in the history of classical Chinese poetry. Li Bai's (also Li Po, Li Tai-po, etc. 701–762) "Song of the Hengjiang River" says: "People say Hengjiang is good, / But you say Hengjiang is evil. / The river wind can blow down a hill in three days; / Its white waves are higher than the Waguan tower". In the face of such a breath-taking and spectacular scenery, what do you think of the Hengjiang River? Is it good or evil? It forces you to understand the world by yourself. The Tang poetry is thus always fresh, even read 100 times. It is the fresh understanding that helps the Tang poets to have described the mountains and rivers of our home country so magnificent and gorgeous. As a part of Nature, mountains and rivers are almost the same through thousands of years; however, why are they so fascinating in the Tang poetry? That's why I particularly love the Tang poetry.

China is known as a country of poetry, and the Tang poetry is the most beautiful flower in it. Its abundant creativity and fresh understanding are artistic achievements in the splendid ancient Chinese culture we are always proud of. We do not read the Tang poetry today for imitation, because imitation will never make people feel the originality. Innumerous people imitated the Tang poetry, but their imitations have already been forgotten for long. However, the Tang poetry is still so fresh. We read the Tang poetry to make our mental state reinvigorated, powerful, and full of vitality. Such a mental state is helpful for our understanding of the world around us, which is limitless and infinite. The Tang poetry, therefore, like every beautiful classical artistic creation, has been inspiring all the people throughout history.

Originally published in *People's Daily*, 21 June 1982

Foreword to the Chinese edition
Lin Geng's Poetic Thoughts and Academic Contributions

Zhong Yuankai

Born in Minhou County, Fujian Province, Lin Geng (1910–2006), alias Jingxi, was a famous modern poet and a scholar in classical Chinese literature. After graduating from the Department of Chinese Language and Literature of Tsinghua University in 1933, he began to work at his alma mater as a teaching assistant of Mr Zhu Zhiqing. Once a professor at Xiamen University and Yenching University, and in the Department of Language and Literature at Peking University, he had major academic interests in *Chuci*,[1] the Tang poetry, and the history of Chinese literature. His works include *A Study of Poet Qu Yuan and His Works*, *A Comprehensive Study of Tang Poetry*, *A Brief History of Chinese Literature*, and *Talks on Journey to the West*.

A distinctive feature of Lin Geng's lifelong career is that his life of new poetry writing was closely accompanied by his academic career. Among modern scholars, only a few are simultaneously engaged in creative works.[2] However, Lin Geng stands out not only for his long life of creative writing, but for his idea that creation and academics are not unrelated fields. Instead, consciously starting from the creation of new poetry, he integrated the two and drew experience and nutrients from the academic study on literary history. He admitted that he "had a career in teaching but was devoted to writing" and that his research interests were "devoted to the mystery of literary and artistic creation in the field of classical literature research".[3] As early as in the 1940s, he said that "creating the future has a greater responsibility than studying the history", and that "all the discussions of the past are

---

1 *Chuci*, variously translated as *Chu Ci*, *Ch'u Tz'u*, *Elegies of the South*, *The Songs of the South*, *The Songs of Chu*, etc., is an anthology of ancient Chinese poetic songs traditionally attributed mainly to Qu Yuan (340–278 BCE) and Song Yu (c. 298–c. 222 BCE).
2 It is nearly 70 years from 1932 when Lin Geng started with his poem collection "Night" as his graduation thesis to 2000 when his poem collection *Reverie in Space* in his late years was published by Peking University Press.
3 Lin Geng. "Mourning Brother Zuxiang", *Historical Materials of New Literature*, 1995 (1).

just a mission for the future, and all the understanding of arts is beneficial to writing".[4] In the 1990s, he reiterated,

> Scholars studying classical literature in past dynasties mostly focused on the past. However, I aim for the future in writing literary history to promote new literature. I experienced the New Culture Movement (mid-1910s to 1920s) after the May Fourth Movement (4 May 1919). I write new poems, and my major interest is in new poetry. In fact, the history of Chinese literature is centred on poetry. Its study provides an ideal window and examples to explore the mystery of poetic aesthetics and the development of poetic language. Thus, in studying classical literature, I always hope to find a practical and valuable way for the development of new literature, especially new poetry, and to enrich our creation today with the help of ancient cultural heritage.[5]

If creativity requires talent, then the communication between academics and creative writing needs more ambition and wisdom. However, such talent, ambition, and wisdom are beyond ordinary scholars. As a poet who grew up under the enlightenment of the May Fourth New Culture Movement, Lin Geng's faith in new poetry has always been unswerving. New poetry based on vernacular Chinese originally appeared as the opposite of classical Chinese poetry. Therefore, the communication between new poetry writing and academic studies on classical poetry is naturally endowed with a profound significance on how to make reality and tradition, innovation and inheritance, phenomena and laws achieve a dialectical integration in the process of bringing forth the new through the old. It is this process that has made Lin Geng's academic character and academic contribution outstanding and extraordinary.

Lin Geng was a tireless cultivator and explorer in the field of new poetry. He persists in theoretical thinking while writing. His perception of writing and theoretical insights are combined into his unique poetic thoughts, from which many of his academic achievements are crystallised. Therefore, starting with his poetic thoughts, we can more clearly identify his academic lines of thought and understand his academic achievements and significance.

The vitality of poetry originates from the creation of life, which is the most philosophical aspect of Lin Geng's poetic thoughts. He believed that poetry "is, therefore, a call to life, enlivening all the lifeless with the source of life, and awakening the feelings of life in all the most uninteresting places" (269);[6] "Art is not the ornament of life, but the awakening of life; artistic

---

4 Lin Geng. *Asking for Directions*, Peking University Press, 1984, 190.
5 Lin Geng. *Metrics of New Poems and the Poeticisation of Language*, Economic Daily Publishing House, 2000, 162.
6 Cited from the Chinese edition of this book. The following page numbers from the Chinese edition will be cited in-text without additional notes.

language does not aim to be more elegant, but more primitive as if the language is newly born" (282). Of course, his words contain his understanding of creation. The joy of life that the creation of new poems brought to him is unforgettable. He has fondly recalled the "unparalleled excitement" after writing his first poem "Night", and the bitterness and sweetness in writing "Dawn". Such perceptions of creation make "the creation of life" accumulate into the core of his poetics. He wrote a motto for himself after the completion of "Night": "A little spark can start a fire that burns the entire prairie / Too much ash is useless / I will explore why a little spark burns a prairie / And trace the beginning of all beginnings", which vividly demonstrates his firm will in exploring the origin and mystery of the creation of life. This ideological core not only runs through his new poetry creation, but determines his academic interests, value orientation, and academic paths and methods. His research on classical Chinese literature focuses on creativity. He once said that "In studying literary history and classical literature, I look into its creativity with 'my heart in creation'", and that

> I am most excited in the era with the strongest creativity, believing that it is the most promising time for literature. I put creation in the first place, so when I collect materials of literary history, I also search for those that best explain creation.[7]

For example, his *A Brief History of Chinese Literature* takes creativity as an important yardstick for choosing the level of detail. Lin Geng took Qu Yuan's *Chuci*, and the Tang poetry as his research focus all his life. In an interview, he said, "Even my study of *Chuci* at the earliest was done from the angle of literary creation to explore what role *Chuci* played in the whole history of poetry development".[8] Similarly, the Tang poetry also became his research focus because of its "rich creativity". Striving for creativity, Lin Geng put the texts of works first while the writers second in his study of literary history, because "only literary works embody the writers' literary creation" and "writers are determined by their works". Creativity has become an important yardstick for choosing and evaluating different works in his academic research.

Lin Geng held that poetry mainly expresses the inner feelings rather than the external world, and the pursuit of ideals should be an essential character of poetry. Lin Geng once said that among the three elements of literary works, the first is "the fundamental human emotions that are unchanged from ancient times; therefore, when we read the masterpieces, we will feel the same emotions with the ancients".[9] He also said that "more permanent

---

7 Lin Geng and Zhang Ming. "The World is Searching for the Traces of Beauty", *Literature and Art Research*, 2003 (4).
8 Ibid.
9 Lin Geng. *Asking for Directions*, 172.

and universal sentiments are hidden behind temporary emotions" in poetry, and that the universality of arts lies in "the permanent sentiments beyond time and space" (329). Lin Geng's new poetry writing focuses on this. In the 1930s, when he was confronted with criticism that his poetry could not "grasp the reality" or "achieve an accurate social understanding", he wrote an article, replying that "I think 'content' is the most fundamental emotion of life; it is an affection for freedom, love, beauty, loyalty, bravery, and innocence, or sadness without them; the sadness, even desperate, shows that it is uncompromising, and forever facing the precious soul!"[10] Obviously, "the fundamental emotion of life", the expression of the spiritual world, is the core of poetry, and the transcendence of ideal over reality is essential and inherent in poetry. He said that "the purpose of art is to bring people to a higher ideal, rather than to make them dependent on life" (359), that "literature and art, therefore, do not await but create the time. Thus, poetry is a lofty feeling of the time", and that "the vitality of poetry... must be achieved from the lowest to the loftiest" (268, 269). Emotions are related to the category of "loftiness", which shows that Lin Geng attaches more importance to transcending the ordinary emotional texture and emotional intensity. Some critics also found from this point of view the value of his poems at that time in that "The Youth Spirit prevalent in the May Fourth Movement generally declined in the 1930s; however, in Lin Geng's poems, it showed a new vigour and advancement".[11]

Lin Geng concentrated his ideal of poetic beauty into a phrase, that is, "a fresh sense of understanding",[12] which mainly refers to the perfect combination of "its energetic spirit" and the "simple but profound language" in poetry (1). The function of poetry is to make us "always have new emotions in our lives, and always be affected by the tide of emotions" and to bring back the "joy and reasons of life" that have long been lost (266); thus, the real charm of poetry is "the soberness of emotions, the vitality of senses, and the sensitivity to all new things" (287). Lin Geng often uses "the Youth Spirit" to refer to the grandeur of poetry. If its connotation is "vigorous, creative, upward, youthful, even sad and painful, it still belongs to the youth", then it is, in fact, an aesthetic concept similar to "the fresh sense of understanding". However, "the Youth Spirit" as a poetic metaphor more highlights its spiritual characteristics.

When new poetry was in its infancy during the May Fourth Movement, modern romantic literary thoughts greatly helped the poetry circle to innovate at that time, and these thoughts became the conceptual backbone and

---

10 Lin Geng. "Spring Wilderness and Windows: Self-Postscript", quoted in Peng Qingsheng and Fang Ming. "The Annalistic Record of Lin Geng's Works", *Journal of Huaiyin Normal University*, 2003 (4).
11 Sun Yushi. "On the Spiritual World of Lin Geng's Poems in the 1930s", in *A Collection of Nourishing Rains*, People's Literature Publishing House, 2005, 286.
12 Lin Geng and Zhang Ming. "The World Is Searching for the Traces of Beauty".

foundation of Lin Geng's poetics. For example, his understanding of the nature, expressions, and functions of poetry, his view of creativity as the touchstone of art, and his idea of naturalness as an important criterion for weighing the value of poetry are closely related to the trend of romanticism. Lin Geng claimed that "I belong to the romantic school, which is probably the best and most normal school in the history of poetry".[13] However, the essence of romanticism lies in its special promotion of subjects' spirit, that is, emphasising the spiritual temperament and spiritual characteristics of poetry, and all those contained in poetry such as the full, youthful disposition, the extraordinary ideal, and the heroic characters that inspire and strengthen the will of life, which are considered the fundamentals for the fresh understanding of poetry. Lin Geng wrote in his own preface to *A History of Chinese Literature* published in Xiamen University Press that

> I think the characteristics of the time should be the forms of thoughts and the emotions of life. The High Tang (713–766) and the Northern Song Dynasty (960–1127) are both peaceful and prosperous times with little difference in life. However, the Tang people's sentiment of emancipation, lofty pursuit and longing in the journey of life were not seen in the Song Dynasty (960–1279); this caused the division in literature and arts between the Tang and Song Dynasties.[14]

Lin Geng's poetic thoughts have made his study of the Tang poetry a comprehensive interpretation of the poetic peak from the romantic poetic viewpoint. His modern interpretation of the High Tang poetry is based on his grasp of its most distinct spiritual temperament and his overall comprehension of the aesthetic grandeur it has reached. In elaborating the inheritance and development of the High Tang Atmosphere on the basis of the Jian'an Spirit and the essential characteristics of the High Tang poetry, he has grasped its inner spirit mainly from his aesthetic perceptions. For example, he believes that the spiritual essence of the Jian'an Spirit is a "free-running romantic temperament with bright images full of prospect", and the "power of emancipation" it reflects thus constitutes the backbone of the High Tang Atmosphere, which "is a more abundant development of the Jian'an Spirit" (34–36). If the keynote of Jian'an literature is "characterised by the desolate and high-pitched singing" of "'the bleak autumn wind' and 'the sad wind on the high terrace'" because of its time (238), the High Tang shows "a kind of self-confident and delightful prospect (35)". Thus, the High Tang Atmosphere refers to

---

13 Lin Geng. *Metrics of New Poems and the Poeticisation of Language*, 159.
14 Lin Geng. *A Brief History of Chinese Literature*, Peking University Press, 1995, 726.

the burgeoning atmosphere in poetry, which is not only due to its grand development, but more importantly, the characteristic burgeoning ideas and feelings which cannot be separated from that era. The High Tang Atmosphere is, therefore, a reflection of the spirit of the High Tang.
(28)

Chen Zi'ang, as a bridge between the Jian'an Spirit and the High Tang Atmosphere, became "the pioneer of the High Tang poetry circle" and began its prelude because his poems enhanced the "heroic temperament for breaking through the status quo" with "a passion for ideals" (31–32).

This spirit was peculiar to the High Tang. "This kind of melody is rare before. However, in the Tang poetry, it has become the major theme with heart-moving affection", while "the melody of spring since the Mid-Tang (766–835) and Late Tang (618–907) has been shrouded in a weak tenderness and dreamlike pursuit" (240). In the Song Dynasty, "a kind of middle-aged men's need of personal integrity and a mood close to the pure autumn atmosphere have become the common keynotes of poetry, prose, drawings, and even philosophy such as Neo-Confucianism" (362).

Lin Geng's understanding of the spiritual essence of the High Tang Atmosphere is based not only on a diachronic historical examination by tracing back to the Jian'an Spirit until Chen Zi'ang's tradition, but on a synchronic comparison of different typical poets in the High Tang, specifically represented by Li Bai, Wang Wei (also Wang Mojie, 699 / 701–761), and Du Fu (also Tu Fu, 71–770). They have their typical characteristics at the peak of poetry: Li Bai is "a typical model at the height of the poetic era", Wang Wei is "a more comprehensive model" (117), and Du Fu is "an epitome and the last great poet in the High Tang poetry" (151). "If Li Bai is a typical model in pursuit of what will be available, then Wang Wei is a general reflection of what is available" (124). Different in styles and achievements, the three representative poets also expressed the common youth melody of the High Tang.

In *The Poet Li Bai* published in 1954, Lin Geng highlighted the spirit of the High Tang represented by the poet. Because of his "sense as a commoner" and independence, Li Bai intensively expressed "the lively singing of the common people emancipated from the aristocratic literature, and the free and unique singing emancipated from the feudal ethics" (212). Li Bai's "optimistic and high-spirited quality, enlightening prospects, unquenchable thirst for liberation, rich and distinct imagination, plain and heavenly expressions, and profound thoughts in simple language" (229) became the strongest voice of that era. In the early 1950s, the study of Li Bai was once in a state of "aphasia", but Lin Geng was not restrained by the trend at that time. He vigorously praised Li Bai's romantic spirit and called it the "emblematic singing" of the High Tang (229). He cultivated a new field and played a leading role in the study of Li Bai. After its publication, it was reprinted nine times in only a few years. In 2000, Shanghai Chinese Classics Publishing House wrote in the "Note for the New Edition" that "the basic issues about Li Bai's works since the reform and opening up of China have all been derived from this short but fruitful and lasting book", demonstrating its considerable academic weight.

Lin Geng's interpretation of Wang Wei and Du Fu embodied his unique insight and understanding. Wang Wei has long been regarded as a landscape poet represented by the *Rim River Collection* in his later years; however, Lin Geng thought that "these lonely works in his later years were just a part of his poetic life, not representing all his achievements at that time" (130). Wang Wei wrote many frontier fortress poems, such as "Song of Longxi", "Song of Youth", and "Song of Longtou", in which "such romantic and heroic feeling of these young roaming swordsmen running to the frontier fortress is the embodiment of the Youth Spirit of the High Tang" (120–121). Even his landscape poems are not constrained in a quiet corner, but have a broad space, lively vitality, and fresh spirit. Lin Geng pointed out that in general works on literary history, "to classify the High Tang poets into landscape poets and frontier fortress poets would have hindered us from understanding a poet in an all-round way" (120). The reason why Wang Wei is a "comprehensive model" in the High Tang is that in his poems, "everywhere is the lively spring, and everywhere is the fresh green, which is seen in the air and drizzle, constituting the overall atmosphere of Wang Wei's poetry" (126). Since the Song and Yuan (1280–1368) Dynasties because of historical reasons, people "have long lost a comprehensive understanding of Wang Wei's poetry" (130). However, Lin Geng restored the poet's original features closely linked with the time. Du Fu's poems after the An Shi Rebellion (755–763) have been well known for reflecting the suffering of the time. Lin Geng, however, sensed the persistent pursuit and hope of spring in the chaotic period from his poems such as "Happy at the Spring Night Rain", "Washing Weapons and Horses", and "On the Army's Recapturing of Henan and Hebei". This is a release and echo of the "Youth Spirit" in a special form. For example, "Washing Weapons and Horses" is "literally a long symphonic poem with the melody of spring, bursting out the feelings that were suppressed deep inside", and smoothly forms "a triumphant and everlasting masterpiece of rejuvenation" (239). Also, "On the Army's Recapturing of Henan and Hebei" sings "an unconstrained song", and "the last flowing water couplet (or complementary couplet) fully demonstrated the poet's happy mood, and the return of the melody of spring to the poet's heart". Lin Geng thus believes that "These rekindled memories of rejuvenation were temporarily suppressed in the An Shi Rebellion but never extinguished" (239–240). Even on the sad autumn songs such as "On Autumn", "Feelings on Ancient Monuments", and "Mount Climbing", Lin Geng's interpretation is that it is "precisely because the hope of rejuvenation had been so strong in his heart that once he saw clearly that it would finally be gone, he would definitely write down such mournful feelings" (240). The three representative poets reflected the universal spiritual outlook of the High Tang through their artistic individuality.

The theory of "the spirit of the time" originated from romantic philosophy. Because the High Tang is a peak era through historical integration rather than a differentiated period of many divergent paths, it is an appropriate theory to illustrate the overall style of the High Tang literature and art, especially of poetry. Through the diachronic analysis and synchronic comparison, Lin Geng made the "High Tang Atmosphere" a vivid and three-dimensional generalisation of the spirit of the time.

This interpretation firmly rooted in the poetic understanding of the texts is full of flesh and blood rather than pale and empty. Lin Geng, as a poet, demonstrated his superior ability beyond that of ordinary people. His poetic creation made him deeply realise the characteristics of poetic language, that is, "to understand all the potential forces in language images, and to combine these potential forces with the meaning in concepts", and "full of affection and inspiration, it is not constrained by words" (301–302). Therefore, the key to poetry interpretation lies in grasping "the abundant potential capacity" of the poetic language (284). For example, in his quotation of Li Bai's "Song of the Hengjiang River": "People say Hengjiang is good, / But you say Hengjiang is evil. / The river wind can blow down a hill in three days; / Its white waves are higher than the Waguan tower". His commentaries are: "Facing the dangerous surging waves, he wrote out such a spectacular scene, making it a grand song of the era, similar to the soul-stirring 'Hard are the Trails of Shu,'" and "the overwhelming brilliant image shows the growth of an era's character that can withstand the surging waves" (50). Li Bai's "Bringing in the Wine" ends with "And kill with you thousands of years of sorrow". Lin Geng said, "If we think that 'white hair of ten thousand metres,' and 'kill with you thousands of years of sorrow' are only about the huge amount and endurance of sorrow, we are still at the literal level. A deeper understanding of the image should focus on its fullness and vigour, which is the real accomplishment of the High Tang Atmosphere" (51). He also quoted Wang Changling's "Seeing off Xin Jian at the Lotus Tower": "When cold rain came to River Wu at night, / I bid farewell at Mount Chu alone at dawn. / If my friends in Luoyang ask about me: / A piece of ice heart is in a jade pot". His commentary is:

> The High Tang Atmosphere is full and burgeoning because it is abundant in every corner of life; it seems not exaggerating when it uses exaggeration in 'white hair of ten thousand metres', and it seems not small in 'a piece of ice heart in a jade pot.' Just like a small dandelion, it represents the whole spring world. It is exquisite and thorough, but still dense. It is sorrowful in a thousand ways but still open-hearted. Rooted in the great enthusiasm of life and the sensitivity of new things,... it brings sunny, rich, and healthy aesthetic attainments.
>
> (52)

Meng Haoran's "Spring Dawn" seems to rest on a sad sentiment according to its order of words, but Lin Geng's interpretation is "What an invigorating experience of seeing the blue sky after the rain, and how pure it is when the subtle melancholy of the fallen flowers is washed away" (1). The specific emotions expressed in these poems might differ in thousands of ways, but Lin Geng is able to sharply grasp the keynote. His poetic perception has the distinct characteristics of being "not determined by reasoning, or constrained by words" (Yan Yu's *Azure Stream Poetic Remarks*), that is, not weighing and balancing on the literal interpretation, nor sticking to the logical order as in the prose, but directly exploring the most intrinsic characteristics of the "literary mind" and "poetic sentiment" of poetry, that is, focusing on the fullness of emotions, the vividness of images, and the rhythm of melodies at a deeper level, in which the spiritual outlook of the time can be traced and identified. In "Essays on Poems" in the Chinese edition of this book, some appreciation essays are compiled with academic articles. This special editing style shows that the author attaches great importance to the textual interpretation because the only way to understand the spiritual features of poetry is to have an accurate and thorough understanding of the integrity of the sensibility and rationality of the poetic text. However, if completely divorced from sensible interpretation, it is easy to produce a misreading that loses the essence while focusing on the marginal aspects. When Lin Geng interpreted and studied poetry with a "poetic attitude", the grandeur he attained naturally transcended scholars who are accustomed to interpreting and explaining poetry with a "non-poetic attitude". The integration of academic character and aesthetic disposition, the unity of poetic perception and rational analysis, and the mastery of poetry and history have become the distinct academic personality and characteristics of his "academic scholarship as a poet".

To summarise the overall outlook of a poem, Lin Geng proposed "atmosphere", an aesthetic tradition of poetry in ancient China since the Tang and Song Dynasties. Jiaoran and Yin Fan in the Tang Dynasty, and Jiang Kui and Yan Yu in the Song Dynasty all used it to interpret the High Tang poetry. Yan Yu also used "atmosphere" to metaphorise the continuous historical connection between the High Tang and Jian'an, and considered the "Jian'an Spirit" and the "High Tang Atmosphere" as ideal models of poetic beauty. Lin Geng also made a modern interpretation of traditional literary theories when he expounded the "High Tang Atmosphere". For example, Yan Yu's evaluation of the Tang poetry in terms of "interest" and "ingenious enlightenment" is indescribably remarkable, while Lin Geng has demystified Yan Yu's Zen discourse and returned to its simplicity and conciseness with his perception of poetry creation and modern literature and art studies.

> However, in *Azure Stream Poetic Remarks*, the term "enlightenment" is the capture of images, the "disposition" or "interest" is the triumph of imagination, the 'thoroughness' means to directly seek profundity out of simplicity, and the "atmosphere" is about the style and manner. The

word 'dense' is used to show the vitality and fullness of the style and manner, which is the reflection of the High Tang Spirit.

(47)

Yan Yu said that "The Han and Wei poems are not relying on enlightenment" while "the High Tang poets have thorough enlightenment". Lin Geng explained that

> Since the Han and Wei poets did not strive to capture images, the images were simple but complete; thus, "excellent lines are difficult to find"; it's like an unexplored mine or "a chaotic atmosphere". The High Tang poets, on the other hand, endeavoured to capture and obtain the most direct and distinct images. It seems as if the mine of real gold and jade has been explored and is shining with beautiful and extraordinary brilliance, which cannot be chaotic, but is in a dense atmosphere.
>
> (46–47)

The poet's perceptions on writing have provided him with the ability to theoretically control complexity with simplicity and cut off the flow of thoughts to be enlightened suddenly, enabling him to become familiar with the process of changing ancient speeches to thrive in a modern context. This kind of theoretical discourse transformation and the poetic interpretation of poetic texts complement each other and make the poetic aesthetic paradigm of the "High Tang Atmosphere" coruscate with new vigour and vitality.

As mentioned before, the high point and basic spirit of the May Fourth romanticism have become the major background of Lin Geng's poetics, from which he reinterpreted and expounded classical Chinese poetry. He realised the modern transformation of the aesthetic tradition of ancient Chinese poetry from this special perspective. Coincidentally, Wen Yiduo and Lin Geng are modern poets of romantic temperament, Wen's *Miscellanies of the Tang Poetry* and Lin's *A Comprehensive Study of Tang Poetry* have become far-reaching landmarks with great influence in this field because of their achievements in such a modern transformation. As a thought of writing, romanticism has gone through a gradual decay process from the peak after descending, fading, and exile from modern Chinese literary circles. However, Lin Geng, who received its direct inheritance in poetics, persisted in it and relentlessly explored with creativeness, and was shining brilliantly in academia. Such a contrast is thought-provoking.

The exploration of the mystery of poetic language constitutes another important part of Lin Geng's poetic thoughts. Most of his theoretical articles on new poetry are centred on the construction of poetic language. The focus of this poetic thought also brought ground-breaking discoveries and achievements to his academic research.

Poetic language is the focus of the new poetry circle:

Today, looking back at the new poetry circle, we find that many problems arisen are mainly centred around the language. For example, language issues include the controversy between classical Chinese poetry and vernacular poetry in the early period, the argument between free verse and metrical poetry in the late period, and the disputation in the 1950s between the form of "foot" in western languages and the form of "x-character" in Chinese.[15]

Having liberated itself from old style poetry, has new poetry been accomplished? In other words, "does the emancipation of poetic language only suggest prosification?"[16] Although free verse has brought about brand-new emancipation to him, Lin Geng's writing practice and theoretical thinking made him meditate profoundly. He once cited his poem "Nature" as an example. Full of mysterious cosmic consciousness, abstract and metaphysical metaphors, and free sentence patterns, it is perhaps the most modernistic free verse. However, after its writing, the poet himself could not help feeling "narrow and deep", which is in contradiction with "emancipation". Summing up the status quo of the poetry circle at that time, he said that free verse "broke away from the constraints of old poetry while grasping some new progress, in which, however, everything is sharp, deep but radical;... And the sharp, deep, and radical ways, if continue, must fall into the trend of being 'narrow'".[17] Based on this sober reflection, Lin Geng put forward the proposition that the poetic language should be emancipated twice: "since the language of new poetry has been emancipated in the waves of prose, does it still need re-emancipation?" "Re-emancipation" means "to get rid of the inherent logical habits of prose" and "to further find a more perfect form".[18] As for the process of emancipation of poetry from prose, Lin Geng called it "poeticisation".

The two-time emancipation of poetic language is a realistic subject put forward in Ling Geng's writing practice of new poetry. However, his research on the poeticisation of language has opened up a brand-new academic field. On the one hand, he devoted himself to grasping the new rhythms in the language of life, and attempted to write new metrical poems; on the other hand, he traced back the historical experience and laws in the development of the forms of Chinese poetry, and embarked on the ways of exploring the poeticisation of traditional poetic language. It can be seen that it is Lin Geng's attention to the evolution trend of new poetry that activated and promoted his unique "problem consciousness" and perspective in his academic research.

This traditional exploration is based on the belief that the creation of poetic language cannot leave the national cultural soil. Lin Geng said:

---

15 Lin Geng. *Metrics of New Poems and the Poeticisation of Language*, 16–17.
16 Lin Geng. *Asking for Directions*, 1.
17 Ibid., 175.
18 Ibid., 2.

"Accumulated in history, the cultural soil is a crystallization of chances and inevitability, sensibility and rationality in thousands of years", and "language is something with roots in culture".[19] "Of course, the soil should not be limited to language, but poetry is the purest art of language; the soil of language is thus particularly important".[20] In the new poetry circle with the prevailing trend of "Europeanisation", such an understanding is undoubtedly more historical.

Lin Geng discovered: "From *Chuci* to the Tang poetry, the national forms of Chinese poetry did have a similar development. It also obtained certain freedom first in the waves of prose emancipation, and then found the perfect five- or seven-character forms and had more freedom".[21] His research on the process of poeticisation also focuses on this historical period. The key points and highlights of his research on literary history rest upon how the poetic language based on the language of life constantly evolved, innovated, grew up, and matured in a tortuous course, the linguistic achievements and signs at the peak of the poetic country, and the artistic experience that can be learned from today.

In his research, Lin Geng related the "process" of poeticisation closely to the "connotation" of poeticisation. In other words, the development of the process is mainly to understand the essence of poeticisation, so as to learn from the enlightenment and reference of the tradition for today. To outline the necessary ways of transition from the old to the new in the poetry circle, he mainly discussed the maturity symbols of poeticisation from the following three aspects.

The first maturity symbol of poeticisation is the formation of the universal forms in the poetry circle. As a historical reference to new poetry, *Chuci* became the starting point of his study. *Chuci* written at the peak of prose in the pre-Qin Dynasty (2100–221 BCE) was greatly influenced by prosification. Compared with the four-character style of *Shijing*,[22] *Chuci* obviously had great emancipation. However, why did this freed poetic form become an unprecedented and incomparable phenomenon in literary history? Why is it not the form of *Chuci*, but the subsequent five- and seven-character forms that have become the universal forms of poetry? This issue has hardly been touched upon in the past studies of *Chuci* and literary history. After a comparison and contrast between *Chuci* and four-, five-, and seven-character poetry, Lin Geng pointed out that *Chuci*, a prosified product of the

---

19 Lin Geng. *Metrics of New Poems and the Poeticisation of Language*, 175–176.
20 Ibid., 2.
21 Lin Geng. *Asking for Directions*, 3.
22 *Shijing*, also known as *Shih-ching*, translated variously as the *Classics of Poetry*, the *Book of Songs*, the *Book of Odes*, or simply as the *Odes* or *Poetry*. It is the oldest existing collection of classical Chinese poetry, comprising 305 works dating from the 11th to seventh centuries BCE. It is one of the "Five Classics" traditionally said to have been compiled by Kongzi (also Kong Fuzi, usually as Confucius in English, 551–479 BCE).

Foreword to the Chinese edition xxi

poetic language, brings a brand new rhythm to the poetry circle, that is, the three-character rhythm in a large number of poetic lines. Compared with the two-character rhythm of the four-character poetry in *Shijing*, this is a new leap. Different from the expression function in *Shijing*, the Chinese character "兮[xī] (a carrier sound)" in almost every line in *Chuci* functions as a pause and musical note, dividing each line into two symmetrical parts. The following five- and seven-character poetic lines inherited the characteristics of "half-pause" and three-character rhythm in *Chuci*. Nevertheless, the forms of poems in *Chuci* are not the same. There is not only the improved form of *Shijing* in the "Ode to the Orange", but the regular form closer to the later seven-character poetry in "Nine Songs", showing that *Chuci* is a kind of transition and bridge with a new rhythm that is far from being finalised. Because it did not finish the task of "construction", the forms in *Chuci* did not become the universal forms in classical poetry. Although it can be said to be a "strange pioneer" of five- and seven-character poetry, *Chuci*, a peak of singing, is lack of follow-ups.

In the following Han Dynasty, there were both five- and seven-character poems with the basic rhythm of "the three-character end", indicating that they were from the same origin, i.e., the same new rhythm of *Chuci*. This is why five-character poetry and four-character poetry are in different eras though they differ only by one character, while five-character poetry and seven-character poetry are in the same era though they differ by two characters. Five-character poetry is a combination of the three-character pattern of *Chuci* and the two-character pattern of *Shijing*. On the original tradition and length of *Shijing*, it was more easily accepted at an early stage than seven-character poetry. Thus, it became dominant in the poetry circle at first, but it did not make the poeticisation reach its peak. It was not until the emergence of a large number of lively and fluent seven-character poems that brought full-scale prosperity to the poetry circle, because seven-character poems with an essentially simpler and more thorough three-character rhythm are more vernacular and easier to follow than five-character poems.[23]

The period from *Shijing* to *Chuci* until the Tang Dynasty when five- and seven-character poetry became fully mature spanned nearly a thousand years. This long period of historical observation provided convenience for summarising the development laws of the Chinese poetic language. Obviously, Lin Geng's academic research is synchronous with his thoughts on new poetry. For example, the proposition of the "half-pause law" began with the study of punctuation in "Crossing the River" of *Chuci*. Wen Yiduo thought that the original bamboo slips were in disorder, and could not punctuate properly, while Lin Geng thought that the half-pause law can be applied to solve the problem, and then further extended to the punctuation function of "兮" in *Chuci*. However, it is only after "the confirmation in new poetry" that it

---

23 Lin Geng. *Metrics of New Poems and the Poeticisation of Language*, 75, 99–109, 128–137.

rises to be "a general characteristic of Chinese poetry".[24] In the same year of 1948, he published two articles, "The Nature of the Character '兮' in *Chuci*" and "The Forms of New Poetry Revisited". The former put forward a new interpretation of the rhythmic function of the character "兮" in *Chuci*, while the latter proposed the "half-pause law" of poetry for the first time, positing that "if a poetic line has a 'pause' in the middle, it can have rhythm". "When poetry can establish new patterns of language, it can have a new universal language, and poetic lines can have endless but steadfast forms".[25] Both of them confirm each other and develop each other, which not only strengthens Lin Geng's understanding that the language development of new poetry should focus on the issue of "construction of poetic lines", but helps him discover in an academic way the evolution rules of the forms of classical Chinese poetry centred around the form of "x-character". Scholars have studied different styles of poetry in various ways, but Lin Geng is exceptional in that he not only focused on the fixed forms, but directly explored the mystery of the growth and development of different types of poetry, from which he summed up the basic composition law of Chinese poetry, the "rhythmic pattern". Such an academic achievement is inextricably linked to his academic approach embracing the topics of the time.

The second maturity symbol of poeticisation is the visualisation of language or the abundance of images. If "the maturity of poetic forms is only a most superficial symbol of the poeticisation of language" (95), then the poeticisation of vocabulary and grammar is also worthy of great concern. The poeticisation of grammar such as the simplification or omission of function words and the formation of special syntax is conducive to the refinement and flexibility of poetic language and the foregrounding of images. The poeticisation of vocabulary is "the most intrinsic link in these steps, and it seems to be a poetic catalyst that makes a breakthrough at one point but develops into a comprehensive one" (295). From the perspective of poetic "images" to explain the poeticisation of vocabulary, Lin Geng brought brilliance to the theory about "the visualisation of language".

The perspective of "images" is also related to Lin Geng poetics. It was the 1930s when he entered the poetry circle and reached his creative peak. The modern poetic trend in that period in China, which drew on the artistic concepts and creative experience of Western Symbolism, Imagism, and Modernism, had a significant influence on his poetic creation and poetic ideas. At that time, one of the leading journals *Modern* published the translation and introduction of English and American imagist poetry, and illustrated the poetics of Imagism. This poetic trend emphasised "modern emotions in modern life" and replaced the "feelings" expressed in confession with the inner "emotions" condensed after sublimation, and

---

24 Lin Geng. *Metrics of New Poems and the Poeticisation of Language*, 157.
25 Lin Geng. *Asking for Directions*, 208–210.

substituted the spontaneous flow of passion with the combination of images and emotions. Several poetry anthologies that Lin Geng published in the 1930s were included in modern poetry by literary historians.[26] In his published article "Rhythm of Poetry", Lin Geng said: "A literary work has three basic elements: basic human emotions, the content, and feelings, which are about how an emotion falls on something, or how something produces an emotion". He also said that "a great element (of poetry) is about emotions, but the development of feelings is what a gardener does in the field of human spirits". Here, the "emotions" and "feelings" refer to the "new sentiment and feelings" pursued and captured by "free verses such as Symbolist poetry".[27] In the 1940s, he published "Vitality and New Prototypes of Poetry", in which he emphasised "the new feelings on new things", and reflected on the tradition of classical Chinese poetry through image symbolism, from which he expounded the importance of "new prototypes". Deep impressions of modernist poetry are obviously seen here.

With a deep understanding of the images in classical poetry and the sensitivity as a poet, Lin Geng is greatly at home flying in the world of images of ancient poetry. In fact, the "new prototypes" mentioned above are "new images". Images have to rely on new feelings to enter the poetry circle and become "poetic yearnings". Their maturity has a historical accumulation process, which is an important aspect of "language poeticisation". For example, the "zither" accompanied five-character poems and the "flute" became the bosom friend of seven-character poems, while the "wind" became the pride of the poetry circle in Jian'an and the "rain" became more and more emotional in the Tang poetry. In *ci* poems, such images as "pavilion", "bridge"," "swing", and "railing" became prominent images for some time. These were originally used as proof of how new poems acquired new prototypes; however, they opened up a new garden.

Lin Geng has combed many times the historical tradition of the evolution of images in classical poetry. For example, Qu Yuan made the mythical "Nine Songs" more poetic rather than storytelling. After Qu Yuan's creation, "autumn wind", "the Dongting Lake", and "wooden leaves" have become the most sentimental words in the poetry circle. The "willow" has already appeared in "Minor Court Hymns: Picking Vetches", and developed deep national feelings in "Of yore I went away, / Willows would not say bye", "Verdant grass grows along the river banks; / Green willows in the garden are flourishing", and "Lush orchids grow under the window; / Plenteous willows are before the hall". Then, it had a layer of complex sentiment in the folk song "Song of Plucking Willows" in the Northern Dynasties (386–581). In the Tang poems, the willow was not only interwoven with the complex

---

26 Sun Yushi. *On the History of Chinese Modernist Poetry*, Peking University Press, 1999, 123–155.
27 Lin Geng. *Asking for Directions*, 167–168.

mood of "youth is happiness; parting is bitterness", but related to the nostalgia of the homeland in the frontier fortress and the yearning for spring (249–251). The images such as the "pass", "mountain", and "moon" accumulated considerable life history from the Qin and Han Dynasties to the Tang Dynasty. The depth and breadth of life feelings they aroused inspired Wang Changling's famous line "In the passes of Han under the moon from Qin", which predominated over all the frontier feelings in a thousand years.

The creation of images contributes to the emergence of perceptual factors in poetic language, which is fully demonstrated in the article "On 'Wooden Leaves'". Beginning with an investigation into the historical development of a specific language image, this article makes an accurate and detailed analysis of the rich connotation of the poetic language that is based on concepts and transcends concepts, or its perceptual characteristics. The term "wooden leaves", taking the place of "tree leaves", becomes the poets' favourite without making any difference in concept. However, in the field of artistic images, one word is worth a thousand pieces of gold. "Wooden leaves" and "tree leaves" are different in that the former are sparse and scattered, while the latter are usually luxuriant and lush; the former have a yellowish and dry feeling of falling leaves, while the latter are moist and not drifting. However, Du Fu and Huang Tingjian further created a term "falling wood", which "cleaned up the denseness suggested by the word 'leaves'". Thus, the term "wooden leaves" in "Nine Songs" is quite profound, because "it is the unity of 'wood' and 'leaves,' the interweaving of sparseness and denseness, and a distant, an affectionate, and a beautiful image", while "falling wood" is so spacious that it will "cut off the tenderness". Thus, the creation of language visualisation by such poets as Qu Yuan, Du Fu, and Huang Tingjian (also Huang Shangu) is understood and received a detailed and discerning elaboration.

Lin Geng related the poeticisation of the seemingly micro language images to the evolution of the macro history, and re-evaluated the writer's historical values from the perspective of the creation and influence of poeticisation. Why can Song Yu's "Nine Arguments" be unique among the numerous imitations of Qu Yuan? Lin Geng holds that "Nine Arguments" inherited and developed Qu Yuan's steps of poeticisation. From the breakthrough of "autumn wind", "Nine Arguments" further combined "Impoverished men lost their official positions and felt unfair" with "How sorrowful the autumn atmosphere is". Thus, it gained adherents in the poetry circle, pioneered the "Song of the Autumn Wind" by Emperor Wudi of the Han Dynasty (202 BCE–220), inspired Cao Pi's "Song of the Yan", and enlightened the Jian'an era (196–220) and even later. Therefore, Song Yu is different from those ordinary imitators and should have his status in literary history (288–296).

Lin Geng also extended the research method of "image analysis" to the discussion of the significance of landscape poetry and frontier fortress poetry. He pointed out that landscape poetry flourished for the great progress of image capturing in poetry. It is not only inspiring but combined with the poet's political aspiration, official life away from home, wandering, travelling, and home thoughts. Thus, it goes beyond ordinary subject matters and becomes "more closely related to a general national form" (81). As a new symbol of the image language, the emergence of landscape poetry has also promoted the further visualisation of allusions in poetry. "Since the development of landscape poetry, the images in allusions began not to rely entirely on the original story, but on all the objects in Nature directly taken from the living environment" (92). The significance of frontier fortress poetry lies not in a specific battlefield or battle, or in a specific time and place, but in a wide range of time and space to sing about the frontier fortress as an entirety. It is actually "an expansion of the traditional theme of wanderers, political vision, as well as landscape and scenery" (66). It is a new image of poetry that emerged in expressing the passion of the time.

"The theory of imagery" has aroused heated discussion and concern in the academic circle and the poetry circle in the 1980s. However, 20 or 30 years earlier, Lin Geng had used this method to systematically analyse the language images of classical poetry. This unprecedented study had given a freshly enlightening and pioneering theoretical explanation to an important part of language poeticisation.

The third maturity symbol of poeticisation is the realisation of the language accomplishment or aesthetic model of "profundity out of simplicity". Lin Geng summed up the language styles and achievements of the Tang poetry with "profundity out of simplicity", which is not a simple comment and description of his impression, but reflects his own aesthetic ideal, which was born and sublimated from his observation and summary of the differentiation and disputes in the new poetry circle. Shortly after the birth of the new poetry, there were two different tendencies of "profundity" and "simplicity". The vernacular poems represented by Hu Shi's *Trial Collection*, with the aim of "being plain and clear" and "writing poems like writing essays", belonged to the school of simplicity, while the early symbolic poems represented by Li Jinfa belonged to the school of profundity for their obscurity and mystery. In the 1930s, with the rise of modernist poetry, there were once again debates about "clarity" and "obscurity", and "intelligibility and unintelligibility" regarding poetic expressions. Lin Geng summed up the New Poetry Movement by dividing its development into three stages: the first is the period of getting rid of the old poetry; the second is the period of "writings centred on the journal Modern and numerous poets' free verses" when the modernist poetry was in full swing in the 1930s. This is a period of shedding the imitations from Western poetry, in which "the authors delve into profound knowledge and explore hidden things to have their own creation"; thus, "it's a period of profundity". The third stage should be a period of "going back to simplicity from profundity" and "casting off unintelligibility". Lin Geng believed that "profundity out of simplicity is a natural order and a supreme ideal".[28] His attempt to shift from the "narrow and deep" new free verses to new metrical poetry was probably driven by this ideal.

---

28 Lin Geng. *Asking for Directions*, 202–203.

This aesthetic ideal enriched and deepened Lin Geng's understanding of the Tang poetry, especially the linguistic model of the High Tang poetry. To reach the grandeur of "profundity out of simplicity" needs many conditions. In terms of language, it's necessary to find the universal forms of poetry at first, because "the universality of forms is the emancipation of forms so that expressions can have profundity out of simplicity".[29] "When poetry can establish new patterns of language, it can have a new universal language, and poetic lines can have endless but steadfast forms. Then, in terms of form, profundity and simplicity can have new emancipation and unification".[30] Profundity out of simplicity is certainly inseparable from the visualisation of language. "Profundity" includes what is "deeply rooted in the field of images" (99). Nevertheless, the realisation of the grandeur of "profundity out of simplicity" depends, on the one hand, on the accumulation and inheritance in history, and, on the other hand, on the great creation of contemporary poets, so that poeticisation can blossom brilliantly on the traditional branches and produce fruitful results.

Lin Geng's study of the poeticisation grandeur of "profundity out of simplicity" is characterised by his discovery and exposition of the Tang people's creativeness. Lin Geng believed that classical Chinese poetry had all the forms in the Tang Dynasty, and the Tang people's creativeness was best represented in quatrains and seven-character ancient poems. Though existed before, these two forms of poetry became the pride of the poetry circle in the hands of the Tang people. Quatrains develop from folk songs; although the shortest, they have a more pure language compared with five-character ancient poems inevitably with more prose elements; the poems the Tang people have been singing are mainly quatrains, indicating that their characteristics of spontaneous flow of emotions are integrated with the language of life; it often "makes a breakthrough at one point but develops into a comprehensive one", reflecting a strong leaping, and "the abundance and freedom of the leaping nature" are beneficial to "the richness of poetic lyricism". Seven-character ancient poetry was a kind of new chanting poetry popular since the Sui and Tang Dynasties. It's different from five-character ancient poetry because the first half of the latter still has the rhythmic nature of four-character poetry, and is still used to long-term transitional expressions. However, seven-character ancient poetry has a brand-new three-character rhythm, and frequent change of rhymes in the Tang people's hands. Thus, "the sweeping changes and coherent style make the seven-character ancient form the most personalised and liberating" (115). The unique path of "singing" of seven-character ancient poetry and quatrains "shows that poetry was really liberated from the aristocratic parallelism of the Six Dynasties (220–589) and returned to the simple and natural language" (221). Led by them, regulated poems also stand out from long

---

29 Ibid., 205.
30 Ibid., 210.

regulated poems along the path of simplicity and plainness. They are much more refined and flexible than long regulated poems, which is exactly in line with the characteristics of quatrains and seven-character ancient poems. All these suggest that "the peak of the whole poetry circle is based on the spontaneous flow of emotions in quatrains and seven-character ancient poems" (63). And the most outstanding works in the unique "frontier fortress poems" happen to be seven-character quatrains and seven-character ancient poems. After the Mid-Tang, the poetry circle had the differentiation of "plain and easy" and "hard and difficult". Profundity and simplicity were combined and flew towards ci poems (159–160). Lin Geng's elucidation not only more clearly presented the linguistic model of profundity out of simplicity of the Tang poetry, but highlighted the creative historical achievements of the Tang people.

Lin Geng's study of poeticisation focused on "the general language level at a time"; thus he did not confine himself to specific writers and works, but assessed the general situation of the whole poetry circle and even the literary circle. Before the Tang Dynasty, the process of poeticisation swept through the literary circles of the Wei, Jin, and Six Dynasties for about 400 years. In this period, proses and *fu* (also poetic exposition, rhapsody) gradually became similar to poetry in the process of poeticisation. *Fu* in this period broke away from the track of Han fu, and almost all their content and language "were developing around poetry as the centre" (89). The poeticisation of prose was highlighted in the unprecedented and unmatched *pianwen* (also parallel prose) of the Six Dynasties. Though flourishing in the Six Dynasties, *pianwen* declined and disappeared like *fu* in the Tang Dynasty when the poeticisation was mature. This shows that the predominance of *pianwen* is "a great wave around the rapid development of the poetic language, ebbing after the completion of poeticisation" (89). In this way, genres like prose, *fu*, and poetry were no longer genres unrelated to each other, but contained the in-depth evolution message of the literary language in their ups and downs. The commanding of the overall development of artistic language from a macroscopic and comprehensive perspective while breaking the stylistic boundaries was rare in previous studies. Thus, the literature of the Six Dynasties, which was simply denounced as "flowery" that people cherish not from the perspective of the traditional orthodox literary theory, regained new significance. As Lin Geng said, "The development of poetic language from the Jian'an era to the Sui Dynasty (581–618) paved the way for the Tang poetry, as the steepest Three Gorges helps the Yangtze River vigorously rush down a thousand *li*" (94). It shows his deep and keen sense of history to grasp the development of poetry. Of course, the Six Dynasties were still "at the stage of deliberate poetic pursuit" while "the traces of skills still existed", and the full maturity of language was yet to be achieved. However, in his discussion, Lin Geng not only reasonably explained many unique literary phenomena in the Six Dynasties, but traced the historical context of the Tang poetry that made it a high peak rather than a lonely peak, and thus it is significant and inspiring for future researchers.

The confluence of the maturity of poetic language and the maturity of the Tang society produced the peak of the Tang poetry, and created the ideal of ancient Chinese poetry: "it is distinct, open-hearted, simple but profound; the vivid images, rich imagination, and abundant feelings are united into rich and endless expressions with ideological and artistic achievements. This is also known as the 'dense' style of the High Tang Atmosphere" (53). Why did the Tang poetry become the peak in the country of poetry? What lay behind its prosperity? Many scholars have been searching for answers, but only Lin Geng has answered this difficult question based on the integration of the life content, spiritual outlook, and high maturity of poetic language in the Tang Dynasty. Especially, he made a convincing exposition on how the poetic language matured through a long poeticisation process, thus having thoroughly explained the reasons leading to the prosperity of the Tang poetry from the perspective of poetics.

For nearly a century, new poetry has always been facing the pressure of fighting on two fronts. On the one hand, it must resolutely undermine the position of classical Chinese poetry, and be highly vigilant against the return of old poetry; on the other hand, it must learn from the modernisation experience of world literature, and, at the same time, guard against the denial and disregard of the tradition with a "Complete Westernisation". Lin Geng transformed such a sense of pressure and adversity into his own writing practice and theoretical thinking on new poetry, and then extended it for his inner drive of academic research on the poetic tradition. Inheritance, reference, and creation are not only the themes of Lin Geng's new poetry writing career featured by "asking for directions", but the centre of his diligent academic career. They contain a conscious sense of mission and lasting confidence in the construction of new poetry, and a keen aspiration for the prosperity of new poetry. It is this far-sighted approach of establishing the new from the old that makes Lin Geng's study of the history of poetry go beyond ordinary "academics" and become more distinct in contemporaneity, innovation, and originality. When his theory came out, it always aroused great concern and heated discussion in the academic circle.

Since the May Fourth Movement, the creative transformation of tradition has become an unavoidable and serious issue in the ideological, cultural, and academic circles. If we agree that "the genuine creativity and originality can only be obtained in the tradition of creativeness",[31] then Lin Geng's academic significance lies in his creativeness. It is beyond doubt that his achievements will continuously enlighten future generations with varying originality.

---

31 Lin Yusheng. *Creative Transformation of Chinese Tradition*, SDX Joint Publishing Company, 1988, 193.

Translator's notes

A Comprehensive Study of Tang Poetry is translated from a wide-reaching and creative Chinese masterpiece on the Tang poetry in the Golden Age of Chinese poetry (618–907). The first Chinese edition was published in 1987. In 2011, it was selected into the Masterpieces of Chinese Modern Academic Series and published by the Commercial Press with the support of the National Publication Fund.

Focusing on the poetic language, metrical patterns, landscape poetry, frontier fortress poetry, and the four greatest poets Li Bai, Du Fu, Wang Wei, and Bai Juyi, it has in-depth and refreshing discussions about the Ji-an'an Spirit, the High Tang Atmosphere, the Youth Spirit, maturity symbols, poeticisation, poetic vitality and new poetic prototypes with thousands of classical Tang poems themed in the love and friendship, aspirations and seclusion as well as travelling and home thoughts of people from all walks of life in that period when ancient China was the most civilised country in the world.

The original book includes three parts. The first part, "the Peak of the Tang Poetry", is particularly relevant to the book title; the second part, "Far Notes of the Tang Poetry", is related to the literature before the Tang Dynasty, many of which have little to do with the Tang poetry, or only have distant relationship and influence; the third part, "Essays on Poems", contains the literature of the Song Dynasty.

According to the opinion of the reviewers for the Chinese Fund for the Humanities and Social Sciences that the content should match the book title, I translated the preface "Why Do I Particularly Love the Tang Poetry", the "postscript", "Mr Lin Geng's Academic Chronology", and the foreword Zhong Yuankai's "Lin Geng's Poetic Thoughts and Academic Contributions". Moreover, the first part, "the Peak of the Tang Poetry" totalling 265 pages, was fully translated, with seven essays on the Tang poetry covering 17 pages in the third part. The translation was divided into two volumes with necessary editing and emendation.

As a matter of fact, Mr Lin Geng is highly accomplished in fields such as literature, philosophy, and poetry. Regarding poetry research, he is an expert not only in the Tang poetry, but in *Chuci*. A small number of essays that were not translated in this book should have opportunities to be translated in other monographs.

This year coincides with the 110th anniversary of Mr Lin Geng's birth. Our translation project team members sincerely wish that his academic thoughts would be disseminated around the world and have great influences on generations to come!

Finally, I would like to express my heartfelt gratitude to Prof. Kelly Washbourne at Kent State University for his meticulous editing of the manuscript, to Prof. Ni Chuanbin at Nanjing Normal University, to Prof. Yang Junfeng at Jilin International Studies University, to Prof. Liu Junping at Wuhan University, to Prof. Xu Mingwu at Huazhong University of Science and Technology, and to Prof. Tian Chuanmao, Prof. Xi Chuanjin, Prof. Tan Honghui, and Associate Prof. Ma Yan at Yangtze University for their constant support of this national translation project.

All mistakes are mine and mine alone.

Wang Feng
Yangtze University
June 2020

1 The four great Tang poets

The four great poets of the Tang Dynasty we will discuss are Wang Wei, Li Bai, Du Fu, and Bai Juyi (772–846). Li Bai and Du Fu are the greatest poets in the Tang poetry circle. Their greatness lies in their vigorous pursuit of ideals and their tenacity to face the darkness. In feudal society, there are always struggles between the bright side and the dark side even in a flourishing age, only that the former has the upper hand. Therefore, Li Bai always took a critical and contemptuous attitude towards the forces that hindered social development, and always proposed higher requirements on the time, which is the embodiment of his ideal and confidence. Even in the An Shi Rebellion, Li Bai did not lose his confidence. He firmly believed that the An Shi rebels and the evil forces in the royal court would end together, and on this basis, everything would have a new beginning. A new court would be more vibrant, and he would be vigorous in realising his great ambition and in implementing his political ideal of "making the world secure and united". Therefore, Li Bai spent his whole life enthusiastically eulogising his ideals and became the most heroic poet in the High Tang. Du Fu also struggled for his ideals all his life. Living in the whirlpool of the An Shi Rebellion, he wrote many poems reflecting the war, even though he always hoped to return to the High Tang. With great confidence in their brilliant poems, they illuminated the entire poetry circle with such lines as "The southern chief surrendered to the northern saint", "The five royal tombs always have the best fortune" ("Sorrow for the Emperor's Grandson"), "How can the fate of Hu people last? / The royal tie should not be cut off", and "What a great cause of Emperor Taizong / Whose achievements are truly magnificent" ("Northern Expedition"). However, each poet has his merits in the whole poetry circle. Other prominent representatives of Tang poets are Wang Wei and Bai Juyi, second only to Li and Du. Wang Wei, fond of a simple life, became a hermit in his old age, as he states in "In my later years, I was quiet, / And I didn't care about anything" ("Presented to Privy Treasurer Zhang"). In his later years, Bai Juyi became the "Hermit in the Fragrance Hill", also called the "Drunken Chanter", living a "half secluded" life. What he did has a foundation from the ancient time, as shown in "when successful, you should benefit the world; when poor, you should cultivate yourself". Li Bai, therefore, says:

> I'm fond of Master Meng Fuzi, / Whose talent is famed in the world. / Rose-cheeked, he quit his official career. / White-haired, he lies under pines and clouds. / Often drunken with the moon like a saint, / He serves flowers more than the Emperor. / How can I adore his peak-high virtue? / Here I can only honour his grandeur.
>
> ("To Meng Haoran")

Du Fu says: "The noble Right Minister Wang not seen, / Hills and valleys in the Blue Field grow cold vines" ("Twelve Poems on Boredom Killing"). They were related to "peak-high virtue" or "the noble". It can be seen that at that time their seclusion was beyond reproach, and we shall not be too critical about them.

Wang Wei and Li Bai were born about ten years before the High Tang. At the beginning of the High Tang, they were in their adolescence, facing the vigorous High Tang, and singing its hearty sounds. Each represented the various achievements in the poetry circle. Li Bai is such a prominent figure that as soon as we begin to read his works, we will immediately feel an extraordinary power. Therefore, he is a typical model at the height of the poetic era. Wang Wei is a more comprehensive model. He has earned his fame at the beginning of the High Tang, reflecting the universal prosperity of the entire poetry circle, on which more outstanding poets like Li Bai appeared. Thus, we might as well discuss Wang Wei first.

I Wang Wei's comprehensive artistic talents

Wang Wei is a comprehensive model, first because he fully reflects the prosperous atmosphere of the High Tang, which has not only sufficient political and economic development, but a high degree of cultural achievements. His profound accomplishments in various arts made him a universal representative. Well versed in music, he was once a Music Aide in his early years. Legend has it that he once wrote a *pipa* tune "Gloomy Ring Robe", and was able to play it himself. According to the *Complement to the National History* and the new and old *History of the Tang*, someone had the "Drawing of Music Playing" while not knowing the name of the music. Wang Wei pointed out that it's a painting of the first part of the third refrain of the "Tune of Rainbow Skirt and Feather Robe". It was proven true after musicians were summoned to play the music. Although these legends are not fully believable, they are widely spread, at least showing that Wang Wei's musical accomplishment has been well known. Wang Wei is proficient not only in music, but in painting. His achievements in painting are more recognised nationwide.

His "Occasional Writings" No. 6 states: "I was a poet in my last life / And a master of painting earlier". Obviously, he is quite self-assured in painting. These various artistic accomplishments made Wang Wei able to achieve successes in the field of arts, so he became a perfect representative of the High Tang culture, i.e., a comprehensive model. In poetry creation, Wang Wei further showed his comprehensive artistic talents.

The primary forms of the Tang poetry are five-character and seven-character, while few excellent works are in the form of *Chuci*. However, Wang Wei has extraordinary poems such as:

> Boom! Bang! Drums are beaten
> At the foot of the Fish Mountain.
> Blow bamboo flutes;
> Look far at the waterside.
> The witches come in
> And begin to dance.
> What a gorgeous feast
> With wine clear and fine!
> The sad wind comes with the night rain,
> But the goddess may or may not come,
> Which makes my heart bitter and cold.
> —"Song of Welcoming the Goddess" from "Songs of the Goddess Temple at the Fish Mountain"

> She comes in to worship at the hall's front.
> Her eyes gently fall on the grand feast.
> She comes silently, saying nothing.
> She invites the night rain to the empty mount.
> Flutes of sorrow are played quickly;
> Numerous chords are echoing around.
> Her spirit drives away as in a whirl.
> Clouds are gone, the rain is over,
> Mountains are green, and water is rippling.
> —"Song of Seeing off the Goddess" from "Songs of the Goddess Temple at the Fish Mountain"

> Staying late is the Northern Star.
> I feel sad for things against us.
> I stop my horse between two trees.
> In the green mount I won't be back.
> — "Looking at the Zhongnan Mountains: A Song for the Imperial Secretary Xu"

They might be unsurpassed masterpieces after "Nine Songs". If Li Bai was mainly influenced by "Li Sao", then Wang Wei inherited the tradition of

"Nine Songs". "Li Sao" is dramatic, while "Nine Songs" are more poetic, which shows the two poets' difference. As for the five- and seven-character poetry at that time, Wang Wei achieved a great deal in both poetic forms. Among the High Tang poets, Li Bai wrote fewer regulated poems, Du Fu wrote fewer quatrains, while Wang Wei balanced his talents and achieved universal success. If the High Tang poetry has all the forms, then they are all reflected in Wang Wei's poetry.

Wang Wei wrote poems about every subject. We usually think that Wang Wei is a landscape poet, and that his landscape poems are deep, quiet, and lonely, represented by his poems written about the Rim River (also Wangchuan) in his later years such as "None is seen in the empty mount; / Only a human voice is heard. / Sunlight breaks into the deep forest, / And shines on the green moss again". However, as a matter of fact, Wang Wei's popularity among people at that time was not dependent on such poems. *Fraternal Remarks at Cloud Stream* states:

> (Li) Guinian once sang at a banquet for the Royal Emissary to central Hunan: "Red beans in the southern land / Grow several twigs in spring. / I ask you to gather a few more, / As they are symbols of missing.

He also sang, "In the moonlit wind, yearnings attack me. / You've been in force for more than ten years. / The day you went, I advised you in tears / To send me more letters when geese come back". These poems were written by the Right Minister Wang and have been sung by the operatic circle till now.

In *Anthology of Poems: Spirits of Mountains and Rivers*, poems from the year of the First Tiger (the second year of Kaiyuan, 714) to the 12th year of Tianbao (753) were selected, and Wang Wei was recommended as the top contemporary spirit. However, even he was paid much attention to, his works in seclusion were not emphasised in the collection. It can be seen that Wang Wei's influential poems at that time were not mainly about seclusion, so we might as well talk about his frontier fortress poems first. There are more than 30 surviving frontier fortress poems by Wang Wei. By contrast, Li Qi, commonly known as a frontier fortress poet, has extant poems fewer than ten, and Wang Changling has just over 20 in existence. To classify the High Tang poets into landscape poets and frontier fortress poets would have hindered us from understanding a poet in an all-round way. It seems that Wang Wei's representative frontier fortress poem has only two lines: "In the vast desert a lone smoke rises up; / In the long river the setting sun is full" in "Envoy to the Fortress" because it describes the landscape. In fact, Wang Wei's poems on frontier fortress are not only numerous but also excellent, as in:

> For ten *li*, the steed kept running.
> It ran five *li* with each whipping!

> The chief's army letter arrived:
> The Huns are attacking Jiuquan.
> The flying snow on Mount Guanshan
> Has blocked the beacon fire and smoke.
> —"Song of Longxi"

How lively is the tense life on the frontier fortress! Also in:

> Horns are blown to summon soldiers,
> Who make great noises in marching.
> In sad Hu flutes, horses are neighing
> And rush to cross the Golden River.
> At twilight by the desert fortress,
> The war sounds are in smoke and dust.
> — "Army March"

There is neither exaggeration nor exclamation here. It seems emotionless, but its emotions are in the poem. Such writing has its own style in the frontier fortress poems of the High Tang. His "Song of Youth" reads:

> The New Home wine worth ten thousand is so mellow,
> Enticing young roaming swordsmen in Xianyang town.
> They drink heartily to their spirit and renown,
> Leaving their steeds by a high inn to weeping willows.
> They served the state, promoted to be royal guards,
> And first fought in Yuyang with the knights' general.
> Who doesn't know the hardships in the frontier fortress?
> Even they are dead, their bones as knights mark their fame.

In "A youthful swordsman from the capital Chang'an / Mounted the guard tower to watch the Star of War. / The moon far from Lin'guan shines above Longtou, / On which a soldier is playing the flute at night" ("Song of Longtou"), such romantic and heroic feelings of these young roaming swordsmen running to the frontier fortress are the embodiment of the Youth Spirit of the High Tang. Also in:

> Strong soldiers in Zhao, Wei, Yan, Han were plenty.
> How robust the youthful swordsmen in Guanxi were!
> ...
> Painted halberds and carved daggers cooled the white sun.
> Big banners and flags were lost in the yellow dust.
> The beating drums stirred up the ocean waves afar;
> The echoing sound of flutes moved the Tianshan moon.
> —"Song of Mount Yan"

6 The four great Tang poets

The vivid and compelling images are comparable to the famous lines in Li Bai's "Fighting in the City South":

> Soldiers washed their blood on the Tiaozhi Ocean
> And herded steeds in the snowy grass of Tianshan.

How vigorous it is in:

> At Heaven's order, the Star of War is moving.
> The green willows in the Han land are improving.
> Copper dippers ten thousand *li* far away sing,
> When the three armies are marching out of Jingxing.
> — "Seeing off Commander Zhao to Daizhou, with an end rhyme -ing"

Of course, the life at the frontier fortress is hard, as in:

> Yellow clouds cut off the colours of spring;
> The painted horn evokes frontier blues.
> In the North Ocean, you will stay for years,
> The Cross River flowing out of the frontier.
> — "Seeing off Judge Ping Danran"

There are also feelings of injustice on the frontier fortress.

> The old general of Guanxi was worried,
> Sitting on his horse and listening with flowing tears.
> ...
> Su Wu's talent was wasted on a vassal state,
> His hairy sceptre broken in the west of the sea.
> —"Song of Longtou"

Here it is related to political injustice, similar to his political poems with metaphorical writing such as "Song of an Old General". His "Watching Hunting" reads thus:

> In the strong wind, the bow-like horns shouted
> When the general hunted in Weicheng.
> Prey in dry grass can't hide from the falcons;
> The snow melted, horses were running fast.
> In a flash, we passed the New Home city
> And returned to the camp by fine willows.
> Looking back at where the eagle owl was shot,
> At dusk clouds of thousands of *li* were quiet.

How brisk and swift! These are the singing centred around frontier fortress poems. And his popular "Song of Weicheng" says:

> My friend, raise a toast with wine! One more cup!
> West of the Sunny Pass no friend cheers you up.

With "one singing and three sighs", it became the "Triple Singing of the Sunny Pass", which is closely linked to the atmosphere of the frontier fortress. The feelings on the frontier fortress are reflected in many aspects of Wang Wei's poems.

In political poetry, Wang Wei elaborated his liberal political demands in general opposition to dignitaries. He says:

> Rich men are often from the wealthy Jins and Zhangs
> For their fathers' deeds and noble kings' early grace.
> From childhood, they live dainty lives without learning,
> While talents are not commended to the monarch.
> ...
>
> —"Chanting of Four Worthy People in Jizhou"

His "Chanting of Unrecognised Talents" observes:

> I wrote to the northern court but got no reply.
> I farmed at the southern hill with no harvest at times.
> In a meeting of hundreds, I was not valued.
> I was not willing to flatter those powerful men.
> I went to Heshuo to live in a friend's mansion,
> But was worried about my households in Maoling.
> Let's climb the mountains and face the rivers again,
> Asking not why the spring breeze is swaying willows.
> Most people are selfish, not caring for others.
> I have been unhappy, and you should have known it.
> I hope to help people in the world first and retire.
> How can I be a common man in my whole life!

His "Pouring Wine for Pei Di" also notes:

> I pour wine for you; please feel free from worries.
> Human relations are constantly changing like waves.
> People guard with their swords from youth until white-haired.
> Those rich and powerful flick their crowns and scorn others.

Such feelings of injustice embody the general injustice the commoners and poor scholars are facing. He complains:

> The chariots and crowns are so costly
> That commoners would never understand.
>
> — "Fables" No. 1
>
> People should know poor scholars' bitterness,
> Never boasting of the warmth of white-fox clothes.
>
> — "Fables" No. 2

These thoughts and feelings are often revealed in Wang Wei's political poems. However, after all, the High Tang is an upward developing era, and its mainstream is inspiring. Although there are resistances, which may happen at any time, some of his poems are so unrestrained that the disappointment of official career seems inevitable in life, and should be dealt with ease, as in "Farewell":

> I dismount for a drink of wine,
> "Hi, my friend, where are you going?"
> You say for the unpleasant life,
> You'll retire by the Zhongnan Mountains.
> Take care! I will not ask again.
> The white clouds there are without end.

However, the feelings of injustice are there without being said. His "Queen of the Xi State" argues:

> Think not that today's favour will make me
> Forget the old kindness I was given.
> Facing beautiful flowers, I'm in tears,
> And will never talk with the king of Chu.

This popular and famous poem just explains how many good wishes the poet has. The spirit and emotions are self-evident without any exaggeration. This, of course, is partly due to Wang Wei's personal qualities. He seems to be a pure and simple singer in that era, never highlighting himself. However, Li Bai is a prominent figure capable of overturning rivers and seas at the peak of poetry. He is riding the strong wind of the High Tang to break thousands of miles of waves. He is always pursuing higher ideals. As ideals are always higher than reality, there are inevitable contradictions with reality, which make his poetry more powerful, more concentrated, and more dramatic. Wang Wei, however, lacks such a strong personality. His life lacks dramatic events, and his poems are written about ordinary everyday life. He does not go beyond the time, but conveys the fresh atmosphere of the time in every aspect of daily life. If Li Bai is a typical model in pursuit of what will be available, then Wang Wei is a general reflection of what is available. Both of the two kinds are undoubtedly needed in the High Tang.

Wang Wei seldom wrote about special subjects, nor did he care about the special parts of a subject. He wrote about the common pulse of the time, which endowed his poetry with more general significance. For example, "Looking at the Sunny Wild after Rain" narrates:

> The sunny wild is vast after rain,
> Without any mist or dust in sight.
> The city gate close to the ferry pier,
> Trees in the village grow to the stream mouth.
> White water shines outside of the land;
> Green peaks stand out of the mountains behind.
> No idle people in the farming months,
> Since all are farming in the southern land.

In "White water shines outside of the land; / Green peaks stand out of the mountains behind", the feelings about the landscape are not only clearly written and thought-provoking, but mingled with the daily life. About the red beans, we read:

> Red beans in the southern land
> Grow several twigs in spring.
> I ask you to gather a few more,
> As they are symbols of missing.
>
> —"Red Beans"

Here, it may be about love, or friendship, or homesickness. It contains very general ideas and feelings, but not too ordinary, which is manifested in the general characteristics of the High Tang poetry known as "profundity out of simplicity". Another example is his "Seeing off Yuan the Second to Anxi". As the first two lines "A morning rain has washed Weicheng so clean, / The inn looks thriving in fresh willows green" include "Weicheng", the poem was later called "Song of Weicheng", as if the specificity of the original title were completely forgotten, leaving only the richest universality, and the poem became the most typical singing in farewell poems in the Tang Dynasty.

The High Tang is a time of triumph and vigour, full of vitality in life. Therefore, excellent poetic lines seem at hand. The ancients considered Wang's poems "gentle as the breeze" as if they were fresh air flowing silently at any time and anywhere. This is precisely because of its close linkage with the atmosphere of the time. Therefore, Wang Wei's poems are always extremely fresh. For example, "To a Friend Faraway" says:

> Those years I waited behind closed curtains,
> Dreaming of Guanshan when departing.
> I see not mails at the feet of wild geese,
> But the crescent moon is like your eyebrow.

This might be the world's newest moon, as it seems to appear for the first time and be acquainted with people for the first time, so that the whole poem's sentiment at once ascends beyond the general bitterness of missing, and goes into a new poetic realm. Life is not always a joy. Is there no sorrow in youth? After all, this is the sorrow of the youth so that we can have such an original feeling. Wang Wei's poetry impresses us with the invigorating spirit of the youth. "In the Same Rhyme Scheme as Cui Fu's Answer to his Younger Brother" says:

> Lower-Yangtze soldiers sometimes pass by Yangzhou,
> And play the flute before the ancient Lanling town.
> Going back by night fires to the out-town Fuchun,
> They hear storks cry in the Stone City in autumn wind.

The poem seems to live in the freshest air. Instead of describing specific scenes or noting down the travel and routes, Wang Wei wrote down his feelings on the journey and created coherent poems with such refreshing breath running through. For example,

> Few passengers wait at the ferry by willows
> For the boatman paddling to the Linyi town.
> My missing is like the spring colour, seeing you
> Off along the south and the north of the river.
> —"Seeing off Shen Zifu Returning to the River East with an Excuse of Disease, and Presented to Li Bai"

Everywhere is the lively spring, and everywhere is the fresh green, which is seen in the air and drizzle, constituting the overall atmosphere of Wang Wei's poetry. In his words:

> At Heaven's order, the Star of War is moving.
> The green willows in the Han land are improving.
> —"Seeing off Commander Zhao to Daizhou"

> They drink heartily to their spirit and renown,
> Leaving their steeds by a high inn to weeping willows.
> —"Song of Youth" No. 1

> Let's climb the mountains and face the rivers again,
> Asking not why the spring breeze is swaying willows.
> —"Chanting of Unrecognised Talents"

Falling flowers are silent among singing birds;
Green willows are waving towards river-crossers.
—"Written on the River Bank at the Cold Food Day"

How much breath of the spring is manifested in the green willows in these poems! This is the exact breath of the High Tang. The landscapes in the poems are more than landscapes! Wang Wei's landscape poems are not limited to one style. For example, "The Hanjiang River View" observes:

Chu fortress adjacent to the Three Xiang,
Mount Jingmen overlooks the nine branches.
The Hanjiang River flows out of the sky;
The peak colours are hidden in the mist.
Towns and cities are floating on the fords;
The waves are rippling at the far horizon.
In the soft and gentle wind of Xiangyang,
I would get drunk with the mountain hermits.

"Seeing off Governor Li of Zizhou" states:

Ten thousand dell trees are touching the sky,
Cuckoos singing in thousands of mountains.
A night of rain in the mountains becomes
Hundreds of tiny springs on the twig tips.

Another two examples are:

In sunset, the rivers and lakes are white;
When the tide comes, the sky and earth are blue.
—"Seeing off Xing, Governor of Guizhou"

Black colours span thousands of *li*;
A few peaks pierce into the clouds.
—"To Brother Governor Cui Jizhong of Puyang at the Front Mount"

How lofty and sublime the atmosphere is! Still another three poems depict:

The green mountain outside the door is like my home.
The eastern water flows to the western neighbour.
—"Visiting Hermit Lü at Xinchangli with Pei Di on a Spring Day Without Seeing Him"

> Pine and fir trees by the waterfall have raindrops
> That turn to haze when the sun sets on the greenness.
> —"Seeing off Fang Zunshi back to Mt. Songshan"

> No rain is on the mountain trails;
> The empty green wets people's clothes.
> —"In the Mountain"

How natural and vivid they are! It is through all aspects of nature that the pulse of the time is seized. Therefore, his landscape poems are in a vast world, rather than in a quiet corner. Their liveliness and fresh breath are in harmony with the pulse of the whole time, thus joining its chorus.

As for the hermit poetry, it is also a popular theme in the High Tang, but it is more than loneliness. Here follows Wang Wei's "Song of the Peach Blossom Village" written in his early years:

> Fishing boats chasing water love the mountain spring.
> The peach blossoms on both banks are along the ford.
> Seated, I couldn't know how distant the red trees go;
> I walked to the end of the green stream, finding none.
> ...
> When spring comes, peach blossom water is everywhere.
> Oh, where to trace the fairy Peach Blossom Village?

Is it full of the atmosphere of spring? Even after secluding in the mountains, Wang Wei often shares his feelings that "In happiness, I go there alone, / And I enjoy being myself" ("My Villa in the Zhongnan Mountains"), showing that he is not willing to live a lonely life. Other examples are:

> The sound of bamboos calls washing girls back.
> The lotus moves to greet a fishing boat.
> Though the beauty of spring has subsided,
> Royal men still linger for the autumn.
> —"Autumn Twilight in the Mountain Residence"

> Seeing off his friend in the mount,
> The wood gate is half-closed at dusk.
> The spring grass will be green next year.
> Will the Emperor's grandson return?
> —"Farewell in the Mountain"

Isn't there some news of spring here? Wang Wei issues his answer:

> Hibiscus buds at the twig tips
> Are blooming red in the mountain.

With no one in the still valley,
The flowers bloom, and then wither.

—"Xinyi Dock"

Even in emptiness and stillness, an endless liveliness is interlinked with the universe.

Wang Wei's faith in Buddhism in his later years definitely encouraged many quiet and solitary works, such as:

The Fragrance Temple is hidden
A few *li* from the peak in clouds.
No trails among ancient trees, but
Somewhere the sound of bell is heard.
The spring wanders over steep stones;
The green pines are cold in the sun.
At dusk by a deep empty pool,
A Buddha rules a vile dragon.

—"Passing the Fragrance Temple"

These poems have achieved relatively high artistry, which just shows that Wang Wei is a more comprehensive poet. But, is there any lonely corner in the High Tang?

Wang Wei has long been regarded as a landscape poet represented by his *Rim River Collection*, mainly because of the history after the Song and Yuan Dynasties. Since that time, the orthodox poetic language has been increasingly distinct from the daily life language, and creativity has become increasingly exhausted. However, landscape painting gradually flourished along with the development of landscape poetry in the Tang Dynasty. Since the Song and Yuan Dynasties landscape poetry has lost its excellence, and landscape painting, not limited by language, replaced landscape poetry in arts and had a widespread development. However, since the Song and Yuan Dynasties, China's feudal society gradually declined, and social contradictions became increasingly complex. Generally speaking, people of vision often felt lonely, thus yearning for a lofty and quiet state. In this way, more and more literati paintings since the Song and Yuan Dynasties turned to reclusion-centred themes, and even landscape paintings tended to have more ink than green mountains and blue rivers. In this case, the quiet and lonely artistic realm in Wang Wei's later poems naturally merged with his landscape paintings. In *Ten Thousand Quatrains by Tang People*, even the four lines "I was a poet in my last life / And a master of painting earlier. / Unable to give up my practices, / I become known by the people" in "Occasional Writings" were opted out into a quatrain entitled "On the Paintings of the Rim River". Moreover, Wang Wei was regarded as the ancestor of the Southern School of painting by later generations. Therefore, his landscape poems, especially those in his later years, were increasingly loved and valued. But that happened after the Song and Yuan Dynasties, and these lonely works in his later years were just a part of his poetic life, not representing all his achievements at that time. We have long lost a comprehensive understanding of Wang Wei's poetry. Moreover, we should have a re-evaluation of his landscape poetry.

II Li Bai's emancipating sentiments

Li Bai's poems are magnificent and passionate with feelings of injustice, giving full play to the romantic tradition to "be passionate to show their styles; be forthright to find out their fortes" in the Jian'an era, and bringing more development in the High Tang poetry circle, which represents the spiritual strength of the High Tang. The Jian'an era is undoubtedly full of strong sensations of inequality and passion of lamentation when the political and economic forces at that time were constantly developing. Chen Zi'ang is a pioneer of the High Tang poetry and an advocate of the Jian'an Spirit. His "Song of Mounting the Youzhou Terrace" has been read from ancient times:

> Before, no ancients were seen;
> After, no followers will be seen.
> How vast the sky and earth are;
> Alone, I feel sad and shed tears.

It's a strong song with a broad vision and passion with feelings of injustice. This passion is due to the gap between ideal and reality, posing a higher demand on time. As shown in "The commoner in Dantu is / Passionate beyond measurement" ("Two Poems for Captain Zhang at Princess Yuzhen's Villa in the Bitter Rain"), Li Bai and Chen Zi'ang are quite similar in this respect, as shown in "The Roads are Hard" No. 2:

> King Zhao's white bones are tangled by weeds that creep.
> The Gold Terrace for talents none will sweep!
> Furthermore, Chen Zi'ang in "King Zhao of the Yan" complains:
> Mounting the Monument in the south,
> I looked at the Gold Terrace afar.
> The hills are covered with tall trees.
> Where is the King of Zhao, alas?
> Now that his great empire has gone,
> I have to ride my steed back home!

They come down in one continuous line. Full of confidence in reality, thus they have higher ideals and pursuits that may not be realised and satisfied. However, they show the vigorous and upward forces in the High Tang. Li Bai's heroism is reflected in "Riding the long wind to break the waves one day, / We hang up cloud sails to march to the vast sea!" ("The Roads are Hard" No. 1). Moreover, Li Bai sighs:

> The roads are as bright as the sky,
> But I cannot reach out that high!
> —"The Roads are Hard" No. 2

He complained by saying "But I cannot reach out that high". However, why did he say that "The roads are as bright as the sky"? This shows the contradictions between reality and ideal in the High Tang, which is unified in this era as well as in Li Bai himself. Therefore, Li Bai exclaims, "Cut water with a sword, it faster flows. / Drink wine to ease sorrow, it deeper grows!" At the same time, he also sang a jubilant song that "All of us have vigorous thought endless, / Almost near the sky to touch the bright moon" ("Farewell to My Uncle Collator Yun at Pavilion Xie Tiao in Xuanzhou"). This is a good description of Li Bai's passion with feelings of injustice.

In the High Tang, the development of Chinese feudal society reached its peak in politics, economy, etc., which aroused general enthusiasm and confidence in the future. Although Li Linfu killed many talents out of jealousy, the general situation was not immediately altered. The enlightened politics provided a variety of ways for scholars to take official positions, the most important of which is the imperial examination.

However, Li Bai did not want to take this ready-made road. He would rather ascend the sky at one step, accomplishing the cause of assisting the monarch in one fell swoop. Afterwards, he would leave abruptly with a flap of his sleeves, and become a recluse among the rivers and seas, thus creating a miraculous career. Such confidence, enthusiasm, and longing for miracles continued throughout his life. Even after returning home for his failure in the capital Chang'an, he still believes:

> We sleep, get up like Xie An in Mount East,
> But it isn't too late to rescue people.
> —"Song of the Liangyuan Garden"

He continues to praise Lu Zhonglian and believes that he is Lu Zhonglian.

> A letter on a single arrow
> Can help conquer City Liao.
> —"An Answer to an Old Man by the Wen River when Travelling in the Eastern Lu in the Fifth Month"

In the chaos of the An Shi Rebellion, he often compares himself to Xie An:

> In the stone-like calmness of Xie An of Dongshan,
> Talking and laughing, I'll rid of the Hu tribes' sand.
> —"Prince Yong's Eastern Patrol"

In the water army of Prince Yong Li Lin, he even thought that he is on the Gold Terrace he has been dreaming of:

> As if mounting the Gold Terrace above
> To honour Goddess Purple Glow afar.
> —"Presented to the Officials of the Pavilion Administration at the Water Army Banquet"

Obviously, the An Shi Rebellion did not make the poet pessimistic or desperate, but inspired his ambition to rejuvenate the country in disasters instead. Li Bai thought he could become Lu Zhonglian and Xie An in one fell swoop to accomplish his political ideal of "making the world secure and united". Therefore, he has always been an idealist.

It should be pointed out that Li Bai's ideal is not coming from nothing. It soars above reality; however, it is also based on reality. Although Li Bai finally failed, at that time many people such as Li Bi succeeded. According to the *Old Tang Book: Biography of Li Bi*, Li Bi in his youth was "versed in writing, especially in poetry, and self-conceited as a minister to the Emperor", and was

> unruly in conduct, and ashamed to follow the usual official career. In the middle of Tianbao, he submitted a statement about the current affairs from the Songshan mountain. Emperor Xuanzong summoned him, and ordered him to be a *Hanlin* on Summons in the *Hanlin* Academy and live in the East Palace for summons.

Later, because of Yang Guozhong's "jealousy of his talents in argumentation", "he secluded in a famous mountain to ease him as a recluse". During the An Shi Rebellion, Li Bi took a government post again.

> From the Songshan mountain and the Ying River in the Central Plain, he risked his life in travelling to Hangzhou in the east, finally met the Emperor in Pengyuan Prefecture in the southwest, and elaborated on the keys to success or failure, which won the Emperor's favour. He was often summoned into the Emperor's inner chamber and was frequently consulted,

and "became more powerful than the Prime Minister". Later, he returned to the mountains again because of the suspicion of the Chief Eunuch Li Fuguo. Nevertheless, under Emperor Daizong's reign, he was once again summoned as a *Hanlin* Scholar, and "was quite valued by the Emperor". Li Bi was ever summoned and dismissed by the emperors of three dynasties. Travelling between famous mountains and royal courts, he finally achieved political success, enjoying his special career as either a recluse or an official. This shows that the road Li Bai chose was feasible. We can even say that his ideal was realised in Li Bi's success. The *Old Tang Book: Biography of Li Bi* also commented:

> Bi, open-minded and resourceful in debate, prefers unrestrained words. Since he became a guest of the Emperor's palace, he frequently aroused powerful officials' jealousy. However, he always protected himself from scourge for his wisdom, eventually succeeded with his eloquence in enlightening the Emperor, and became the Prime Minister.

Li Bi's temperament and experience as a political strategist are very similar to those of Li Bai, but in the end, Li Bi succeeded in assisting Emperor Suzong whereas Li Bai failed because he stood on the side of Prince Yong Li Lin. However, Li Bi's success at least shows that Li Bai's ideal of "fighting for the king and flying to the highest heaven" ("Dredging Alone") is not a great but improper fantasy. We cannot judge heroes by their successes or failures, let alone deny the vigorous and optimistic tone of the time because of Li Bai's final failure. Li Bai was a prominent figure at the peak of the High Tang. His passion with feelings of injustice represented a higher demand for the time, and thus also embodied the High Tang Spirit of never being satisfied but constantly forging ahead.

Li Bai's life is full of surprises and changes, and his emotions are also filled with ever-changing ups and downs. He had been to the royal court and received Emperor Xuanzong's courtesy, but later he was treated as a criminal and exiled to a small minority state Yelang. He enjoyed travelling like an immortal or a chivalrous swordsman; he was once a hermit and a registered Taoist. Now and then, he talked eloquently about the conquerors' strategies, but sometimes he was engaged in the fishing business. Not long ago, he wasted money like water; then, in the twinkling of an eye, he only had an empty pocket. These dramatic changes and unusual life shaped Li Bai's character and constituted the ups and downs of his emotions in poetry. His "The Roads are Hard" told of the sadness of poor scholars who were dejected and frustrated:

> I would cross the Yellow River, but ice blocked it;
> I would ascend Mt. Taihang, but snow covered it.

But in a sudden, he sang in a high-spirited melody:

> Riding the long wind to break the waves one day,
> We hang up cloud sails to march to the vast sea!

In this short poem, emotions move from one extreme to another, as if from the bottom of the valley to the peak, with great ups and downs. Therefore, if Wang Wei's poems seem to be fresh air, clear and transparent, then Li Bai's poems form a magical scenery with strong wind and great waves, as he says in "Singing on the River":

> Being tipsy, I write and shake the Five Mountains;
> Poems written, I'm proudly laughing beyond Changzhou.

Li Bai seems to be a wave-rider at the peak of the time. His poems braving the turbulence of the time are full of strong and unique artistic power, which makes him a prominent figure and a typical model of the High Tang.

The typicality of Li Bai's poetry is first reflected in the anti-dignitary aspect. This is the general characteristic and essence of the poor scholar's literature. However, Li Bai's poems are the most typical and strongest; his distinct sense as a commoner and his independence, his heroic feeling as a minister beginning from a commoner, and his criticism and contempt for the dignitaries all showed the typical characteristic, thus pushing the poor scholar's literature to a summit. Many stories were told among people about Li Bai's arrogance and disdain for the dignitaries. Although some of them are exaggerated or fictional, they described the general impression Li Bai left, which is largely derived from his poems. For example, "Thoughts on a Cold Night while Drinking Alone: An Answer to Wang the 12th" opines:

> You can't follow cockfighters to use scaring grease and gold claws,
> And be spoiled by success with your nose blowing out the rainbow.
> You can't learn from General Geshu Han,
> Striding across Qinghai with a broadsword at night,
> And blood washing the Stonefort to be a purple-robed hero.
> Reciting poems and writing *fu* under the north window
> Isn't worth a cup of water, even if ten thousand words.
> People in the world hearing these would turn around,
> Like the east wind blowing in and out of a horse's ears.
> The fish's eyes have also come to mock me,
> Boasting that they are bright as the moon.
> A thousand *li* steed refuses to be fed with knees bent,
> But lame donkeys neigh proudly in the spring breeze.
> ...
> Holding your hand, I'll tell you what's in my heart:
> For me, honour and disgrace have long been away.
> Sage Kong Fuzi was sad about the injured phoenix and unicorn.
> The admired Dong Long was sworn to be like a chicken or dog!
> ...

The idea of anti-dignitaries has already been at the top of the mountain, incisively and vividly displayed. Another example is the famous lines in "A Parting Song on Travelling in Dream in the Tianmu Mountain":

> Why lower my head and bend to serve the nobles in power.
> That makes me lose the pleasure I treasure!

Scorning the dignitaries, Li Bai maintains his independence and dignity as a commoner and poor scholar. This represents a democratic requirement in the feudal era, which has never been interrupted in the literary tradition represented by poor scholars, but it is Li Bai who has the strongest singing voice.

The poetry of all dynasties has anti-vulgarity content because real poets are incompatible with vulgarity, and Li Bai cannot tolerate even a little bit of vulgarity. He opposed the dignitaries in order to maintain the backbone and integrity of a commoner and poor scholar. Highly motivated by his lofty aspirations, he laughed at pedantic Confucian scholars. "Ridiculing Confucians in Shandong" satires:

> Old Shandong men moot on Five Classics'
> Words and phrases till white-haired.
> Asked of governance policies,
> They are all lost in smoke and fogs.
> Their feet wear shoes for long distance,
> Their heads wrapped with Fangshan towels.
> Walking slowly on a straight road,
> They raise dust clouds before they move.
> ...

Li Bai is even more contemptuous of those incapable and servile followers who play up to people of power and influence. For example, "Ancient Style" No. 24 records:

> On the way, I meet cockfighters,
> Whose crowns and cap are radiant!
> Their noses blow out the rainbow,
> And pedestrians are frightened.
> The candid Xu You lives no more;
> Who can tell a sage from a thief?

Moreover, "The Roads are Hard" No. 2 promises:

> I'm ashamed to follow Chang'an philistines,
> Who gamble about cockfights, dogs, and stakes.
> Playing the sword and singing complaint songs,
> Or grovelling are never what I like.

Li Bai's ideal of life is to be free from all the shackles of the secular world, and become an independent and free man between heaven and earth; thus, all vulgarity will bring him sharp pain, and arouse his evil-hating personality. However, these demonstrate Li Bai's greatness.

The Tang Dynasty is a time of great achievements for poor scholars. Thus, their political demands are highly reflected in Li Bai's poems. With the grand ideal of "making the world secure and united", Li Bai either did nothing or directly looked into the world's great affairs, always believing that he is able to realise this ideal. This brings a heroic spirit to his poetry. Therefore, even sorrowful and indignant, his poetry is bold and unrestrained. Even he failed, he is still a hero. Li Bai always has the image of a heroic warrior. "Warriors wonder at their frosted hair; / Tears are full of exiled courtier's clothes" ("Feelings Shared with Deputy County Head Chang of Nanling"). Thus, his poems are magnificent, reflecting the developing forces of the High Tang. Moreover, this power is reinforced because of his imagination. This rich and innocent imagination is another aspect of Li Bai's poetic typicality.

Li Bai's poems are so imaginative that they are almost heavenly. Like a child, he imagines the moon following him all the way down the mountain.

> At dusk I go down from the green mount;
> The mountain moon returns with me.
> —"Lodging and Drinking Wine when Going Down the Zhongnan Mountains and Dropping by Mountainman Husi"

He imagines the moon as a companion, drinking and dancing together.

> With a pot of mellow wine among flowers,
> I'm drinking alone without any friend.
> Raising my cup to invite the bright moon,
> With my shadow, I'm in a group of three.
> ...
> When I sing, the moon is lingering on;
> When I dance, my shadow is in motion.
> Sober, we three have a good time together.
> Tipsy, each of us goes on its own way.
> Forever we tour, with no affection,
> Around the River of Stars in the sky.
> —"Drinking Alone under the Moon"

He has really personified the moon, as in:

> The curtain's rolled up,
> Opened by any one?
> The bright moonlight shines
> On my pure heart.
> —"Dredging Alone"

The moonlight comes in with no scruple as if it were an uninvited visitor, yet it is so bright and clean that you need not suspect and guard against it. This way of dealing with the moon has neither predecessors nor successors. Additionally, he sometimes imagines that the moon is hanging on a tree as if it were forever.

> I have a big mansion of yore
> On the Fairy Peak of Songshan.
> A moon is always shining there,
> Hanging on the Eastern Stream pines.

With "a big mansion of yore" and "A moon is always shining there", he emphasises the eternity of time as if the moon hanging on the pines is also eternal. Another example reads:

> The strong wind blows my heart west till
> It hangs on a tree in Xianyang.
> —"Seeing off Wei the Eighth in Jinxiang to Xijing the West Capital"

Surprisingly, the heart is also hanging on a tree like the moon above. Such imagination is heavenly rather than an exaggeration. It is because of his heavenliness as pure as a child's heart that he is able to keep the fresh imagination, free from the limitations of common sense, as shown in "Sitting alone in the Jingting Mountain":

> Many birds fly away, so high,
> Leaving a single lonely cloud stray.
> Who are never bored with each other?
> Only the Jingting mountain and I.

How heavenly is that not only the poet is looking at the mountain, but also the mountain is looking at the poet. It seems like a world of fairy tales: everything has life, and everything is full of spirit. He also writes about the wine:

> Hanshui afar is green as a duck's head,
> Also like grapes just brewed but not filtered.
> If the river were turned into spring wine,
> The fermented rice would be a huge dome.
> —"Song of Xiangyang"

> It's better to remove the Junshan Mount,
> So that the Xiangshui River flows flat.
> The endless wine in the Baling water

Will make the autumn of Dongting drunken.
—"Three Poems after Accompanying my Uncle the Chamberlain in Touring Dongting and Getting Drunken" No. 3

Then, everything in sight has become the wine. As for the two poems, the former about the river was written in his early years, while the latter about the lake was composed in his later years. However, the heavenly imagination is consistent, which has become a typical expression in Li Bai's poetry. Thus, regarding mountains and rivers, Wang Wei writes about ordinary ones that can be seen everywhere, while Li Bai writes about extraordinary ones, as shown in "Enjoying visiting famous mountains all my lifetime" because these famous mountains and rivers can especially stimulate his imagination and arouse his enthusiasm in writing. On the waterfall in Mount Lu, he exaggerates:

The falls flying straight down three thousand feet are like,
The huge galaxy falling from the Ninth Heaven.
—"Looking at the Falls at Mount Lu"

On the Yellow River, he imagines:

The Yellow River falls from the Heaven,
Rushing into the sea with no return!
—"A Song at the Cloud Tower of the West Mountain to Taoist Danqiu"

As for his "Hard are the Trails of Shu", it even "makes gods and ghosts weep". How powerful is such imagination! The poets in the High Tang have a vast vision and liberal open-mindedness, and Li Bai has boundless impetus. "Autumn wind cannot blow away / Soldiers' missing at Yumen" ("Wu Songs at Midnight"). Furthermore, the frontier and passes have always been dangerously steep places as they mark geographical boundaries.

Why should the Qiang flute complain of willows?
The spring breeze does not break through the Yumen Pass.
—Wang Zhihuan's "Song of Liangzhou"

The Yumen pass at the fore frontier is still blocked.
Soldiers have to follow light chariots and fight.
—Li Qi's "Ancient Army March"

However, Li Bai declares:

The long wind of thousands of *li*
Is blowing through the Yumen Pass.
—"The Moon on the Guanshan Mount"

Under Li Bai's pen, the vast and mighty wind of ten thousand *li* sweeps away from the Yumen Pass, unimpeded. The long wind is really strong, so are the high waves:

> The river wind can blow down a hill in three days;
> Its white waves are higher than the Waguan tower.
> —"Song of the Hengjiang River"

The Yangtze River and the Yellow River also have roaring currents and surging waves.

> Ascending high to view the vast sky and earth:
> A great river flows away and never returns.
> —"Song of Mount Lu to Censor Lu Xuzhou"

> The Yellow River falls from the sky to the East Sea;
> In ten thousand *li*, it goes straight into our hearts.
> —"To Pei the 14th"

What breath of mind and vision do they have! These are the fearless heroism over great billows, similar to "I will be integrated with Nature; / My spirit will be mingled with the original one" ("Song of Sunrise and Sunset")!

Therefore, Li Bai sings the high-pitched melody full of emancipating sentiments beyond the keynote of the High Tang poetry. His magnificent impetus and spirit similar to the long wind of ten thousand *li* and great billows make him a figure standing against the highest waves and strongest wind in the High Tang Atmosphere, and a most typical model at the peak of poetry.

III Du Fu's maturity and conciseness

Du Fu, the last great poet in the High Tang, is also an epitome of the High Tang poetry. He adopted an inclusive and learning attitude towards his preceding poets, and thus epitomised in his poetry writing the artistry of the High Tang era. Appraising the four great poets in the Early Tang, he remarks:

> Four poets Wang, Yang, Lu, and Luo wrote in new styles,
> Which were mocked endlessly by shallow commenters.
> Even when their bodies and fame have turned to dust,
> The rivers continue to flow for ten thousand years.
> —"Six Quatrains for Fun"

Summing up his poetic pursuit, he concludes:

> I love the ancients, and cherish modern poets;
> Simple words and elegant lines are neighbours.

(Ibid.)

He also suggests:

> To tell pseudo styles from the classic traditions
> And to learn from various teachers are the right way.

(Ibid.)

The above poems reflect the epitomising tendency of the High Tang poetry. He also makes comments:

> Yu Xin's essays and poems are much more mature
> In various themes with a vigour beyond cloud.

(Ibid.)

Although a comment on Yu Xin, it is even more appropriate for Du Fu. His poems are mature and concise, or "profound and forceful" as he himself says, which is the natural style formed in the epitomising process.

Du Fu draws his passion and inspiration from the vigorous spirit of the time. He stands out with the ideal of:

> I think I'm better than others,
> And aim to be a key figure.
> The king better than Yao and Shun,
> Customs are purified again.
> —"Twenty-Two Lines Respectfully Presented to the Left Deputy Minister Wei"

It is the same as Li Bai's enthusiasm of becoming a minister directly to assist the Emperor. The difference is that Li Bai has a strategist's style, so he has been unrestrained for a lifetime, mingling with fishermen and merchants; Du Fu was born in a family respecting Confucianism and authority. He was influenced by Confucianism from an early age, and his own family was a heavy burden, making him more mature and composed in character. Therefore, despite his admiration, Du Fu has some kind advice for Li Bai who has an arrogant character:

> Drinking too much and singing wildly for nothing;
> For whom are you so intransigent and rampant?
> —"To Li Bai"

Therefore, Li Bai's poetry is ethereal and heavenly, while Du Fu is concise, profound, and mature. However, Du's poems are also easy and vigorous, which is precisely based on the High Tang poetry characterised by profundity out of simplicity as well as a broad vision, which are developed on the Jian'an tradition. Li Bai notes:

> Your Penglai writing has the Jian'an bone.
> —"Farewell to My Uncle Collator Yun at Pavilion Xie Tiao in Xuanzhou"

Du Fu also praises:

> Cao Zhi's poems and essays are grand and powerful.
> —"A Reply to the Late Governor of Shuzhou Gao Shi on the Human's Day"

Du Fu's poems are often "passionate and forceful to the air" as in:

> Whales swimming in the billows break the sea.
> —"A Short Song Presented to Monsieur Wang Sizhi"

> Sorrowful wind comes for me from Heaven.
> —"Song of Tonggu County"

Doesn't Du Fu have the same heroism as Li Bai? The answer is in his "A Song in Drunkenness":

> All the others ascended to key positions,
> But Monsieur Guangwen held a low position.
> The fortunate were fed up with delicious food,
> But Monsieur Guangwen even lacked cooked rice.
> His morality beyond that of Emperor Xi,
> He's more talented than Qu Yuan and Song Yu.
> The respected generation is often luckless.
> What is the profit of fame of ten thousand years.
> I, the wild man from Duling, am much more despised
> For the short and narrow brown clothes and silky hair.
> Once, I bought from the Royal Store a gallon of rice,
> And visited Elder Zheng of the same interest.
> With money, I would oft find him,
> And purchase some wine beyond doubt.
> Calling his name casually,
> Yet, I learn from him while drinking.
> In cold nights, we drink the spring wine and watch over
> Lighted drizzle from the roof falling like flowers.
> Our singing seems to be heard by ghosts and gods;
> Who cares about burial when starved to death?

> Talented Xiangru used to wash plates in public;
> Sinless Ziyun jumped to death from a high tower.
> Tao Yuanming wrote about his reclusion of
> Living near a stone field in a straw house with moss.
> What is the meaning of Confucianism to me?
> Confucius and the evil thief Zhi are in dust.
> I don't need to hear that and feel bad about it.
> Let's cheer and drink for our meeting while still alive.

Regarding their passion with feelings of injustice, Du Fu and Li Bai are exactly the same. Therefore, Du Fu has never been away from the peak of the High Tang. Li Shangyin from the Late Tang learnt conciseness from Du Fu, but he was a little feeble. Later generations learnt maturity from Du Fu, but they were inevitably dull, just because they were away from this poetic peak. Therefore, Du Fu's conciseness and maturity are naturally formed in the process of summing up the natural and enlightening poetic style of the High Tang. The epitomisation of the High Tang poetry naturally marks its end.

In the Tang poetry, quatrains are usually subtle, and seven-character ancient poems often unrestrained. Moreover, conciseness is the most difficult in regulated poems, especially in the middle two couplets. It's obvious that even Li Bai has such unnatural poetic lines as "Household smoke cools tangerine trees; / Autumn colours old parasol trees". The regulated poems in the Early Tang developed from longer five-character regulated poems. Therefore, although there were seven-character regulated poems in the High Tang, most of them were five-character, while Du Fu showed his skills in writing seven-character regulated poems. Especially after entering the Shu region, he had an excellent poem in almost every writing. For example, his "White Emperor City" says:

> The rapids rushing down the steep gorge thundering,
> Ancient trees and green vines dim the moon and the sun.

"A Night at Xige" finds:

> The sound of drums and horns before dawn is solemn,
> The stars mirrored in the Three Gorges flickering.

Vigorous and unconstrained, such poetic lines are extremely concise! Almost every word suggests an image, resulting in a relief effect, which forms Du Fu's special style. Another example is "On Autumn":

> Fragrant rice peck at several parrots grains;
> A green tong-tree perches on a phoenix twig.

Bright colours and rich aroma are condensed in these two lines. All the functional words in the original Chinese poem are removed to reach the highest density. The normal expression is "several parrots peck at fragrant rice grains; a phoenix perches on a green tong-tree twig". However, the word order is even reversed to emphasise the "fragrant rice" and the "green tong-tree". It pushes the continuous poeticisation of poetic language since the Six Dynasties to an extreme, which is the result of the epitomisation of the High Tang poetry. In "Feelings on a Travel Night", we read:

> Hanging stars make the level field look vast,
> The moon seems flowing in the big river.

How many scenes are written in the original short lines! The river under his eyes, the sky above his head, the stars in the sky, the moon surging in the river, the moonlight, and the boundless wilderness before the poet are all presented lively as if the whole universe under the night sky were enclosed in the two poetic lines. We can compare it with Li Bai's "Farewell at Jingmen", which states:

> The mountains merge into the level field,
> The river flowing into the vast wild.
> The moon is like a mirror in the sky;
> Clouds are forming mirages on the sea.

The river view under the sky is the same; however, the four lines actually correspond to the two lines in Du's poem. Of course, this is not describing the same world, but obviously its brightness in images is different from the conciseness in Du Fu's poem, which is not only embodied in his regulated poetry but also in other types of poems. Thus, Du Fu's style is uniform and consistent, as shown in his seven-character ancient poems such as:

> Triumphant news at night was the same as morning one.
> —"Washing Weapons and Horses"

> It dwarfs all the common horses in ten thousand years.
> —"Song of a Painting"

In a flexible and unrestrained manner, he still keeps his consistent concise style of writing as follows:

> Away like dragons in deep mountains and great water,
> In the shady wild with spring cold after sunset.
> —"Seeing off Kong Chaofu back to the River East with an Excuse of Disease, and Presented to Li Bai"

It is precisely in the vigorous and unrestrained manner that the spirit of profundity and forcefulness is echoing. His "Sorrow by the Riverhead" is on the same subject as Bai Juyi's "Song of Everlasting Regret", but the latter was written after the event, mingled with legends, whereas the former was written in Chang'an at that time as an immediate event. The final lines are:

> Where are Concubine Yang's bright eyes and snow-white teeth?
> Her blood-stained soul is wandering with no return!
> The Wei River flows east, far from Jian'ge he lives.
> The Concubine left no news for the Emperor.
> For the emotions in life, our tears wet the chest.
> Is there an end to the river grass and flowers?

Furthermore, this is exactly what Bai Juyi says in the last two lines of "Song of Everlasting Regret":

> The sky and earth are long enduring, hard to change;
> This regret will be lingering, without an end.

Both poems focus on the love story between Emperor Ming of the Tang Dynasty and Concubine Yang, but "Song of Everlasting Regret" follows the narrative sequence to the peak step by step, while "Sorrow by the Riverhead" is written in the lyric style, with great leaps in structure. For example, Du Fu writes about their visit to the South Garden in the past,

> Women with bows and arrows are walking before
> Chariots driven by white steeds with a gold harness.
> They bend towards the sky and shoot at the white clouds;
> Two birds fall down, making the Concubine smile with joy.

The last line is originally about one of the events in their tour to the South Garden, but it is also a pun (the couple will fall through like the two birds falling down) suggesting the tragic ending of Emperor Ming and Concubine Yang. After this hint, it quickly turns to:

> Where are Concubine Yang's bright eyes and snow-white teeth?
> Her blood-stained soul is wandering with no return!

The whole incident of hanging Concubine Yang at the Mawei Slope was omitted, and it directly leapt to the peak of the tragedy. It fully displayed Du Fu's vigorous and concise writing style.

Du Fu didn't write many quatrains, but among which he used to show his consistent style of conciseness and maturity. For example, in "Four Quatrains" No. 3:

Two yellow orioles are singing among green willows;
A row of egrets is flying to the blue sky above.
A window frames the west ridge snow of a thousand years.
At gate moors a boat for Dongwu ten thousand *li* away.

A total of four lines describes so much content, making it very different from other quatrains. Therefore, some people say that the poem "is originally a marvellous seven-character regulated poem, but written as a quatrain". Other people say that this poem is a "semi-regulated poem". In short, it is precisely because of its conciseness. Du Fu's conciseness plays a more special role in five-character ancient poems, which are unique precisely for their conciseness, thus making a new achievement. In the High Tang poetry, five-character ancient poems are far less active than seven-character ancient poems. Chen Zi'ang advocates "the Han and Wei Spirit" and praises "the sound of the beginning", which is the tradition of five-character ancient poems centred on Ruan Ji's "Poems on Feelings". After Ruan Ji, from Guo Pu's "Poems on the Wandering Immortal", Tao Yuanming's "Imitating Ancient Poems", "Miscellaneous Poems", "Poems about Poor Scholars", and "Drinking Wine", Bao Zhao's "Imitating Ancient Poems", and Yu Xin's "Imitating Poems on Feelings", to "Feelings" respectively by Chen Zi'ang and Zhang Jiuling, and Li Bai's "Ancient Style", all are traditional writings focusing on expressing feelings. However, by the Tang Dynasty, these have become the end of five-character ancient poems. Thus, it is still seven-character rather than five-character ancient ones that represent Li Bai's style and creativity, although he wrote as many as 59 "Ancient Style" poems. There had been no new world for five-character ancient poems until Du Fu appeared. Du Fu also used the form of writing that combines narration with discussion since his "Feelings on Ancient Monuments". However, poetry is to express feelings. Adding narrative and argumentative elements will weaken the power of feelings and make the poem long and dull, if not handled well. This happened before, and it was often unavoidable when people were learning from Du Fu's five-character ancient poems, as shown in Li Shangyin's "A Hundred Rhymes after Traveling to the Western Suburb". However, even with his affecting poetry talent, he was a little dull and boring in learning Du Fu's "Northern Expedition". Nevertheless, Du Fu, with his epitomising talent and the liberatory sentiment and vigorous spirit of the High Tang, turned the discussions in his poems into natural voices from his mind. Moreover, because of his concise writing, his narrations are close to the truth of details, which is a creative approach in novels rather than in poetry. However, Du Fu's narrations, more detailed than meticulous or lengthy, can integrate the narrations of trivial things by his side with his discussion of the world's major issues, constituting the outstanding characteristics of his five-character ancient poems. Due to the truth of details, he can give people a sense of immersion and seems to make people see and hear the objective scenes in his description. Therefore, he not only narrates objectively, but also shows his own image in his works such as "The Stone Moat Officer" and "The New Safety Officer", all of which exhibit a complete image of Du Fu through many images, not only in five-character ancient poems but also in seven-character ancient ones. For example, "Song of Soldiers and Chariots" describes:

> The passers-by on the road asked the marchers, but
> They only complained of the excessive recruitments.

The "passers-by on the road" actually include the vague image of Du Fu. To quote:

> Although the elderly asked why,
> The recruited dared not complain.
> ...
> They would not have a baby boy,
> But wish to have a baby girl.
> A grown girl can still be married to a neighbour;
> A man recruited will be buried in grasses.

It's more obvious that the "elderly" has Du Fu's image. The reason why Bai Juyi's new *yuefu* ballads are not so profound as Du Fu's poems is that the former lacks such an image of himself.

Usually, our discussion emphasises the critical spirit in Du Fu's such poems, which are thus called realistic works. However, it is the truth of details that is really the first feature of realism, while criticism is common in his general writings. Romanticism also has a critical spirit. Aren't they critical when Qu Yuan's "Li Sao" blames King Huai, and Li Bai's "A Poem on Redressing Slanders for my Friends" and "Thoughts on a Cold Night while Drinking Alone: An Answer to Wang the 12th" condemn the aristocrats in anger? Du Fu was unfortunately involved in the turbulence of war during the An Shi Rebellion and experienced all sorts of disasters. First, he was trapped in Chang'an, as noted in "At dusk, the city's dust was stirred by Hu riders. / We left for the South, but have to ride for the North" ("Sorrow by the Riverhead"). After the recovery of Chang'an, he unexpectedly encountered the turning war in Xiangzhou. In a chaotic situation, he was anxious about the future. Such a reality was naturally reflected and criticised in his works. However, Du Fu did never lose confidence in the time of the An Shi Rebellion. Once the situation improved, his depression and uneasiness turned into triumphant singing in such enthusiastic poems as "Washing Weapons and Horses" and "On the Army's Recapturing of Henan and Hebei". Isn't that particularly romantic? The strong reflection on the Rebellion is never seen among other Tang poets. Du Fu's famous works include a large number of romantic masterpieces. Even his realistic five-character ancient poems are not entirely critical. For example, his

"To Counselors Wei the Eighth", "Song of Pengya", "Three Poems on the Qiang Village" No. 2, and many lines in "Northern Expedition" either narrate the journey or the friendship, or write about the immediate view to express his inner feelings. They are still considered realistic, precisely because they have the truth of details.

In short, Du Fu's five-character regulated poems initiated a new way of writing, which soon gained self-conscious followers. From Yuan Jie's "Song of Chongling" to Bai Juyi's "Songs Written in Qin", there is no exception. As for Bai Juyi, he achieved less in new *yuefu* ballads in seven-character ancient style than his "Songs Written in Qin" in five-character ancient style. About half of the poems such as "Light Fur-Coats and Well-Fed Horses", "Heavy Taxes", "Buying Flowers" and "Singing and Dancing" are famous in "Songs Written in Qin". Among the 50 new *yuefu* ballads, successful works such as "Carbon-Selling Old Man", "A White Haired at Shangyang", "A Broken-armed Old Man at New Home", and "Red Thread Blanket" account for only about one-tenth. Of course, this is because new *yuefu* ballads begin with a theme, tending to be conceptualised, and the poems in "Songs Written in Qin" are deeply touching because the feelings are provoked by sceneries. However, this also shows that five-character ancient poems are more suitable for combining narration with discussion. Besides "Songs Written in Qin", Bai Juyi's five-character ancient poems include "Watching Wheat-cutting", "Lodging in the North Village of Mt. Purple Pavilion", "Living in Bitterness and Cold in a Village", and "A Newly Weaved Coat". They are all well-known works, which are obviously inseparable from Du Fu's influence. In a word, Du Fu, the epitome of the High Tang poetry, inevitably has an impact on future generations, and there are always laws to follow. Yan Yu's *Azure Stream Poetic Remarks* opines: "Shaoling (a nickname of Du Fu) writes like Sun Wu and Wu Qi, / While Li Bai composes like Li Guang". Li Guang uses troops like a god out of people's expectation, but famous militarists Sun and Wu have commanding laws. Writing poems like Sun and Wu, Du Fu thus became a model for later generations. Du Fu's achievements in five-character and seven-character regulated poems had a direct impact on the writing of the Ten Talents in the Dali period. Thus, regulated poems gradually became popular and finally became the favourite of the poetry circle. However, once the conciseness typical in Du's poems is not based on the keynotes of "profundity out of simplicity" and "spontaneous flow of emotions" in the High Tang poetry, the school of "Bitter Chanting" represented by Han Yu and Meng Haoran came into being. For example, "Two lines are acquired in three years, / Two lines of tears fall in chanting" shows a deliberate way of seeking novelty. That is to say, Du Fu inspired not only the school of Yuan and Bai, but the school of Han and Meng, so it can be said that the development of the whole Mid-Tang poetry is under Du Fu's influence.

Du Fu is an epitome of the High Tang poetry. His "Missing Li Bai in Spring" asks, "When can we drink together and / Enjoy a discussion with you?" which shows that he has been exploring this aspect for a long time. The style formed in such epitomisation has been fully displayed since he entered Chang'an. In the author's words:

> The thoughts drift out of cloud and fog,
> Metrics surprising ghosts and gods.
> Details in poems are flawless,
> With a grand and mature spirit.
> —"Twenty Lines Respectfully Presented to Advisor Zheng"

This is, in fact, the ideal poetic standard in Du Fu's mind. Is it not the same mature style as his self-claimed "profound and forceful" style? ("A Prose on the Vulture") Indeed, "maturity" is Du Fu's style and his character image. Before he turned 40, Du Fu had already called himself "a wild old man at Duling" ("To the Scholars in Xianyang and Huayuan Counties"). Since then, in many different poetic lines, he considered himself old. Later generations then called Du Fu "Old Du", which seems unique in the history of poetry. *Constellation Kui above the Fairy Yingzhou: Essence of Regulated Poetry* comments: "Poetry written by Old Du reaches the summit". It also concludes:

> As for the Old Du, his poems at Hu'nan are better than those at Kuizhou, which are better than those at Chengdu, which are better than those at Guanzhong and Sanfu regions. His poems are better and better; the older, the more concise.

In short, he is inseparable from the word "old". *Constellation Kui above the Fairy Yingzhou: Essence of Regulated Poetry* is mainly about regulated poetry. Its specific opinions are not necessarily right, but this "old" character image is Du Fu's common impression to people. "Poetry written by Old Du reaches the summit" shows that the peak of the Tang poetry has developed to a stage completely necessary for a summary. Does not the "maturity" mean that it is already ripe enough to foresee the end? Du Fu, therefore, is an epitome and the last great poet in the High Tang poetry. This identity is the reason why Du's poems are unprecedented and unparalleled. It is also the reason why they have never been created before and can never be learned by later generations. Du Fu stood at the end of the High Tang and made a compelling summary, which established his irreplaceable position in the poetic history. Therefore, looking back at Wang Wei and Li Bai, we can see a clear and discernible development outline of the High Tang poetry. Wang Wei's youthful atmosphere, Li Bai's heroic spirit, and Du Fu's maturity and conciseness symbolise the magnificent development of the High Tang poetry and make representative illustrations of this peak.

IV Bai Juyi's profundity out of simplicity

After Du Fu, the peak of poetry in the kingdom gradually declined. To get new vitality in the poetic language, fresh blood should be drawn from the language of life again. The appearance of formal ancient vernacular in the Song and Yuan Dynasties shows that the language of life in the Tang Dynasty is constantly developing. The poetic language is once again faced with the problem of how to become more popular, and it is Bai Juyi who vigorously welcomed this development. At the same time, when the upsurge of the feudal society began to slow down, the orthodox literature centred on the political lyric poems on aspirations was gradually losing its excellence, and the emerging civic literature began to flourish. Bai Juyi's most representative achievements are his satirical poems, "Song of Everlasting Regret" and "The *Pipa* Tune", as recorded in "'Song of Everlasting Regret' is romantic. / Ten poems of Qin are close to the tradition" ("After Compiling my Poems into 15 Volumes, I Wrote at the End and Happily Presented to Yuan the Ninth and Li the 20th"). These two different types of works just illustrate in the poetry circle a major turning point, at which Bai Juyi is a representative.

Historically, the passing of the High Tang marks the decline of China's feudal era. The real reason is the crisis inside the feudal society. An important feature of Chinese feudal society is that land, the main means of production, can be bought and sold. What does this mean? It means that China's feudal society contains elements of commercial capital. In the normal development of feudal society, the commercial capital and the natural economy in the countryside can be coordinated and mutually promoted, which is conducive to the unity of the whole feudal society. However, commercial capital, after all, is a foreign object in the feudal society. When it develops to a certain extent, it will destroy the natural economy in the countryside. Therefore, there has been a policy belittling and controlling commerce since the Han Dynasty. In the Tang Dynasty, commerce became more active with the development of the handicraft industry. People like Li Bai have been mingling with fishermen and merchants. Thus, after the An Shi Rebellion, the contradiction between the development of commerce and agricultural production began to intensify. Poets such as Bai Juyi and Zhang Ji all attacked merchants in their poems with the same voice. "A Salt Merchant's Wife" in Bai Juyi's *New Yuefu* notes:

> She was a small family's daughter in Yangzhou,
> But married a rich merchant in the West River.
> How many gold hairpins are in her black hair bun!
> On her plump and white wrists, silver bracelets look tight.
> She shouted at male servants, then swore at her maids.
> But why did she become so rich and arrogant?
> Her husband has been a salt merchant for fifteen years,
> And doesn't belong to the county but the Emperor.

> When profits were turned in each year, few were handed
> To the government, but most owned by the merchants.
> The official profit is poor while the private rich.
> The minister of salt and iron far knows not.
> ...

The development of commerce not only seriously affected the natural economy and complicated the contradictions in the feudal society, but caused the vicious development of rural land annexation and drove more peasants to insolvency. Therefore, many poets at that time deliberately contrasted peasants' poverty with businessmen's wealth, as in Zhang Ji's "Merchants' Pleasure":

> For profits, he drifted from west to east each year;
> His name was not registered in the county's list.
> Farmers have to pay high tax, and work hard and long;
> He gave up farming to be a merchant of goods.

In Liu Yuxi's "Lyrics of Merchants", we read:

> Merchants never have constant routes
> For they only aim for profits.
> Mixing good and bad to deceive,
> They seize chances to make profits.
> They care for slight differences,
> And make fake scales to weigh the goods.
> Never giving up humble works,
> They increase their wealth day by day.
> ...
> Why on earth should peasants work hard
> In hunger and cold all years round?

To quote from Zhang Ji's "Song of a Wild Old Man":

> The old peasant lived a poor life in the mountains,
> Farming only half an acre of mountain land.
> After heavy tax, his sparse paddy left little.
> The rice given to warehouses turned into soil.
> At yearend, he had to plough near his empty house,
> And call his children to gather mountain acorns.
> Merchants at the West River have millions of pearls,
> While their dogs in the boat always have meat to eat.

There is a serious confrontation between merchants and peasants, urban and rural areas, the commercial capital and natural economy. Therefore, the implementation of the Two-Tax Law in the first year of the Jianzhong era under the reign of Emperor Dezong changed the former system of land equalisation based on household registration, and the amount of property became the taxation standard. This shows that the expansion of the rural annexation forces and peasants' insolvency reached a degree that cannot be ignored; the rapid development of urban commerce was in an uncontrollable state, and then the feudal society's economy had a serious crisis. This is the real reason for the decline of Chinese feudal society. The An Shi Rebellion that occurred at this time weakened the ruling power within the feudal society; nevertheless, commerce was further developed; thus, the An Shi Rebellion naturally became a boundary marker dividing the ages. The rebellion itself is nothing but a betrayal led by a foreign frontier general. Li Bai's "Ancient Style" No. 46 exclaims: "In one hundred and forty years, / How impressive is the nation!" A single warlord's rebellion is not enough to change the overall smooth development of the Tang Dynasty of more than 100 years. In the seven-year An Shi Rebellion, the rebels had occupied the capital Chang'an for only two years and were confined to He'nan and Hebei with limited impact in the remaining five years. After the An Shi rebels withdrew from Chang'an, sharp contradictions emerged within them, and it was quite obvious that they could not take hold. In retrospect, during the seven years from Wu Zetian's death to the enthronement of Emperor Xuanzong, there was the Autocracy of Queen Wei, which led to the death of Emperor Zhongzong and the chaos in the royal court. As a result, the states in the Western Regions turned against the Tang Dynasty one after another and caused serious consequences. Nevertheless, it did not hinder the development of the following High Tang. Why? This is because the feudal society was still full of vigour, political and economic forces were constantly rising, and short-term incidents could not have a decisive impact. After the An Shi Rebellion, the High Tang disappeared with no return. The main reason is that the economy of the feudal society was in crisis and the Chinese feudal society began to decline. Moreover, these can only be gradually recognised after the suppression of the An Shi Rebellion. Therefore, during the Dali period, people's hearts were still full of the hope of revival. The poems of the Ten Talents in the Dali period were anthologised in *A Reviving Collection of the In-between Spirits*, which shows the general mood of this period. In the Yuanhe era, the newly throned Emperor Xianzong was regarded as the master of revival. Faced with various social problems, and out of the desire for the revival of the time, there appeared Yuan Zhen (779–831) and Bai Juyi's satirical poems and Han Yu's ancient prose movement in literature. This is the last time that the orthodox literature was radiating with brilliance.

In the feudal era of China, the orthodox literature mainly refers to the literature represented by poor scholars, which is centred on the political lyric poems expressing their bosom feelings. Chen Zi'ang became the pioneer of the High Tang poetry precisely because he advocated "metaphorical writing" and embodied the positive tradition of poor scholars' broad literary vision and vigorous spirits. However, the poor scholar's literature is based on the feudal rule after all; after the upward strength was lost in the feudal society, it cannot help but go downhill. Bai Juyi, in the turn of the time, concentrated on writing satirical poems, which became the last effort of the orthodox literature. Many excellent satirical poems such as "Buying Flowers" and "Heavy Taxes" can show his broad mind of serving people nationwide for his duty and his social responsibility as a poor scholar. However, such writing did not last long. When his dream of "revival" was shattered, Bai Juyi gave up writing satirical poems. Therefore, his political depression in his later years was the result of his disappointment with the feudal rule, which correspondingly showed that he was closer to the emerging civic literature. Therefore, the decline of the orthodox literature became an irreversible trend. At the same time, the ancient prose movement initiated by Han Yu since the Dali period was also the last effort of self-salvation for the feudal orthodox literature. Faced with the disintegration and various social problems at that time, the feudal government lost its unifying power. Hence, Han Yu issued a clarion call, trying to rebuild the unifying power by respecting only Confucianism, and relied on a belief to save the declining time. This campaign has a universal practical significance and ideological basis with the quotation of "praise and satire" from the Han Confucianism in Yuan Zhen and Bai Juyi's satirical poems.

However, the turning point of the time was quickly reflected in literature after all, and it was precisely after the Dali period that civic literature flourished universally. For example, *Bianwen*, a form of talking and singing literature in the Tang Dynasty, flourished after that. Zhao Lin's *Records of Former Talks* records: "A monk called Wenshu once gave talks in public. Though faked as from scriptures, what he said was nothing but obscene and contemptible things. However, ill-intentioned scoundrels turned to support him. Benighted men and coquettish women liked to hear what he talked about. His listeners filled up temples to worship him and called him a Buddha. The Royal Academy of Music composed songs by imitating his tones". These listeners, the "benighted men and coquettish women", were certainly urban residents. It's precisely due to the citizens' promotion that popular talks gradually broke away from Buddhist stories to present popular themes. In addition, puppet plays and military plays became popular in the marketplace and won the favour of citizens. For example, the puppet plays in the Dali period were recorded in *Mr Feng's Records of Anecdotes* by Feng Yan of the Tang Dynasty. We read:

> On the burial day of Taiyuan Governor Xin Jingyun, other governors made people worship, and the tallest was the sacrificial camp of Fanyang County, in which carved woods were used to imitate the fighting between Duke Weichi Jingde and Turkic generals, whose actions were no different from life. When the fighting was over, the hearse wanted to pass, but the envoy said, "The fighting is not finished". Then the hearse

stopped. The worshippers set up the scene of Emperor Gaozu of the Han Dynasty meeting his opponent Xiang Yu at Hongmen and played a long time.

As recorded in *Fraternal Remarks at Cloud Stream* by Fan Shu of the Tang, comedians Zhou Ji'nan, Ji Chong, and his wife Liu Caichun were all friendly to Yuan Zhen, and they all "had expertise in military plays". At the same time, civic novels began to rise. *Tang Decrees and Regulations* Volume IV records: "In the tenth year of the Yuanhe era (815),... Wei Shou, the Crown Prince's tutor, was dismissed. Shou liked comedies and had expertise in civic novels". It can be seen that civic novels have already had an impact on literati. Therefore, it is precisely after the Dali period that the creation of legends reached a pinnacle. A large number of influential works such as *A Dream on the Pillow*, *Biography of Li Wa*, and *Biography of Yingying* appeared one after another. Among them, the theme of *Biography of Li Wa*, authored by Bai Juyi's younger brother Bai Xingjian, is directly derived from folk talks. Yuan Zhen's "A Poem of a Hundred Rhymes Written for the *Hanlin* Scholar Bai Juyi" self-noted that: "I have been listening to *A Flower* in the Xinchang Residence for about six hours, but I still have not finished it". In *Lotus in the Black Mud* by Mei Dingzuo of the Ming Dynasty (1368–1644), a note of the *Biography of Li Wa* also says that the former name of Li Wa was "A Flower". Bai Juyi himself was inevitably affected by this tendency. Zhang Hu once compared Bai's long narrative poem "Song of Everlasting Sorrow" to "Mulian Rescued His Mother", which was recorded in Meng Qi's "Stories in Poems":

> The poet Zhang Hu never knew Bai Juyi. While Bai was the Governor of Suzhou, Zhang Hu began to visit him. Soon after they saw each other, Bai said: "You have my long admiration as I remember your poem of questions". Hu was surprised and asked, "What does Your Excellency mean"? Bai said, "Where will the gold belt of mandarin ducks be thrown? / Whom will the robe with beautiful peacocks be given to? Aren't they two questions?" Zhang Hu nodded, smiling, and then looked up and replied, "I also remember Your Excellency's 'Mulian Rescued His Mother'". Bai asked, "Which lines?" Hu said, "High up the blue sky or low down the Yellow Spring, / It's not seen in the two places for the dead people. Isn't it similar to "Mulian Rescued His Mother"? Then they feasted till the end of the day.

Moreover, Bai Juyi's friend Chen Hong directly adapted the subject matter into a legend and wrote *A Biography of Everlasting Regret*. This general interest in stories reflected the citizen's preference, interests and demands. Can it be accidental that this tendency was formed after the Dali period?

Given that civic literature is mainly interested in stories, Bai Juyi's "Song of Everlasting Regret" became quite widespread. The poetic line that "'Song of Everlasting Regret' is romantic" is just built on this basis. Although the interest of civic literature is not in poetry, the upsurge of poetry brought about new creations such as Dunhuang *quzici* (or Dunhuang song lyrics), which provided a precedent for the popularisation of poetic language and the renewal of themes. Wei Yingwu, Zhang Zhihe, Wang Jian, Bai Juyi, Liu Yuxi, and others were sensitive to this new trend. Among them, Bai Juyi and Liu Yuxi's efforts were particularly prominent. Singing together *ci* poems like "Missing the River South", they were the earliest in introducing *ci* poems into literati's writing and daily communication, thus having changed the tendency of the era.

The emergence of civic literature has brought forth new contents and sentiments. One of their common features is that women are protagonists. This is a common feature of folk literature. However, in civic literature, heroines are more active. Needless to say, the singing of love in *ci* poems is natural, while in legends, women like Li Wa and Huo Xiaoyu have also become positive images of honour, which has opened up a new field outside the orthodox literature. In China's feudal society, the higher the social class of women, the more heavily bound by feudal ethics, and thus less freedom. On the contrary, women in urban and rural areas are relatively free because they directly undertake productive labour and have a certain economic status. Therefore, few women protagonists exist in the orthodox poor scholar's literature, except in such themes as wanderers, women missing their husbands, and palace complaints that are vaguely political poems containing metaphorical writing. The theme of true love is seldom involved. However, folk love songs and love stories have a long history, and the heroines are extremely active. From "A Quiet Girl" and "The Common People" in "Airs of the States" to "A Military Officer", "Roadside Mulberry Trees", and "A Peacock Flying Southeast" in the Han *Yuefu* until "Song of Mulan", "Midnight Song", and "Music of No Worry" in the Songs of Wu and Jiangling, women are always main characters with positive images, which is also true in the Dunhuang song lyrics. Since then, *ci* has developed into *qu* (also song, melodies) and is finally integrated with the traditional opera, which is a typical civic literature. Later, all the important operas such as *The Western Chamber*, *The Peony Pavilion*, *The Palace of Eternal Life*, and *The Peach Blossom Fan* featured women as main characters. After accepting this trend through civic literature, Bai Juyi and others imported the themes of love and women's liberation into their literary creation. Their "Bamboo Branches" and "Willow Branches" are all songs of passionate and lasting love. In "The *Pipa* Tune", the feeling that "We are fallen humans at the end of the earth" reflects the new concept brought by civic literature, which is in contradiction with traditional feudal ideology. This contradiction is reflected even in Bai Juyi's writings such as the "amorous poems" in the "Yuanhe Style" in which Bai Juyi and Yuan Zhen write and reply in poems with the same rhyme sequence. Although often writing about the images of women, they have a playful attitude towards women, displaying coarse expression from the standpoint of feudal scholars. Yuan and Bai's writing and replying in poems are actually a disguise of the palace poetry, but the background moved from palaces to entertainment houses. Thus there was a popular saying that "The Yuanhe style, / The Changqing style, / Poets would look down upon". The reason why "poets would look down upon" is just for its frivolity and impurity. However, Bai Juyi and Liu Yuxi accepted the brand-new influence of civic literature in the singing of folk lyrics, which is the singing of love between men and women on an equal footing. Therefore, Bai Juyi's real poet friend in this respect is not Yuan Zhen, but Liu Yuxi. Their poetic creation contributed to the transformation of poetic concepts, forming a new beginning.

To have new development, the epitomised Tang poetry has to constantly draw fresh blood from the language of life. Bai Juyi's poems strive to be simple and popular, understandable for any old lady, which is precisely the fine tradition of the Tang poetry seeking profundity out of simplicity and natural revelation. After Yu Xin, an epitomised writer in the Southern and Northern Dynasties, the Tang poetry exhibited a new world with a profound and simple poetic language. As a master of poetic language, Du Fu seems to be aware of another requirement of profundity out of simplicity in his epitomisation; thus his poems have very colloquial lines even though his general style is mature and concise, as in "As the geese are yellow like wine, / Drinking wine, I love the new geese" ("Geese in Front of the Boat"), and "Fish swimming out in the drizzle, / Swallows fly slantly in the breeze" ("Two Poems Expressing Feelings at a Waterside Hall"). The two Chinese characters "燕子[yànzǐ] (swallow)" seem very common in later *ci* poems. However, they were rarely seen in past poems. Instead, only the first Chinese character "燕[yàn] (swallow)" was used. In Du's poems, more than ten lines used the two Chinese characters meaning the "swallow", as in "The fishermen drifted on the boat for two nights; / The swallows in clear autumn were flying around" ("Eight Poems of Autumn Expression"), and "Though familiar with my thatched cottage small and low, / Swallows from the river still used to visit it" ("Nine Quatrains of Casual Thoughts"). As for other two-character Chinese words ending with "儿[ér] (a sound added to syllable(s) in spoken Mandarin Chinese)" such as "鹅儿[éér] (goose)" and "鱼儿 [yúér] (fish)", they are the forerunners in the development of ancient vernacular Chinese. This trend is more common in *ci* poems like "正莺儿啼; 燕儿舞, 蝶儿忙[zhèng yīngér tí; yànér wǔ, diéér máng] (The orioles are singing, the swallows dancing and the butterflies flying)" (Qin Guan: "Burning Incense"). Another example is "I remember spring came to my garden afar", "They were laughed at by plum blossoms every year", and "Tipsy, I will sing the song 'Fisherman Proud'" (Qin Guan: "Fisherman Proud"). Obviously, many lines are colloquial in this short *ci* poem. Moreover, Qin Guan is not the only *ci* poet writing in this way. *Ci* poems are gaining a new power of expression by constantly drawing fresh blood from spoken language. The era in which Bai Juyi lived required a new breakthrough in poetic language, so the emerging *ci* poetry became a breakthrough. This means that the peak of poetry creation would eventually turn from poetry to *ci* poems. Bai Juyi's sensitivity and vision were also displayed here as he straightforwardly welcomed this development. Relatively speaking, the poetic school of Han and Meng took a difficult road and added unique splendour to the poetry circle in terms of poetic arts. However, Li He, the most successful poet of this school, notes in his "Song at the Riverview Pavilion":

> The water by the pavilion flows to Jiangling.
> The autumn wind in the carp month makes lotuses old.
> At dawn, I dress up; hairpins talk to the south wind:
> "It only costs her husband one day to sail back".
> ...
> Drinking newly brewed wine, I feel feeble and weak.
> Acres of waterlilies in the South Lake turn white.
> I'm missing my dearest a thousand *li* away,
> When Little Jade opens the screen for mountain colours.

Doesn't it have a similar sentiment to "Dressing up, I lean on the Riverview Pavilion alone" in a *ci* poem? Following Li He's poetic style is the further development of Li Shangyin and Wen Tingyun, while Li Shangyin's large number of love poems are unique in the Tang poetry. Moreover, Wen Tingyun became the chief *ci* poet of the "Collection among Flowers", and his status in *ci* poetry is far greater than that in poetry. This shows that no matter how tortuous the road is, it will eventually go to the same place via different routes. Profundity and simplicity were combined and developed towards *ci* poems together. The decline of the orthodox literature and the rise of civic literature were inevitable as general trends. Bai Juyi and Liu Yuxi took the first steps forward as in Bai Juyi's "Willow Branches":

> Each household is singing "Green Waist" and "Water Tune";
> "White Snow" and "Plum Blossoms" are played everywhere.
> Never be troubled by those old and ancient songs,
> But listen to the newly composed "Willow Branches".

Similarly, "Bamboo Branches" notes:

> The cold mist is low at the mouth of the Qutang Gorge;
> The moon on the White Emperor Wall is facing west.
> When the sound of "Bamboo Branches" is sadly sung,
> Cold apes and dark birds can't help crying for a while.

Moreover, Liu Yuxi's "Bamboo Branches" muses:

> By green willows and flat river water,
> I heard you singing songs on the river.

Sunrise in the East while rain in the West,
Is it mercy or at the mercy of Heaven!

They are consciously pursuing new developments rather than accidentally. Bai Juyi's "Missing the River South" exclaims:

The River South is fair,
The scenery familiar.
The sunrise makes the river flowers redder than fire.
In spring the river water is green as orchid leaves.
How to stop missing the River South?
Liu Yuxi's "Missing the River South" sighs:
Spring goes away,
Saying goodbye to people in Luocheng.
Weak willows seem like raising their sleeves in the wind.
Orchid clusters with dewdrops are like shedding tears.
She is sitting alone with knitted brows.

Another example is Bai Juyi's "Always in Yearning" that opens up a new world for poetic language:

The Bian River flows,
The Si River flows,
To the ancient ford in Melon County.
Mount Wu is dotted with sorrow.
Thoughts are lingering,
Regrets are lingering,
They would not stop until you come back home.
I lean by a moonlit tall house.

In the Song Dynasty, *ci* poetry developed further and separated from the orthodox poetry. For example, Ouyang Xiu and other poets are quite different in writing poetry and *ci* poems. Apart from the differences in content, they have more language differences. Poetry at this time still follows the traditional poetic language, travelling farther and farther from the language of life, thus losing vitality more and more. *Ci* poetry, however, gained new vitality in the language of life, thus representing the new direction of poetry development. After the Southern Song Dynasty (1127–1280), expressions close to the four- or six-character parallel prose gradually appeared in the slow tune, and *ci* poems embarked on the road of elegance. Therefore, except for a small number of bold and unrestrained works, *ci* poetry gradually ended its life in the Southern Song Dynasty. Then, *ci* poetry had to develop into *sanqu* (or casual melodies). The problems here are closely related to the development of poetic language so that we can understand the full significance of Bai Juyi's efforts for colloquialism in the poetic language.

In a word, the Mid-Tang poetry circle began to have a historical turn, which is the ending of the orthodox literature and the rising of civic literature. Poetry had new changes not only in contents but in language. Besides a large number of political satirical poems, Bai Juyi, on the one hand, reflected citizens' common interest in stories and completed eternal masterpieces of narrative poems in a profound and simple language in his "Song of Everlasting Regret" and "The *Pipa* Tune", which became important themes in later traditional operas. On the other hand, he vigorously promoted the development of *ci* poems, holding an indispensable position in this great transitional trend. The Mid-Tang is a turning point in the Tang Dynasty, and the Dali period is only its beginning. The entire Mid-Tang poetry circle showed dramatic changes and diversified schools. It was not until the Late Tang that this turning tide became calm, and the whole trend moved from the traditional wave to another wave. Bai Juyi is the most comprehensive representative in this process, and most directly welcomes this historical change in literature, which marks the end of the High Tang.

The report was released in Qingdao in the summer of 1957 and revised,
9 September 1985

2 The poet Li Bai

The realistic significance of Li Bai's poetry

I On the peak of the era

The Tang Dynasty marks the peak in the development of classical Chinese poetry, and also the most glorious and most desirable era of the Chinese nationality in ancient times. Standing on the peak of the era, the greatest poets singing about the spirits and destinies of the whole nationality are undoubtedly Li Bai and Du Fu, although they are 11 years apart in age and are active in different times. Li Bai is active mostly before the An Shi Rebellion,[1] while Du Fu is after it, but they share the same breath and destiny with the Tang Dynasty. The An Shi Rebellion, the most important boundary marker of the Tang Dynasty, divides the dynasty into two completely different periods: the way up and the way down. The two superstars in the realm of poetry are standing side by side on the summit of the era, but in different moods. Li Bai has just walked up to the peak, looking around the vast land and feeling exalted, as expressed in his poetic line "Almost near the sky to touch the bright moon",[2] while the other poet Du Fu has seen the lurking signs on the downhill road. Even though he feels delightful on the peak, he is awaited by the unhappy future. When he goes up to the peak, he seems to have only noticed the sky, so he cannot bear to leave, as shown in his poetic lines "The pen of colours has been aspiring, / Old and grey, bending in sadness, I sing".[3] The two superstars in the country of poetry stand on the summit of the time side by side, facing the reality of two stages in different moods.

---

1 The rebellion took place from 16 December 755 to 17 February 763. Also known as the An Lushan Rebellion, it resulted in a huge loss of life and large-scale destruction, and thus weakened the Tang Dynasty.
2 "Farewell to My Uncle Collator Yun at Pavilion Xie Tiao in Xuanzhou". (In this chapter, all poems are by Li Bai, unless otherwise stated.)
3 Du Fu. "Eight Poems of Autumn Expression" No. 8.

II The realistic significance of Li Bai's poetry

The era of Li Bai is not only the highest peak in the Tang Dynasty, but also the peak of the healthy development of the whole feudal era in China. The subdued class conflicts and rapid development of productivity during this period are reflected in Du Fu's poem "Remembering the Past":

> Look back upon the best Kaiyuan era:
> A small county has ten thousand houses.
> Millets are white, rice is like fat in fluid.
> Filled are public and private warehouses.
> Free of tigery robbers, roads in Cathay are
> People need not choose a day to travel far.
> Silk from Qi and Lu States in carts is ample,
> Men till land; women make silk. They are loyal.

The unprecedented economic and cultural spectacle has brought about boundless promises and outlooks for the future. To describe such a peak, and to tell the longings and pride that people have towards their home country at that time and towards future generations, poetry is the best vehicle in all the arts, and it is later remembered by the following generations as "the High Tang Voice".

After the reunification in the Qin and Han Dynasties, China became a strong nation; thus its people were called "the Han people". Then it was called "the Tang people" because of the unprecedented economic and political development, great cultural contribution to all the other Eastern nationalities, and its great power in national defence. It has been the most advanced nationality in the feudal society in the world, walking towards the peak of prosperity. Her infinite vision brings forth free and boundless imagination, the liberatory spirit of youth, and the love and praise of the home country and local lands. She needs to sing to her heart's content, which is the common desire of the people. Countless poets have tried to satisfy people's desire, and reigning supreme among them is Li Bai.

Li Bai is undoubtedly a prominent figure among all poets. His prominence originates first in his strong longing for liberation, which is reflected in his thoughts and feelings about society. At that time, the North-South split was ended, the shackles of the noble family conception derived from the Six Dynasties were also ended, and there emerged a large number of land-holding peasants and city craftsmen who later became the townspeople, which is the voice of the era. Li Bai sets the trend of the era like a pioneer surfing on the top of overwhelming waves. His innocence is an utter innocence from his patriotic heart; his enthusiasm is an unrestrainable force. He says:

> The Yellow River falls from the Heaven,
> Rushing into the sea with no return![4]

---

4 "Bringing in the Wine".

Every man who has read such a poem will be affected by the power of breaking through all restraints. Some people say that once they read such lines, they will feel the great verve of mountains and rivers of the country, which is more typically sung out only in the artistic peak of the era, and Li Bai is the typical singer. As for the following lines,

> The road is as bright as the sky,
> But I cannot reach out that high!⁵

Every repressed man will be encouraged to cast out the injustice that lies in his heart. He says:

> The strong wind blows my heart west till
> It hangs on a tree in Xianyang.⁶

No poet in history has ever written such innocent and vivid lines, but the innocence really makes his feelings more authentic. He objects to the flowery style in the Six Dynasties, because it is decorative and superficial. The reason why he has said that "Starting from the Jian'an era, / People cherish not the flowery"⁷ is that he needs the authentic and resolute liberating force as shown in the lines "How to have the skills of Chu master? / In a swing, to be an axe master?"⁸ At this point, Li Bai, with Chen Zi'ang, has successively made the same request, which is the essence of the Tang poetry. In practice, he is more forceful and remarkable in achieving this goal and becomes the key poet in the Tang poetry. Thus, in his "Foreword to the *Cottage Collection*", Li Yangbing (?–?) states:

> The Chamberlain Lu Cangyong once said that Imperial Advisor Chen (also Chen Zi'ang) overpowered the decadent trend, and the literary features of the country were suddenly changed. While the poetic forms in the Tang Dynasty still have the court style of the Liang and Chen Dynasties, they are drastically changed because you completely swept it away. Collections of today and the past are not popular, but your writings are as powerful in the universe as Nature'.

The appearance of Li Bai has helped the Tang poetry develop to its peak.

The era of Li Bai witnesses such a reality of increasing development, which is completely in accordance with people's wishes and interests. People take pride in the singing of such wishes and interests to put forward more ideal requirements, to encourage more abundant strength, and to create richer and more vivid images. It is because of this pride that the Chinese nationality has been full of confidence in life and creation for thousands of

---

5 "The Roads are Hard" No. 2.
6 "Seeing off Wei the Eighth in Jinxiang to Xijing the West Capital".
7 "Ancient Style" No. 1.
8 "Ancient Style" No. 35.

years without any interruption or pause, which makes it the greatest miracle among ancient kingdoms in the world. It is because of this pride that we can better understand and better love our history and culture, which endows it with the most realistic significance. Li Bai is the best in accomplishing the mission of this era. Without him, our evaluation of the peak in the Tang poetry would be lower. Without him, the peak of the Tang poetry would also be lowered. This is the realistic significance of Li Bai's poetry.

III People's pride in Li Bai's romantic spirit

Li Bai's poetic temperament is romantic. This romance means a higher liberation, with an overwhelming force that inspires more enthusiasm, and this is the positive and optimistic romanticism. He says: "Heaven-made talents, we weren't made in vain. / A thousand gold coins spent, more we will gain!"[9] The heroic words from a commoner reflect the existence of human liberation in reality, which is the pride of the era. In the historical records of *Brief Notes on Twenty-Two Histories*, "there are just a few good and able men elected from commoners in the Han Dynasty". It is more eye-catching if we compare it with the Western Han society described in Dongfang Shuo's (154–93 BCE) *Answer to a Guest's Enquiry*, which states:

> This is not the case now as the emperor is virtuous ... What is the difference between the good and the bad? ... Honor him, he is to be a general; humiliate him, a prisoner; support him, he is to be above the blue sky; suppress him, under the deep spring; use him, he is to be a tiger; disuse him, a rat! ... If the strategists Su Qin and Zhang Yi were born with me in the world of today, they would not be elected as guards. How could they expect to be a Chamberlain?

This is where the Western Han Dynasty is different from the Tang Dynasty, even though both of them are unified feudal empires. The former has raised a rhetorical question, "What is the difference between the good and the bad?" while the latter makes people believe that "Heaven-made talents, we weren't made in vain". The former has only allowed the noble literature like *fu* in the Han Dynasty serving the royal court to dominate the literary circle, while the latter can nurture the Tang poetry, the singing of ordinary people. Certainly, the talents' liberation in feudal society always has a certain limit; thus, in the above poetic lines, Li Bai confidently put forward a higher aspiration for and demand to the era. He also writes:

> Cut water with a sword, it faster flows.
> Drink wine to ease sorrow, it deeper grows![10]

---

9 "Bringing in the Wine".
10 "Farewell to My Uncle Collator Yun at Pavilion Xie Tiao in Xuanzhou".

King Zhao's white bones are tangled by weeds that creep.
The Gold Terrace for talents none will sweep![11]

Similar to Chen Zi'ang's "Song of Mounting the Youzhou Terrace" and "King Zhao of the Yan", these lines are spirited songs overlooking the past millennium, and a powerful yet romantic exclamation in response to the unsatisfactory circumstances. They protest against the feudal rulers, impose a higher demand on the era, and transform the contradictions of life into a romantic and passionate spectacle. They always inspire people, making people's heart beat more quickly and their blood flow much faster, more powerfully and more excitedly. Even Yuan Zhen who sings highly of Du Fu much more than Li Bai has to admit Li Bai's "romance and passion", which definitely include his passion for wine. Du Fu has also written about the wine that "In broad day we drink hard and loudly sing. / We'll return to our native place in spring".[12] This poem is the most optimistic one in Du Fu's lifetime that reflects the essence of the Tang Dynasty.

Li Bai's "Answers to the Tibetans" has become "Li Bai Wrote in Drunkenness to Frighten the Tibetans" in the form of the novel. Why did he write in drunkenness? It is aimed to make Li Bai more vivid, more powerful, and more full of "romance and passion". The Tang people's drinking of wine is healthy and unrestrained, as the wine is a common thing in people's daily life from ancient times, but it has a different connotation in different eras. The drinking atmosphere of the Wei and Jin Dynasties is like that of the middle-aged. Even though the wine is a stimulant, it cannot inspire more enthusiasm in life; thus, there is no more rich imagination in the wine at that time. People in the Wei and Jin write poetry while drinking wine, but the wine and poetry are two different things. The wine is usually a concept in poem titles, or simply written in poems. It is generally from the Tang people that the wine is thoroughly integrated in the poetic expressions and loudly celebrated in people's singing. The unrestraint of the youth's drinking as shown in "The New Home wine worth ten thousand is so mellow, / Enticing young roaming swordsmen in Xianyang town"[13] and "The grape wine glows in luminous jade cups. / Drink! But the *pipa* calls horseback lineups"[14] is lively, realistic, and passionate. It is on this basis that Li Bai has exaggerated and typified the wine and integrated it into the singing of "A hundred poems for a barrel of wine". In the poetic lines such as "Treasure not jade-fine food with bell-drum tune",[15] "We must drink together three hundred cups",[16] and "Drunken for a

---

11 "The Roads are Hard" No. 2.
12 Du Fu. "On the Army's Recapturing of Henan and Hebei".
13 Wang Wei. "Song of the Youth".
14 Wang Han. "Lyrics at Liangzhou".
15 "Bringing in the Wine".
16 "Song of Xiangyang".

whole month, belittling kings",[17] he emphasises the drinking of wine, but the essence is the singing of "belittling kings". Later, in "Partridge Heaven", Zhu Dunru (1081–1159) sings that "Ten thousand poems, / Thousands of vessels, / My eyes are never on vassals". These lines were widely known in the feudal era, because they weakened the power of the ruling class, increased the power of opposition, and became the pride of the people. People are fond of Li Bai's character and dramatism, and the wine is his percussion accompaniment, although the percussion was not without a certain impurity in ancient times, or even negative elements. However, the wine, the impurity, or even the negative elements have not drowned Li Bai. On the contrary, he increased the worth of wine as the accompaniment. The famous brand of "Taibai Legacy" is seen not only in wine bars, but in remote villages. People are fond of Li Bai as well as of his wine. Of course, the wine should not necessarily be advocated now, nor should it at that time. The idea here is that the wine drinking, as a small part of life, can be healthy, or decadent, while Li Bai's drinking is healthy, unrestrained and liberating, rather than ailing and decadent. Instead of escaping from reality, he bravely challenges the contradictions of reality. In "Song of Resting Crows", he writes:

When the crows rest on the Terrace Gushu,
Fair Xishi gets drunk in the palace of Wu.
Wu songs and Chu dances are on for fun;
The gray mountain is hiding half a sun.
How the silver arrow times gold clock water
Till the autumn moon sinks into the river!
The East grows bright; rapture returns never!

This is what He Zhizhang called a work that "makes ghosts cry".[18] Li Bai presented before our eyes the realistic contradiction between indulgence and sobriety. The language of the poem is vivid, and the traditional meaning is ironic, but in this contradiction, it presents very bright and distinct images. That is why it "makes ghosts cry". In reality, there is always a battle between the light and the darkness, which determines the destiny of mankind. Li Bai is loudly singing out such a destiny. Thus, his romantic spirit is enthusiastic, positive, and in accordance with the real life. This is the people's singing.

17 "Remembering the Past Travels and Sending to Military Councillor Yuan in Qiaojun".
18 Fan Chuanzheng's (?–?) "Foreword to the New Tombstone of Monsieur Li, Left Imperial Advisor and *Hanli* Scholar of the Tang" is very believable. According to Yin Fan's (?–?) *Anthology of Poems: Spirit of Mountains and Rivers*, it is collected as a masterpiece in the Kaiyuan and Tianbao eras. As "Crows Crying at Night" is not in the anthology, the masterpiece must be "Song of Resting Crows". Later, in *Stories in Poems*, Meng Qi noted below "Song of Resting Crows" that "Others say that this poem is written as 'Crows Crying at Night', but it is probably a mistake".

Li Bai's thoughts and struggles

I Li Bai's sense as a commoner

Li Bai is a commoner in his lifetime. What does this mean?[19] This is a concrete manifestation of the political struggles in the feudal society. In a confrontational society, struggles always exist. People are singing of their wishes for happiness, pursuing free lives, yearning for the appointment of talents, and are excited with the country's prosperity. Such powers of light will be arrayed against the essence of darkness in the ruling class. They become a kind of pressure pushing forward the country's social development, which is a form of struggle under circumstances of moderate contradiction, reflected as a more liberating sentiment of the people in victory and an inherent and insatiable exalted temperament. It is one of the two forms of the same struggle in different circumstances, while the other is the exposure of darkness in intensified contradictions.

When various contradictions rooted in economic basis in society are reflected in political struggles, their struggles are unified as the sense of a commoner in the feudal society. The commoner originally refers to the civilians in ancient times. In *Historical Records*, Sima Qian (c. 145–86 BCE) puts emphasis on many "chivalrous commoners", who are swordsmen from the common people. As *Debate on the Monopoly of Salt and Iron* states, "In ancient times only outstanding or old civilians wear silk clothes, while the rest wear common hemp clothes, so they are called the commoners". In "The Song of Feelings on Leaving for Fengxian County", Du Fu writes, "Those bathing are nobles with long-tassels; / Gourmets are not in short, coarse cloth". "Short coarse cloth" is usually worn by the commoners in opposition to the nobles. Thus, in "Fables", Wang Wei says that "The chariots and crowns are for nobles, / Who won't talk with a commoner". Here a commoner is just a poor scholar, belonging to the lower and middle class in society. In light of their origins and interests, they want to have access to the ruling class, and acquire a part of the political status from the noble, rich, royal, and powerful families, so as to achieve liberal politics in feudal times, which are the democratic elements of the time.

According to Karl Marx, "Politics is an intensive manifestation of economics"; thus, it is through such politics that the excessive economic monopoly and exploitation of the ruling class is limited, to ensure the development of productive forces, the accumulation of wealth, and the liberation of society. This is in line with the interests of the common people, and supported by them. If the ruling class accepts such political requirements, it will get the support of the people and have the strength, and the society

---

19 Cheng Dachang's (1123–1195) *Records of Historic Sites*, and Ma Duanlin's (1254–1323) *Survey of Literature* state that Li Bai has not taken any official position. Details can be found in the section "Li Bai's Entry into *Hanlin* as a Commoner".

will be flourishing; if not, it will not get the support of the people and have no strength and the society will be declining. These are historical facts. We should say that the liberal politics is not kindly bestowed by the ruling class, but by the fruits of victory out of people's struggles, without which the liberal politics of more than 100 years from the Early Tang to the High Tang is unthinkable. Any common person who wants to participate in politics has to be an intellectual, so the commoner, in the traditional sense, refers to the intellectuals with political ambitions in the lower and middle class. Their political capital is their opposition status against the noble and powerful class, thus winning the support of the common people. Whether they hold official positions or not, they are always proud of themselves as commoners, which is acclaimed as the backbone or character by people in the feudal society, and the means by which they can meet the kings and nobles as equals. Thus, Cen Sen (c. 715–70) says in a poem that "Come hither as a commoner, / Go away as a commoner".[20] Du Fu writes: "In Duling a commoner good / Grows old, and his mind turns stupid. / How foolish he is! As he would / be like ministers Ji and Qi".[21] In their poems, they are proud of their identity by introducing themselves as commoners.

Of course, military struggles also exist besides political struggles. The peasant uprising at the end of the Sui Dynasty is a determinate factor distinguishing the Tang Dynasty from the Sui Dynasty regarding the political landscape. When the Emperor Wen of Sui (541–604) reunified the states and kingdoms, the situation, in fact, was not far off from that occurred in the Early Tang, except for the peasant uprising as a means of military struggle, which is the highest form of political struggles, but does not often appear. When it is not the time to change the regime, the practical significance of political struggles is to require liberal politics, where the pride as a commoner naturally has a justification.

Therefore, besides the direct struggles of the peasants, the struggles of the commoners often manifest the major contradictions in the feudal society. If the contradiction is well dealt with, the feudal society will be progressive; if not, it will be at a standstill. Here, "well dealt with" means that the progressive party in the contradiction wins out, which is shown in the commoners' victory in the contradiction. In the Tang Dynasty, it is the commoners who have continued the democratic struggles and set themselves on the road to victory after another peasant uprising. At that time, it is economically reflected in the "Equal-Field System", as shown in "Swallows once nested in noble Wang and Xie / Families in commoners' homes reappear".[22] It is also politically reflected in the appointment of imperial censors in the "Prosperity of Zhenguan", and the emphasis on commoners in the "Zhongnan

20 Cen Shen. "Written on the Guancheng Gate for Fun".
21 Du Fu. "500 Chinese Characters of Feelings in my Trip from Fengxian County to the Capital".
22 Liu Yuxi. "Black Clothes Lane".

Shortcut to High Offices". The "Biography of Lu Cangyong" in the *New Tang Book* records the story as follows:

> When Sima Chengzhen once summoned by the Emperor was going back to mountains, Cangyong pointed at the Zhongnan mountains and said, 'there are many beautiful scenic spots in the mountains'. Chengzhen slowly replied, 'In my opinion, it is only a shortcut to high offices.'

(Chengzhen is a good friend of Li Bai, who has written "*Fu* on the Big Bird Dapeng" for him.) What Chengzhen said is on the one hand a satire of those fake commoners, criticising them that they just wanted to climb to higher offices by being hermits in Zhongnan; on the other, it indicates the commoners' political status out of office at that time. If the commoners do not have a high reputation, no one in society will fake them. Of course, fake commoners should be criticised, and it is necessary to distinguish the real from the fake. Almost every time when Li Bai mentioned politics, he also mentioned going back to mountains, which shows a real commoner's attitude of not being unwilling to leave his official post. In light of his fame, his circle of friends, and Emperor Tang Xuanzong's courtesy, he would absolutely have a high position and handsome rewards if he compromised a little with the ruling class. However, Li Bai is finally a commoner in his lifetime, which makes him such a typically prominent figure in the struggles.

The political activities in the Tang Dynasty may be divided into three different types: the first type is related to the royal and noble families, who are certainly important; the second is through the more civilian imperial examination system, in which a successful candidate, *Jinshi*, moves up slowly from the low and middle offices; the third is concerned with the commoners. They are not from the royal and noble families, nor are they willing to move up slowly and humbly because it is like joining in the training class of the ruling class and losing the commoner's spirit when they finally move up. Thus, a commoner is either a minister if successful, or a peasant if unsuccessful. They have a more vivid sense of a commoner and clearer idea of their political attitude than those intellectuals moving up slowly through the imperial examinations. They are identified as politicians out of office. In their political activities, they have to make friends, but to a certain extent, they are "neither humble nor offensive"[23] as Li Bai has boasted. This is the commoner's pride. Li Bai says of himself that

> I have the talents to govern and benefit people, with the characters of the famous hermits Chaofu and Xu You. My writings can change the customs, and my studies explore into Heaven as well as human beings.

---

23 "A Complaint to Privy Treasurer Meng on Behalf of Shoushan".

Without killing a single person, I have the ability to surrender the four oceans of states and kingdoms.[24]

On the one hand, being "neither humble nor offensive" shows that he is not humble to the ruling class; on the other, he boasts about his "ability to surrender the four oceans" to urge the ruling class to let him participate in politics. Li Bai repeatedly compares himself to the hermits Chaofu and Xu You, because the ancient tribe chief Yao would hand over the leadership to them, even though they are commoners. Li Bai certainly would not ask Emperor Xuanzong to hand over the emperorship to him, which is too unrealistic. However, he makes no secret of asking Xuanzong to really let him participate in state affairs. He says, "I am willing to assist in governing the empire, making it peaceful and united with all the seas and counties".[25] He also says, "It's shameful to succeed with help, / But noble to have a blueprint".[26] That is, he wants to participate in making state policies truly related to the people. In fact, even though Li Bai cannot be so honoured like Chaofu and Xu You, Emperor Xuanzong finally invited him to the capital Chang'an as a distinguished guest. However, Li Bai soon became unsatisfied with the invitation as the ruling class is not actually generous. He says, "The still straight pine and cypress / aren't like the pretty peach and plum",[27] and he also says, "Why lower my head and bend to serve the nobles in power?"[28] He is sober about his purpose of going to Chang'an, that is, "to realise the ideals like ministers Guan Zhong and Yan Ying, to design in the ways of kings and emperors",[29] "to support the economic development",[30] "to provide consultations on the relief policy",[31] and "to advise on the rise and fall".[32] But the ruling class requires him to be an ornament instead ("like the pretty peach and plum"), and to flatter the ruling class ("bend to serve the nobles in power"), which shows the contradiction between the commoners and the ruling class. Li Bai's "fame in the universe" and "ability to surrender the four oceans" make Xuanzong "lower the royal carriage and welcome on foot".[33] Xuanzong also says, "I know that you are a commoner. If you do not have great accomplishments in Taoism, how can I respect you so much?"[34] This typically represents the commoner's victory. But in the end,

---

24 "A Self-Written Recommendation on Behalf of Mid-Inspector Song".
25 "A Complaint to Privy Treasurer Meng on Behalf of Shoushan".
26 "To Prime Minister Zhang Gao".
27 "Ancient Style" No. 12.
28 "A Parting Song on Travelling in Dream in the Tianmu Mountain".
29 "A Complaint to Privy Treasurer Meng on Behalf of Shoushan".
30 "A Poem on my Feelings to my Brother Cui Shufeng, Privy Treasurer of Chang'an after Reading *The Biography of Zhuge, Marquis Wu*".
31 "To Elder Wang in the City Ye".
32 "Expressing Feeling to Imperial Secretary Cai Xiong".
33 "A Self-Written Recommendation on Behalf of Mid-Inspector Song".
34 Li Yangbing. "Foreword to the *Cottage Collection*".

Li Bai serves "without killing a single person", which typically represents the essence of the contradictions and struggles between the commoners and the ruling class. These are unified in Li Bai's sense as a commoner.

As Li Bai's "Complaint of a Poor Girl" points out, "When you are a commoner, / You work hard with me. / Once an official as Wulang, / You go for Handan girls". Here he satirises those who forget their origin as commoners once they become officials. The reason why Li Bai remains a commoner all his life is that he is never willing to forget that he is a commoner. In "An Answer to an Old Man by the Wen River when Travelling in the Eastern Lu in the Fifth Month", he writes:

> A letter on a single arrow,
> Can help conquer City Liao.
> But I won't accept awards,
> Ashamed to be a layman.

Why doesn't he accept awards? Because only in this way can he maintain the quality of a commoner, and he will not be ashamed to be a commoner. In "Ancient Style" No. 47, he writes:

> The peach blossoms in the east park,
> Are praising in smiles the white sun.
> Brought up by chance by the east wind,
> They are endowed with sunny traits.
> ...
> How do they know south mountain pines
> Are lonely but free of control.

It is this feeling that makes him proud of himself in face of the ruling class. He says, "The greatness of virtue is not determined by status".[35] This pride is the pride of the people. It is because of this common pride that people are willing to spread his story of ordering the emperor-favoured eunuch Gao Lishi to take off his boots, even though it might only be a tale. Moreover, Li Bai's pride often makes him look down upon the money that the ruling class are proud of. He says, "Why do you think I won't pay enough money?",[36] "Moved by your loyalty dearer than gold!",[37] "Gold was out of my hand to seek pleasure. / Now I'm poor as I used up my treasure",[38] and "Return good for good, as is told. / So belittle thousands of coins gold".[39] Thus, he

---

35 "An Inscription of Missing and Praising the Resigned Governor Han of Wuchang".
36 "Bringing in the Wine".
37 "Remembering the Past Travels and Sending to Military Councillor Yuan in Qiaojun".
38 "To my Nephew Gao Zhen after Drunkenness".
39 "A Poem on my Feelings in Huaiyang".

naturally shouts out the famous line "The breeze fresh and moon bright need no money to buy",[40] which is from the bottom of a commoner's heart.

Li Bai's sense as a commoner is first manifested in the fact that he is well aware of his identity as a commoner. He says, "(Li) Bai, a man in the wild",[41] and "Bai, a commoner from the west of Gansu, is drifting in Chu and Han".[42] He also says, "Throw away chopsticks, take off clothes / For wine and get drunk in the North Hall. / Like a commoner from Dantu, / He is boundlessly generous".[43] Such a commoner is indispensable for liberal politics. He says, "As you can honour the lowest corporals, / The whole world will wait to see good omens".[44] (The *Book of Rites* states: "A corporal's allowance can support nine people". "The first-class peasant can support nine people, the second-class eight, the third-class six, and the lowest-class five. The allowance of a commoner holding an official post follows the same ranking. A corporal governed by a vassal is considered a first-class peasant, and the former's allowance is equal to the latter's farming".) Here "the lowest corporal" refers to the intellectual similar to "a commoner" or "a first-class peasant". Here Li Bai explained his ideal of politics as a commoner, or his ideal of politics for the ordinary people.

However, since Li Bai is conscious of his identity as a commoner, he is inevitably aware of his contradictions with the ruling class. At that time, the Tang society is in rapid economic development, and the civic class has begun to evolve and become quite active. Li Bai is proud of being a commoner, and by chance he was born in a merchant's family; thus, he is the most active and discernible in his ideology as a commoner. He is well aware that his cooperation with the ruling class will not last long because it seems that the contradictions can never be resolved. He says, "Enjoy themselves day and night, / Say they can live a thousand years. / If they don't leave after success, / Since ancient times misfortune falls".[45] "I have observed elites since ancient times. / If left not after success, they were killed. / Zixu's ashes were cast in the Wu River, / Qu Yuan drowned himself in the Xiang River".[46] He also says, "If success, fame, wealth, nobleness always glow, / The Han River would rather Northwest flow".[47] However, commoners cannot take the place of the ruling class, and it is obvious that they cannot cooperate for a long time. Such a contradiction is reflected in his negative view that all things are dreams, as shown in:

40 "Song of Xiangyang".
41 "A Letter to Adjutant Pei in Anzhou".
42 "A Letter to the Vice Governor Han of Jingzhou".
43 "To Security Officer Zhang in a Rainy Day in Princess Yuzhen's Imperial Palace".
44 "On Qian Shaoyang to Censor Pan".
45 "Ancient Style" No. 18.
46 "Ancient Thoughts".
47 "Chanting on the River".

Having fun in life is also the case,
From ancients all are east-flowing water.
Bidding farewell, when can you return here?
Let me put among green cliffs the white deer,
And ride it to visit mountains of grace.
Why lower my head and bend to serve the nobles in power?
That makes me lose the pleasure I treasure!"[48]

This negative element is actually the projection of the dark side of feudal times in Li Bai's poetry. For him, behind the seemingly negative "all are east-flowing water" is the commoners' opposition against the ruling class; thus, it is finally shown in the famous, powerful line "Why lower my head and bend to serve the nobles in power?"

Moreover, if we make a comprehensive survey on Li Bai's enthusiasm in politics throughout his life, his retirement after winning merits is only superficial, in light of what he said in his later years, "All my life I'd work for the Crown, / In hundred ages vie for fame. / These ambitions can't be realised, / How sad I cannot repeat it".[49] On the one hand, it shows his identity as a commoner not indulged in fame and official position; on the other, it mentions the necessary precaution in cooperation with the ruling class. "To Secretary Wei Zichun" contains such lines as:

There is Zheng Zizhen from Gukou
Who is farming in person in rocks.
He's renowned in the capital,
With great reputation in the world.
But this man won't be elected,
Saying that he would lie at ease.
Without a mind to rescue people,
What is the use of being moral?

It is shown that the negative "farming in person in rocks" is actually a positive foundation to politics, a political capital to materialise "the mind of rescuing people". Li Bai once writes in "A Self-Written Recommendation on Behalf of Mid-Inspector Song" that "Zizhen from Gukou was famous in the capital; the Emperor heard of him and was happy to summon him to the royal palace".[50] Obviously, this is Li Bai's practical approach. He repeatedly compares himself to Zhuge Liang (181–234) cultivating in person in Nanyang. He says, "I'm also a man among grass, / with affection for rescuing

---

48 "A Parting Song on Travelling in Dream in the Tianmu Mountain".
49 "To Prime Minister Zhang Gao".
50 "A Self-Written Recommendation on Behalf of Mid-Inspector Song".

things".[51] "I'm also a man from Nanyang, / Often warbling sadly 'Liangfu Yin'".[52] He thinks that it is useless to compromise with the ruling class to engage in politics, as shown in "Serve the other with your beauty, / How long can you be together?"[53] Instead, he believes that they should rely on the struggles as opposition, as shown in "Ancient Style" No. 15:

> Pearls and jade are used to buy fun,
> But husks and chaff to feed genius.
> That's why the yellow crane flies up
> And wanders a thousand *li* away.

"The yellow crane flies up" alludes to Tian Rao's story in the *Unofficial Biographies with Poems by Han Ying*, that is, only when out of power and "famous in the capital", a commoner can manifest his opposition status, forcing the ruling class to extend him courteous reception. If not, the ruling class will use "husks and chaff to feed genius", and never give the commoners opportunities to engage in politics. This series of oppositional political activities in feudal society is well shown in Li Bai's "A Letter to Security Chief Jia" and "Bai will not show any traces of opposition, and is ashamed of being profound or remote ... Why do I market myself in faraway places only for fame?" It shows that Li Bai is well aware of the secret because he is "Famous in the capital ... the Emperor was happy to summon him to the royal" is the specific result of the "traces of opposition". He says, "Take a post to be equal friends with the nobles, flee away from a post to overlook the most-famous hermits Chaofu and Xu You".[54] However, he would "overlook Chaofu and Xu You" to "be equal friends with the nobles" in his heart. Of course, even though Li Bai has the spirit as a commoner to "be equal friends with the nobles", he must leave his political stage and go back to his foundation as a commoner, as he predicted. He says, "Hope not a cloud-high post in the North Court, / I would retreat in Mount East, white-haired".[55] Here Li Bai takes an initiative and makes preparations for a comeback. He says, "Washing my heart to get feelings true, / Washing ears only to buy the fame. / In the end, Mr Xie is with you; / Making people better is your aim".[56] Li Yangbing's "Foreword to the *Cottage Collection*" states, "He (Li Bai) then wandered and got drunk, and became unconscious; he repeatedly sang of Mount East ... the Emperor knew that he would not stay, awarded him with

---

51 "A Poem on my Feelings to my Brother Cui Shufeng, Privy Treasurer of Chang'an after Reading *The Biography of Zhuge, Marquis Wu*".
52 "Departing Minister of War Wang Song".
53 "A Misfortunate Concubine".
54 "Parting Words to the Misty Yuan Yan to Seclude in Xiancheng Mountain in Master Ziyang's Canxia Pavilion in Suizhou at a Winter Night".
55 "Remembering the Past Travels and Sending to Military Councillor Yuan in Qiaojun".
56 "Seeing off Pei Tunan the 18th".

gold and allowed him to go back". This is how he took the initiative. As the "Song of the Liangyuan Garden" goes,

> Thinking of the past, I shed tears on clothes, / Having bought wine with gold, I won't go back. / I gamble with Five-White and Six-Bet on end; / We bet and drink in teams to kill our time. / We sing and sing, our thoughts are far. / We sleep, get up like Xie'an in Mount East, / But it isn't too late to rescue people.

This is about his preparation for a comeback.

Since Li Bai thinks that for a commoner, being in office is temporary, while being out of office is normal, which is the tradition from ancient times; thus, he boasts of being out of office as a holy and noble foundation for mounting opposition. This tradition began from the first poet Qu Yuan, and later a series of works like "The Fisherman", "Divination", "Far-off Journey", and "Summons for a Recluse" were written.[57] Then, Tao Yuanming became a more distinct representative of the opposition. When it comes to Li Bai, he unified the relationship between being in office and being out of office. Every time when he mentioned politics, he also mentioned "boating in the Five Lake" and "playing in Cangzhou" just because they are the backbones of the commoners' engagement in politics, showing that they are more reliable than the royal court.

For the fantasy of ascending to Heaven and travelling like an immortal that developed from Qu Yuan, the tradition of "expressing feelings on earth" in roving immortal poetry (also *youxian* poetry), and the extreme prevalence of Taoism in society at that time, Li Bai did not hesitate to see himself as a "banished immortal". These aspects undoubtedly increased his splendour as a commoner. He repeatedly wrote about the Four White-Haired Hermits, whom he mentioned on several occasions. In poems such as "The Four White-Haired Hermits" and "Passing by the Tombs of the Four White-Haired Hermits", he states that "When I travel to Shangluo city, / I visit immortals secluded".[58] Obviously, the Four White-Haired Hermits are the so-called immortals in his poems. Nevertheless, they are famous for their participation in politics, which is sung of in his poem "Toasts for the Mountainmen". In his later years, Li Bai says in "Feelings Before a Mirror": "The peach and plum have said nothing; / I'll end in the Zhongnan Mounts, white-haired". The "Foreword to the *Cottage Collection*" also records that when Emperor Xuanzong saw Li Bai, he looked like one of the Four White-Haired Hermits. In "A Self-Written Recommendation on Behalf of Mid-Inspector Song", Li Bai points out that "Formerly the Four Hermits were

---

57 It is recorded that "Summons for a Recluse" was written by Liu An (179–22 BCE) under Qu Yuan's influence, while others were written by Qu Yuan himself.
58 "Passing by the Tombs of the Four White-Haired Hermits".

summoned by Emperor Gaozu of Han, but they refused, while they later assisted Emperor Hui. There are destinies in the relationship between emperor and officials. How can this man famous in the universe wither away in such a time? As 'On Biographies of Hermits' states, 'When hermits are promoted, all people will follow him'". This is Li Bai's unification of his roving like an immortal and his participation in politics. "On Qian Shaoyang to Censor Pan" states:

> With eyebrows snow-white as the Four White-Haired,
> He can help the Crown Prince in cordial smiles.
> As you can honour the lowest corporals,
> The whole world will wait to see good omens.

The "Four White-Haired" are "hermits", or "the lowest corporals". All these support the thought of equality when commoners out of office want to "be equal friends with the nobles", and demand for democratic politics in feudal times.

Li Bai's thought represents the thought of commoners struggling on the road to victory. It reflects the political outlook of the High Tang, and the budding thoughts of the civic class. A kind of liberation that demands equality and freedom has become his pride and belief. Some people say that Li Bai is dominated by Taoist thought, which is biased. Li Bai is certainly influenced by Taoism, just like Qu Yuan at his time. Qu Yuan, living in the state where Laozi and Zhuangzi were born, created roving immortal poetry. Works such as "Divination", "The Fisherman", "Grieving at the Eddying Wind", and "Far-off Journey" induced from Qu Yuan are greatly influenced by Taoism; however, we cannot say that Qu Yuan is dominated by the Taoist thought. In the Tang Dynasty when Taoism prevails, Li Bai is naturally influenced by Taoism. However, he says, "With bottles, never say you are poor. / Take the wine to meet your neighbours. / Immortals are really untrue, / Not as true as in drunkenness".[59] He also says, "Since virtuous saints also drink wine, / Why do we seek to be immortals? / Three cups help us see through the Tao, / A barrel unites us with Nature".[60] It seems that he is not really superstitious about the so-called immortals as he thinks that being an immortal is not so good as enjoying the wine in reality. With the wine, he will forget about immortals. His "Song of Sunrise and Sunset" and other poems more clearly show that he does not believe in the immortality of human beings. That is why he says: "He is indulged in elixir, / Making everyone's heart sad. /... / But under the Three Springs, there is / A gold coffin with cold bone ash".[61] Thus, Li Bai's "Not far to find immortals in the Five Summits"[62]

---

59 "Imitation of 'Ancient Style'" No. 3.
60 "Drinking Alone under the Moon".
61 "Ancient Style" No. 1.
62 "Song of Mount Lu to Censor Lu Xuzhou".

is just the fashion of his time. He says, "Recruitment would empty most homes; / Building bridges harms multitudes. / He dreams of island elixir, / Not thinking of farming in spring".[63] He is against the pursuit of immortality when it is in contradiction with people's interests. As the Taoist thought related to Taoism is the tradition of the intellectuals in the Six Dynasties, Li Bai is certainly not immune from it. However, the idea of "small territory and sparse population" has not influenced him, nor has the Taoist thought of "governance with inaction", not to mention that the quiet Taoist thought that "an empty room has more light (to see through Tao)" is totally in opposition to him. Thus, we cannot determine how much Taoist thought Li Bai has. Confucius says, "To live in seclusion to pursue his interest, / And do justice to achieve the Tao".[64] He also says, "If the Tao doesn't prevail, float in a wood raft in the sea".[65] However, it is worthy of research whether Li Bai is dominated by the Taoist thought or the Confucian ideology when he unifies "participation in politics" and "roving like an immortal". Li Bai himself has not thought of clarifying the boundaries as he says, "Confucius is going to the sea, / While my ancestor (Laozi) will go for the drifting sand. / The saints are going for water. / Why sigh when we are at crossroads?"[66] and "How virtuous the immortal was because he changed his form at sixty. ... When Yanling was dead, Confucius sighed with anguish".[67] Obviously, he treats them equally. In his poems, Li Bai mentioned much more about Confucius than about Zhuangzi. He says, "If you judge my ability, / I'm similar to Confucius? / I have never met a great saint. / As a little Confucian, I'm sad".[68] It seems that he considers himself a Confucian. "A Complaint to Privy Treasurer Meng on Behalf of Shoushan" states:

> To realise my ideals like ministers Guan Zhong and Yan Ying, and to design in the ways of kings and emperors, I am willing to assist in governing the empire, making it peaceful and united with all the seas and counties. Then I have worked for the emperor and honoured my parents.

This shows Li Bai's thoughts in his youth, which can be considered Confucian. Since his middle age, Li Bai wrote 59 "Ancient Style" poems, which are quite similar to Ruan Ji's "Poems on Feelings" and Chen Zi'ang's "Thoughts", showing their own thoughts and feelings. Among them, the first poem makes clear the purpose and main theme from the very beginning. He says,

---

63 "Ancient Style" No. 48.
64 Confucius. "The Jis" in the *Analects of Confucius*.
65 Confucius:. "Gong Yechang" in the *Analects of Confucius*.
66 "Ancient Style" No. 29.
67 "Inscription for the Taoist Master Ziyang of Handong".
68 "Feelings Shared with Deputy County Head Chang of Nanling".

> Major Court Hymns not written for long,
> To whom shall I say I'm not strong.
> ...
> Editing is all my doings
> To honour it for a thousand springs.
> I'll, like Confucius the Saint,
> Stop only at a *qilin*'s constraint.

In the whole poem, he encourages himself by a comparison with Confucius. Additionally, in many other lines, Li Bai compares himself with Confucius or calls himself a "Confucian". When he approaches the end of his life, his "Before my End" reads:

> The Dapeng bird flew and shocked all eight ways.
> When hurt, it's powerless in Mid-heaven;
> It remained thrilling for ten thousand years,
> But broke its left wing on Fusang near the Sun.
> The descendants heard what was said,
> But who would cry for him when Confucius was dead!

Still, he cannot forget Confucius. Li Bai has created works like "*Fu* on the Big Bird Dapeng", which is probably from the Taoist thought; however, in the end, it goes back to Confucianism by "crying for Confucius". In China's feudal society, Confucianism is dominant, and no one can totally avoid its influence. Especially, Li Bai cannot be completely divorced from Confucianism because in his lifetime he has been engaging in politics. Thus, the relationship between Li Bai and Taoism represents the fashion of the High Tang.[69] Li Bai's Taoist thoughts represent the intellectuals' tradition from the Jian'an era, while his Confucian thoughts represent the basic thoughts in the whole feudal society. As Li Bai lives in the Tang Dynasty, he inherited the democratic elements in the thoughts of former dynasties. Combined with the contemporary spirit, he has nurtured his belief in the struggles for the commoner's equality and freedom, that is, the liberating spirit and rising democratic ideology in the era.

---

69 Li Bai is invited to the capital between the first and the second year of the Tianbao era, of course, mainly for his fame. So Du Fu says, "His brush pen shocks the wind and rain, / His poems make ghosts and gods shed tears, / More fame, from then on, he does gain. / Though left out, success is now here". But Wei Wan's foreword to *Li Hanlin's Collection* states that, because of the Taoist priest Chiying (also called Princess Yuzhen), he is related to Taoism. Moreover, in the first year of the Tianbao era, Lao-tze is worshipped as Emperor Xuanyuan (mysterious and primordial) in the newly refurbished temple. According to the *Old Tang Book*, the Taoist Wu Yun was summoned to the capital before Li Bai, and recommended him. It may not be credible, but Wei Wan's record is probably real. Thus, in the fashion of Taoism, his relation with Taoism is also related to political activities.

II Li Bai's parentage and democratic demands in class struggles

Li Bai's parentage was noted but not in details.[70] Liu Quanbai's "Late Tang *Hanlin* Scholar Monsieur Li's Stone Tablet Inscription" states: "He was a swordsman in youth with no land, but famous in the capital". He himself says, "Thinking I lack a farming field, / Who cares for the soil and culture?" and "I have no land on my return; / Life makes me poor drifting fleabane". Thus, he probably had no land or field.[71] Li Bai's family wandered afar to Sichuan when he was five years old. Fan Chuanzheng's "Foreword to the New Tombstone of Monsieur Li, Left Imperial Advisor and *Hanli* Scholar of the Tang" also records that his father "did not seek an official position", meaning that he did not work as an official. In feudal society, if one is neither a landlord nor an official, then he is a most thorough commoner. Born a commoner, Li Bai has been a commoner all his life. "Foreword to the New Tombstone of Monsieur Li, Left Imperial Advisor and *Hanli* Scholar of the Tang" also notes: since the Tang Dynasty, Li Bai's family has not been registered. At the beginning of the Shenlong period (705–707), his family secretly returned to Guanghan County and resided there like natives. His father Li Ke named himself "Ke" meaning "guest" because he fled to this county. Li Bai's father was probably a merchant. In other words, he was almost born in the civic class. Because of the rapid economic development in the Tang Dynasty, the civic class was forming, bringing about the emergence of the civic folk literature in literary history since the Mid-Tang. Li Bai's "A Song of Changgan" and "A Song of Jiangxia" can also illustrate this situation. At that time, merchants were very free, as described in "For profits, he drifted from west to east each year. / His name was not registered in the county's list".[72] The aforementioned "since the Tang Dynasty, Li Bai's family has not been registered" can also prove it. However, what is more important is Li Bai's own life most obviously illustrated in his "A Letter to Security Chief Jia":

> Mingling with fishermen and merchants,
> Secluded but not isolated.

---

70 See Chen Yinke. "Questions about Li Bai's Clan", *Tsinghua Journal*, 1935, 10(1), Qi Weihan. *Studies on Li Bai*, Zhonghua Book Company, 1948, and Li Changzhi. *Li Bai*, SDX Joint Publishing Company, 1951.
71 The poetic lines are from "To my Younger Brother Lie" and "To my Elder Brother Hao, Privy Treasurer of Xiangyang". Moreover, Li Bai had another poem "To my Two Children at Donglu": "My home is away at Donglu; / Who farms at the northern Mount Turtle? / Spring planting is no longer in time; / I'm lost, travelling in the river". If we believe the poem suggests that Li Bai had a farming land, then it also proves that Li Bai farmed by himself. Thus, when Li Bai was not at home, no one farmed the land. In the Tang Dynasty, the Field Equalisation System was adopted. According to the household number, a corresponding amount of farmland, gardens, and homestead fields is allotted to each person. Is this what Li Bai refers to? However, the land does not seem to be his property, nor does it identify him as a landlord.
72 Zhang Ji. "Joy of Merchants".

Here the "ordinary life" refers to the life of "fishermen and merchants", or generally the life of the civic class. In other words, Li Bai opened up a new way of living out of office. In the past, the highest form of living out of office is tilling by oneself, which is purely an activity on a feudal land. Li Bai's "mingling with fishermen and merchants" means a new sentiment. Tilling by oneself has a positive evaluation in history. Away from the noisy and annoying city, it is cut off from ordinary life, while Li Bai is "secluded but not isolated". Although these did not basically change his ideology and thought in the feudal era, Li Bai was standing at the forefront of the time, which obviously signified a new budding. Although a budding only, the development gave him new strength, making the commoner's stronghold more expanded and more flexible. It is a better choice for him to live independently in confidence without relying on the ruling class. *Supplementary Biographies of Senior Monks* says: "Monk Daoxian was from the Kangju State, living as a travelling merchant. Between the Liang and Northern Zhou (557–581) Dynasties, he travelled between the Wu and Shu regions, and did business as far as Zizhou". Such monks might be the forerunners of "Mingling with fishermen and merchants, / Secluded but not isolated". In the Tang Dynasty, based on the budding of the civic class, such a custom became the great rear for advancing as well as retreating in commoners' struggles, which increased their confrontation and the thoroughness of their democratic demands. Li Bai most appreciated Lu Zhonglian in politics, as shown in "Ancient Style" No. 10:

> Numerous talents live in the Qi State,
> Among them, Lu Zhonglian is the best.
> Like a bright moon out of the vast ocean,
> He begins to shine dazzling lights one day.
> Resisting the Qin State, he earned his fame.
> Future generations admire his feat.
> Belittling a thousand gold coins given,
> He laughed and left Minister Pingyuan.
> As broad-minded as Mr Lu Zhonglian,
> I follow him to be his bosom friend.

What kind of person is Lu Zhonglian? *The Warring States Policies* records: "I think that all people in this besieged city beg patronage from Minister Pingyuan. From your outlook, I believe you are an exception". The reason why Lu Zhonglian is respected and has prestige in politics is that he is self-reliant and does not act as a dependency of the ruling class. Furthermore, Lu Zhonglian has more than that. *The Warring States Policies* also notes:

> The Qin State abandoned propriety and righteousness, and advocated military force. It used its power to control their officers and took their people as captives. If the ruler claimed himself the Emperor

presumptuously or even controlled the whole world, I would rather die in the East China Sea than live as his dependent.

Lu Zhonglian opposed not only the despotism of military force of the Qin State but especially the politics without democracy and freedom that "used its power to control their officers and took their people as captives". "Rather die than live as his dependent" makes him Li Bai's "bosom friend". Li Bai was born in the Tang Dynasty when the civic class was in its infancy; thus, he had more reasons for self-reliance, freedom, and democracy. Li Bai was also opposed to using force to solve problems throughout his life, so Lu Zhonglian became Li Bai's ideal.

In his "A Self-Written Recommendation on Behalf of Mid-Inspector Song", Li Bai states, "Ancient vassals were praised for recommending virtuous men, and criticised for overshadowing them". This is Li Bai's request of others to recommend virtuous men. In "A Letter to Security Chief Jia", Li Bai says that "I should recommend virtuous people to the country and have faith in this belief; if such words were false, Heaven would punish me", showing that he requires himself to recommend talents. "To recommend virtuous men" and "to recommend talents" are Master Mozi's "advocating the virtuous" and Qu Yuan's "electing the virtuous and rewarding the talented". Such a tradition is precisely a democratic call to open up the regime and liberate talents in the feudal ruling class. Of course, what comes with it are the struggles with the ruling class and their minions. The politics of the Tang Dynasty was relatively enlightened even in the late Kaiyuan era, after which the dignitaries gradually got the upper hand. As a great poet reflecting the reality with political sensitivity, he inevitably expressed his attitude towards it. In ancient times, Qu Yuan once set up a distinctive example in such a struggle, and Li Bai inherited and developed Qu Yuan's tradition in the Tang Dynasty. Li Bai's political career is very similar to that of Qu Yuan in many ways.

Li Bai was slandered and alienated from the Emperor; he was a wanderer all his life, and was later convicted and banished to the remote Yelang. It easily reminds us of the exiled Qu Yuan more than a thousand years ago. Li Bai's mythologised death attracted people's widespread attention, only seen in what Qu Yuan's death caused in the history of poets. However, the similarities between Li Bai and Qu Yuan are not only limited to these aspects, but are more specific. From the most reliable historical records of Li Bai, we can at least sum up the following points:

1   Emperor Xuanzong once "asked about state affairs" and "wanted to appoint him to write royal proclamations". He also submitted "A Grand Plan Magnifying Tang" and drafted the "Proclamation of Sending Out Troops". This is similar to what *The Biography of Qu Yuan* records: "In the royal court, he discussed state affairs with the Emperor and wrote royal orders".

2   He wrote "Befriending the Tibetans" (later Fan Chuanzheng wrote "Foreword to the New Tombstone of Monsieur Li, Left Imperial Advisor and *Hanli* Scholar of the Tang": "He talked about current state affairs, and drafted 'Reply to the Tibetans'"). "A Reply to the Tibetans" is actually "Befriending the Tibetans". Fan Chuanzheng's work came out later and was more general. This is similar to "Out of the court, he met guests and dealt with vassals" in *The Biography of Qu Yuan*.
3   He "secretly drafted royal orders, and no one knew what he had written". In other words, he participated in political secrets, which is similar to what is recorded in *The Biography of Qu Yuan*:

> King Huai ordered Qu Yuan (also Qu Ping) to write an important order. However, before he finished the draft, the Shangguan Secretary saw it and wanted to seize it but was refused. Thus, the Secretary slandered to the Emperor: 'Your Majesty asked Qu Ping to write orders. Now everyone knows what has been written'.

4   "If evil officials and good ones are in the same rank, libel against the good ones will arise. If good advice cannot reach the Emperor, he will alienate the good ones". His being slandered is similar to the story in *The Biography of Qu Yuan* that "the Emperor especially trusted him, but the Shangguan Secretary as his peer contended for favour", and then "the Emperor became angry and alienated Qu Ping".
5   Li Bai was ambitious to make the empire "peaceful and united with all the seas and counties", and others praised him in saying that "Clear about the wars between Chu and Han, / He knows all ways of ruling the country". This is similar to what *The Biography of Qu Yuan* says: "knowledgeable with a strong memory, clear in diminishing chaos and well versed in speech".

The above facts show that Li Bai's political activities are almost the same as those of Qu Yuan. Similar to Qu Yuan, he was also slandered, which makes people feel equally indignant. Internally, Qu Yuan's love for his country and the people lies in his idea of "electing the virtuous and rewarding the talented", and his struggles against "the political cliques of partisan and nobility" in the ruling class. Externally, it rests on his idea of allying with the State of Qi to form a united front against the military aggression of the State of Qin. Li Bai also loves his country and the people. Internally, it is shown in his idea of the commoner's politics, and his struggles against the middle-class and noble groups in the ruling class, who "founded parties and formed groups" and were similar to what Qu Yuan called "partisans". Externally, it is embodied in his idea of objecting to the aggressive policy of militarism while living peacefully with neighbouring countries. Their enlightening propositions and bitter experiences coincided exactly with each other even though they are more than a thousand years apart.

However, Qu Yuan is a progressive aristocrat, demonstrating his rebellious spirit of democratic demands. Li Bai went further, reflecting the confrontation as a civilian and commoner. Qu Yuan had to adopt the "low-pitched manner of talking" while Li Bai was more emancipated, more unconstrained, sharper, and even more presumptuous in using language. Sometimes his anger overwhelmed his respect for the ruling class. "Thoughts on a Cold Night while Drinking Alone: An Answer to Wang the 12th" says:

> Holding your hand, I'll confess what is in my heart:
> For me, honour and disgrace have long been away.
> Sage Kong sad for the hurt phoenix and unicorn,
> The admired Dong Long was sworn as a chick or dog!

Li Bai relentlessly attacked the corrupt forces of "Spending pearls and jade on singing and laughing, / But waste chaff on feeding virtuous talents" in his poems. "Ancient Style" No. 24 says:

> Grand carriages raise huge dust,
> Darkening the field paths at noon.
> High officials have lots of gold;
> Their mansions are touching the sky.
> On the way, I meet cockfighters:
> How splendid and bright their crowns are!
> Their noses blow out the rainbow,
> And pedestrians are frightened.
> The candid Xu You lives no more;
> Who can tell a sage from a thief?

For Li Bai, what the high officials of the ruling class and their minions did are robbery. This is Li Bai's democratic struggle. Such poems were written in the peaceful and prosperous time before the Tianbao Rebellion. Except for Du Fu, only Li Bai wrote such lines. However, Li Bai's thoroughness is more than this. In feudal society, loyalty to the emperor and patriotism have always been blended. Naturally, Li Bai could not completely jump out of this limitation, but his attitude towards the emperor is far more uncourteous than that of ordinary people. When he saw that Emperor Xuanzong in his bones had no sincerity to build a strong state even though he seemed to respect worthy men with courtesy on the surface, he says bluntly:

> I admire the hidden Guest Star.
> Weak people are not worth support![73]

---

73 "Expressing Feeling to Imperial Secretary Cai Xiong". According to Wang Pu, this poem was written in the 12th year of Tianbao, alluding from the *Commentary of Zuo* that "the Emperor was too weak". It suggests that Emperor Xuanzong's weakness failed himself.

In other words, "the wall of dirt and soil cannot be painted", or "it's beyond the power of medicine". Such bold criticism shows that he has no special respect for the Emperor. He can be compared to Mengzi (also Mencius, 372–289 BCE), who visited King Liang Xiang (also King Wei Xiang) and unkindly said, "In appearance, he is not like a king!" However, Mengzi only criticised a king, but Li Bai criticised the most authoritative emperor. Afterwards, when Li Bai saw the country was in danger, he apparently separated patriotism from the loyalty to the emperor and named Xuanzong as a fatuous emperor. "Ancient Style" No. 51 says:

> The Queen of Yin broke heaven rules.
> King Huai of Chu was fatuous.
> Monsters filled the court and the wild;
> Bad weeds grew in noble mansions.

This is the most daring criticism in feudal times. No matter how democratic that era was, people didn't enjoy much freedom, especially when the presumptuous Li Linfu in power framed and killed lots of people. Li Bai once writes in the "Foreword to *Riverside Singing*":

> *Riverside Singing* was written by Minister Cui... In 20 poems, he expressed his frustration and named it *Riverside Singing* after the exiled Qu Yuan. Afraid of treacherous ministers' suspicion, he often hid his writings in bamboo slips; hearing that cruel officials would come, he would hide it in a famous mountain; several times later, worms harmed part of the scrolls. After reading his writings, I felt great sadness. Shedding my tears, I wrote the foreword.

Li Bai's bold criticism undoubtedly embodied his brave fighting spirit.

Influenced by the civic class, Li Bai, of course, has its impure side. For example, activities brought about with the emergence of the civic class such as "playing with singing girls", "watching singing girls", and "spending gold drinking until drunken" were repeatedly written about in his poems. These phenomena became more predominant in the Mid- and Late Tang, which became the basis of civic literature and *ci* poems. *National History Supplement* says: "Chang'an became extravagant in amusement and banquets from the Zhenyuan period". Du Muzhi's "A Sentimental Poem" reads: "Until the end of Zhenyuan, / It's romantic and sumptuous". The most popular poems of Bai Juyi and Yuan Zhen are often the works on amusement, banquets, and romance.[74] Yuan Zhen's foreword to *Bai's Changqing Collection* states:

---

74 See Chen Yinke. *Annotations to Yuan and Bai's Poems*. Chapter IV, "Amorous Poetry and Mourning Poetry", and a supplementary commentary "Yuanhe Style Poetry".

Young people from Bashu and Jiangchu to Chang'an imitated successively and competed in writing new lyrics, asserted as the 'Yuanhe Style'. However, few people knew Letian's (Bai Juyi's courtesy name) poems such as 'Songs Written in Qin,' 'Celebrating the Rain,' and 'Allegory'. However, in the past 20 years, many writings of his poems appeared on the walls of the palaces, temples, and postal services. Moreover, princes, wives, herdboys and horse keepers were talking about them ... Since the creation of literary works, there were no such widely circulated poems.

Which work is the most popular in the forms of writing and talking? Bai Juyi's preface to "A Responsory to Weizhi's Poem to Miss Supple" says:

When Weizhi came to Tongzhou, he noticed several lines on a dusty wall before settling down in a lodge. It's one of my old poems, and the last two lines read: 'On green water, a red lotus is blossoming, / Thus, thousands of flowers and grass are colourless'. Nevertheless, he did not know who inscribed it. Weizhi could not help singing and marvelling at the poem. Afterwards, he composed a new poem and sent it to me with my poem. After checking, I found that the poem was written 15 years ago when I had just passed the imperial examination. It was a quatrain for a singing girl named Miss Supple in Chang'an.

This is what Yuan Zhen says in "A Letter to Monsieur Linghu with My Poem": "In the scenes of wine glasses, I often write small and fragmentary lines for self-singing". The nightlife of drinking and playing with singing girls later became common in some Late Tang poems. Rarely written in the High Tang poems; however, it was popular in real life, as long as we know the new *Jinshi* scholars in the Tang Dynasty used to visit Pingkangli famous for the dancing quarters. Since Li Bai was "mingling with fishermen and merchants", he wrote about it as a forerunner. Although not free from impurity, they were somehow a symbol of new life, as in "Yang Rebel":

You're singing "Yang Rebel," and I
Urge you to drink the New Home wine.
What I care about most? The crow
Of black birds in the white-door willows.
The birds are lost in the flowers, so
You get drunk and stay at my home.
In the double-hill stove when incense woods are burnt,
A couple of smokes soars to the purple sunset.

How fresh and gratifying it is! However, that is not the main element in Li Bai's poetry. With the emergence of the civic class, Li Bai mainly lived an independent and free life, with the liberation of individuality, the free will, and the spirit of romanticism, which were progressive in the historical development at that time and inevitably brought about democratic thoughts; in the whole era, Li Bai stood on the front line of breaking through the feudal ruling culture. To a certain degree, Li Bai developed the commoners' traditional ways of fighting, because he represented the rebellious spirit in the traditional democracy; however, the creation of a new ideology on the basis of the economy, even so weak, helped the sensitive and talented poet to seek freedom and liberation, which became the material basis of Li Bai's more thorough democratic thoughts.

III Li Bai's patriotism and advocacy of peace in national conflicts

Li Bai loves the people. His 17 "Songs on the Autumn Ford" are about the lives of bronze artisans, fishermen, and birds-catchers. His "Lodging in the Home of Lady Xun at the Five Pines Mountain" says:

> Peasants work hard in the autumn.
> Neighbour girls husk in the cold night.

Well aware of the working people's hardship, he is modest with them, totally different from his usual pride. Usually, he would say, "Why do you think I won't pay enough money? / Let's buy mellow wine and drink with you! / Steeds of five-patterns, / Fur-coats of gold threads, / Bring them out and exchange for mellow wine".[75] But here, he says:

> Missing the old washing woman,
> I won't eat though saying thanks thrice!

How much he cherishes the working people's kindness! His famous "Song of Captain Ding" written for boat-trackers says:

> Wu oxen panting under the moon
> Show how hard the boat-trackers are.
> Muddy water cannot be drunk
> As half of the pot is muddy.
> When the "Song of Captain" is sung,
> They, heart-broken, shed tears like rain.

The hearty sympathy, emotionally close to the working people, is a more comprehensive illustration of Li Bai's quality as a commoner.

The political aspiration pursued by Li Bai is naturally out of patriotism, as he says in "Ancient Style" No. 46:

---

75 "Bringing in the Wine".

In one hundred and forty years,
How impressive is the nation!
Five Phoenixes Tower in mist
Stands high before the three rivers.

How enthusiastic he blesses his home country on the road to success. However, since Tianbao the country has been gradually deteriorated. The plundering and exploitation of the ruling class are shown in "High officials have lots of gold; / Their mansions are touching the sky", the dignitaries' tyranny in "Their noses blow out the rainbow, / And pedestrians are frightened", the abandonment of democracy in "Spending pearls and jade on singing and laughing, / But waste chaff on feeding virtuous talents", the debauchery in "The kings have no end to their lust. / How can they be kings of the world? / Feasting the Goddess in the West Sea / And Fairy Fullest in the North Hall", and the abuse of peasants' labour in "Recruitment would empty most homes; / Building bridges harms multitudes. / He dreams of island elixir, / Not thinking of farming in spring".[76] These are the concrete reflections of Li Bai's patriotic calls, his struggle for democratic politics, and the class conflicts.

Essentially, the feudal ruling class wants to occupy the land. When it is related to the outside world, it becomes a policy of border expansion, bringing about national conflicts, and the national crisis, which thus becomes the most direct and concrete manifestation of patriotic struggles. If the greed of King Huai of Chu for the 600 *li* of Shangyu is the beginning of Chu's peril, then this is also the case with the policy of opening up the frontier in the late period of Emperor Xuanzong, which Li Bai strongly opposed. In fact, the frontier fortress during the Kaiyuan era was relatively stable due to the long-term adherence to the policy of peace in frontier defence. That is reflected in "Kaiyuan Prime Minister Song Jing didn't praise / Frontier defence to avoid aggression".[77] In fact, Yao Chong, Zhang Shuo, and other famous Kaiyuan prime ministers have made the same efforts. Of course, the frontier fortress problem cannot be eased down with efforts from one side only, especially in a situation of stalemate, and the greatest conflict is the conflict with the Tibetans. The Tibetan regime caused frontier trouble in the reign of Emperor Taizong, so Princess Wencheng was sent for a peace-making marriage with the Tibetan chief. After that, Xue Rengui did not succeed in his Western expedition to Tibet under the reign of Emperor Gaozong. Thus, the Tibetan regime became the centre of national conflicts during the periods of Empress Wu and Emperor Xuanzong. Li Bai's famous "The Moon on the Guanshan Mount" describes:

---

76 All from "Ancient Style".
77 Bai Juyi. "A Broken-armed Old Man at New Home".

The bright moon rising at Mt. Heaven
Shines over the vast sea of clouds.
The long wind of thousands of *li*
Is blowing through the Yumen Pass.
Han soldiers march down the Baideng Path;
Hu tribesmen covet the Qinghai Bay.
In these places of fights and wars,
Few soldiers survive and return!

The "Qinghai Bay" is the battlefield with the Tibetans. Such a national conflict has been stalemated for more than 100 years and should be solved. However, a solution simply by force is obviously impractical. In the 18th and 19th years of the Kaiyuan era, the Tibetan regime twice asked for peace, so between the 19th and 25th years, there was no fight with each other. At that time, the Xi and Khitan tribes were in the north, and the Tibetans were in the west, causing frontier fortress problems. Especially in the west, the River West Pavilion Administration had strong forces there. It's imaginable that the High Tang poets' frontier fortress poems were mostly about Liangzhou, where the Pavilion Administration was located. Of course, the frontier defence needs military strength, so does peace. Many poets at that time wrote patriotic poems for soldiers defending the frontier, which satisfied people's wishes. However, they had nothing in common with the policy of frontier expansion. To solve the conflict with the Tibetan regime, a solution out of force should be sought; otherwise, many people would be sent to the frontier for sacrifice. At that time, the poets' singing sometimes reflected this aspect, as in "Bones of warriors are buried in the wild each year. / They see grapes sent to the Hans, even overstocked".[78] However, before the problem has become prominent, such reflection is generally unclear. The frontier fortress poems of the High Tang are often interwoven with the yearning for the frontier fortress that was on the passage of peaceful trade at that time, travellers' romantic sentiment in a foreign land, the heroism of defending the country, the long-term hardship of frontier defence, the missing of the homeland, and the desire for peace. All these make the frontier fortress theme a very rich singing, however not directed against a certain conflict. In the later period of Tianbao, the problem of frontier expansion unnoticeably became serious, especially in deepening the conflicts within the country. On the one hand, powerful ministers developed their own forces and excluded dissidents from holding power. On the other hand, the constant consumption of manpower and material resources gradually brought down the economy of the High Tang. At the end of Tianbao, Du Fu says in "Song of Soldiers and Chariots": "The blood of soldiers along the border formed seas, / But Empress Wu's border expansion didn't stop. / Haven't you heard that in two hundred

---

78 Li Qi. "Ancient Army March".

counties in Shandong of the Han / Thousands of villages have grown thistles and thorns". The situation between Kaiyuan and Tianbao was not so serious. However, the development during the following ten years shows that the crisis was hidden. With the love of his home country and a statesman's foresight, Li Bai hopes that his country would be "peaceful and united with all the seas and counties", and cries out the warning: "You know the army is an evil weapon. / A saint would not use it unless has to", demanding that the policy of frontier expansion should not disturb people. He says, "Who were the famous generals? / Weary soldiers were lamentable! / When can the Sky Wolf be shot down, / And fathers and sons enjoy peace?"[79] This is Li Bai's advocacy of peace.

In the 12th lunar month of the Kaiyuan 29th year, the Tibetans captured the Stonefort City. After 12 months, in the first year of Tianbao, Huangfu Weiming defeated the Tibetans at Qinghai. During this period, Li Bai arrived in Chang'an and wrote "Proclamation of Sending Out Troops" and "Befriending the Tibetans", the significance of which is not difficult to understand. It's unknown whether Li Bai's "Befriending the Tibetans" is specifically written for the Tibetans. According to the records in the *New Tang Book*, there was no war against the Tibetans in the successive years except the third year of Tianbao, which might attribute to the effect of "Befriending the Tibetans". Between the third and fourth years of Tianbao, Li Bai left Chang'an, while in the fourth year, Huangfu Weiming and the Tibetans fought in the Stonefort City again. The Vice General Chu Li died in the battle, and the situation changed dramatically. At that time, Li Bai's advocacy of peace and Xuanzong's favour of him were naturally contrary to those dignitaries' ambitions, so slanderous talks gathered like hedgehogs, finally depriving Li Bai of the opportunity to present his ideas. Li Bai says in "A Reply to Mountain Gao, and Presented to Two Officials Quan and Gu":

> I wrote edicts sealed with purple mud
> On ideas for the blue sky high.
> But slanders puzzled the Emperor;
> I was exiled for wicked peers.
> I wander at the lower court steps,
> Sighing about the passing of time.

He also says that "Pointing my hand at flying birds, / I can't tell my zeal for freedom". "The small but constant *Jingwei* birds / Sadly chant in vain with wood chips!"[80] One of the officials who slandered Li Bai is the Emperor's son-in-law Zhang Ji, a representative of the dignitaries, who surrendered to

---

79 "Fighting in the City South" and "Song of a Hu Horserider at Youzhou".
80 "Fables" and "To Pei Tunan the 18th".

An Lushan, one of the two leaders of the An Shi Rebellion. Li Bai was forced to ask for leave from Chang'an with such people's despicable slanders.

In the sixth year of Tianbao, Emperor Xuanzong was determined to capture the Stonefort City. At that time, Wang Zhongsi was not willing to command the troops because he estimated that the city could not be conquered without sacrificing tens of thousands of lives. Dong Yanguang offered himself but was still defeated. In the eighth year of Tianbao, Geshu Han was ordered to lead the army to conquer the west, and tens of thousands of people were sacrificed before the city was captured. At that time, Geshu Han received considerable awards from Xuanzong for his great achievements. What are Li Bai's thoughts about this victory? He writes in "Thoughts on a Cold Night while Drinking Alone: An Answer to Wang the 12th":

> You can't follow cockfighters to use scaring grease and gold claws,
> And be spoiled by success with your nose blowing out the rainbow.
> You can't learn from General Geshu Han,
> Striding across Qinghai with a broadsword at night,
> And blood washing Stonefort to be a purple-robed hero.
> Reciting poems and writing *fu* under the north window
> Isn't worth a cup of water, even if ten thousand words!
> ...
> Did not you know Governor Li of the North Sea?
> But where is his heroic spirit today?
> Did not you know Minister Pei?
> Three-foot thorns grow on his tomb.
> The teenager would have secluded at the Five Lake.
> Knowing this, he would stop seeking wealth and ranks!

No one but Li Bai dared to scold Geshu Han so openly by his name. In this poem, he believes that there is no difference between Geshu Han who sacrificed tens of thousands of soldiers' lives to conquer the Stonefort City and the cockfighters trying to win the favour of the ruling class, and that they are doing the same despicable acts of flattering the ruler. His hatred is powerful and vigorous. Furthermore, these are inseparable from the tyranny and brutality of the dignitaries at that time. Having enumerated many facts including Li Yong's death, Li Bai is deeply aware that all these are the tricks of the ruling class. Most of his 59 "Ancient Style" poems may be written during this period. For example, No. 14 states:

> Hu passes with wind and sand are
> Desolate for thousands of years.
> ...
> The Emperor was furious,
> Sending great troops with beating drums.

Peace was turned into chaos as
Warriors stirred the Central Plain.
Three hundred sixty thousand men
Are shedding tears like falling rain.
They are sad for the recruitment,
Having no time to farm the land.
Not a soldier at the border,
You know not the pain at the pass!

He also says: "The white bones of thousands of years / Are scattered in the wild forest... Li Mu has no successor, thus / Guards devoured by tigers and wolves!" These are Li Bai's reflections on the problems in border expansion.

On the one hand, the policy of frontier expansion reduced peasants' productive forces; thus, "Three hundred sixty thousand men / Are shedding tears like falling rain.

They are sad for the recruitment, / Having no time to farm the land". On the other hand, it made border generals stronger, especially Hu generals such as An Lushan, and competent generals in conquering the Stonefort City in the West such as Gao Xiuyan. Thus, such national conflicts slowed down domestic economy and increased border generals' ambition, resulting in the An Shi Rebellion, the demise of the High Tang, and the invasion of Tibetans, Uyghurs, and other ethnic groups. Li Bai might be among the first who noticed the crisis. "To advise on the rise and fall", as he writes, is exactly what it means.

Nevertheless, the ruling class's policy of border expansion would not cease until it reaches the impassable Yellow River. Another expedition to Yunnan happened in the tenth year of Tianbao. According to the New and Old *Tang Book* and *Comprehensive Mirror in Aid of Governance*, Xianyu Zhongtong first recruited 80,000 elite soldiers, but all of them were killed in wars, and then he recruited soldiers from the two capitals as well as Henan and Hebei provinces. Hearing that Yunnan was riddled with miasma diseases and nine out of ten soldiers died from water- and soil-related problems, people refused to be recruited; Yang Guozhong then ordered many officers to arrest people and send them with shackles to the army. As a result, the recruited were sorrowful and resentful, their parents, wives and children seeing them off crying loudly. In the 13th year of Tianbao, Yang Guozhong ordered Li Mi to lead more than 100,000 soldiers to fight along the Xi'er River, and all of them, including Li Mi, were killed. Thus, he ordered 200,000 brave soldiers from all over the country for an expedition to the South. Such an engagement in military aggression is far more serious than the battle of the Stonefort City, but who dares to boldly and explicitly denounce the problem against the ruling class at that time? None but Li Bai! "Ancient Style" No. 34 says:

Feathered edicts like shooting stars
And tiger amulets reached the town.
Calls of rescuing the frontier
Made groups of horses neigh at night.
The White Sun shines on the Purple Star;
Officials perform their duties.
Heaven and earth are united;
All the Four Seas have no human.
But why did all these things happen?
Due to the conscription of Chu.
Crossing the Lu in the fifth month,
They will expedite to Yunnan.
The timid men aren't warriors;
In hot weather, they'll travel hard.
Crying, they leave their dear parents
When the sun and moon shed pale light!
Weeping tears and then weeping blood,
They become voiceless, heart-broken.
...

This is the original version of Bai Juyi's "A Broken-armed Old Man at New Home". Believing that such wars were initiated entirely by a group of dignitaries in the ruling class, Li Bai demanded to change the policy. At the end of the poem, he wonders "How to dance with a shield and axe / To surrender the Youmiao Tribe". Li Bai's advocacy of peace is always consistent and correct. He was in great grief and anger when he saw the serious crisis in the country but had no power to save it. He says in "Feelings Shared with Deputy County Head Chang of Nanling":

At Yunnan in the mid-fifth month,
Soldiers crossing the Lu often died.
Poisonous grass killed Han horses;
Strong armies captured Qin banners.
Now, along the Xi'er River
Corpses are soaked in flowing blood.
Generals don't win seven times;
Lu maid worries about her greens.
Xianyang, the centre of the world,
Lacks of human for many years.
Decaliters of jade at home
Are not worth a plate of millet.
...
I don't think I can be useful,
So I have never returned home.
Struck at strong men's frost hair,
I, an exile, shed tears on my clothes.

He points out that successive years of war had cooled down the economy to the point that "Xianyang, the centre of the world, / Lacks human for many a year. / Decaliters of jade at home / Are not worth a plate of millet". That is why he "Could not sleep well because of this"! Quoting an ordinary story of "Lu maid worries about her greens", he shows that although he is not in power, he still cannot help caring about national affairs in stating that "Struck at strong men's frost hair, / I, an exile, shed tears on my clothes". Li Bai has never forgotten his duty for the rise of his home country.

However, the failure of the Yunnan Expedition weakened the national strength and increased the economic crisis, which led to An Lushan's strengthening in the North and the An Shi Rebellion afterwards. After the wars, Li Bai recounts the situation at that time in "To Jiangxia Governor Wei Liangzai":

> Xuanzong gave up the North Sea,
> Sweeping the world with An Lushan,
> Who breaths like a whale in the ocean,
> Strong enough to upturn Mt. Yanran.
> I know I'm not trusted, so I
> Hide in the fairy Peng and Ying.
> Bending the bow at the Sky Wolf,
> I dare not shoot at it, afraid.
> I shed tears at the Gold Terrace,
> Crying for King Zhao in Heaven.
> But no one treasures powerful steeds,
> Who only prance and snort in vain.
> Even Yue Yi were reborn,
> He would have to flee away today.

The destiny of the country was finally destroyed in the hands of the ruling class, and Li Bai had to flee south. He also has five poems entitled "On the Way of Fleeing", one of which depicts:

> The Han'gu Pass is like Yumen.
> When can I be back home alive?
> Luoyang is like the Yi River;
> Mt. Songshan is thought as Mt. Yanshan.
> Folks speak like the Hu and Qiang;
> Their faces have traces of sand.
> Shen Baoxu cries, heart-broken;
> His hair turns grey in seven days.

Seeing helplessly the destruction and fall of the country, Li Bai compares himself to Shen Baoxu to save the country from peril. He says, "Who can reunite the country? / You know exactly my thoughts". [81] He also says:

---

81 "To Censor Chang".

76 *The poet Li Bai*

> I can beat armies in talking,
> But am estranged by the noble.
> With a feathered arrow in my mind,
> I will win wars like Lu Zhonglian.[82]

Facing the suffering of his home country, he has no intention to retreat. On the contrary, his usual advocacy of peace becomes a brave embrace of battles. He believes: "Poison has soaked the country, and indignation is rising to the sky; this is the time for brave men to fight with their swords and ministers to map out their strategies".[83] He has a poem "Farewell to Brother Yu Di the 11th and Pei the 13th after Visiting Fortresses":

> You perform Chu dance for me;
> I reward you with a Chu song.
> I will explore the tiger's den in the desert,
> And cross the Yellow River, whipping my steed.
> Shamed to cry by the Yi River,
> I shed my tears at a crossroad!

What was the situation then? With emotion, Li Bai writes down "A Poem Expressing my Feelings when Missing old Friends":

> White bones were piled up into mounds,
> But what sins people committed?

How angry Li Bai is about people's poor situation at that time! He also has "To Governor Cui of Xuancheng before Leaving for Shanzhong after the Turmoil":

> Men of Four Oceans missing Chang'an
> Knit their brows and seldom smile as
> Common people are falling leaves
> Or white bones greeting each other!

The misery of numerous common people's death was pushing the country into an abyss of suffering, but the Central Government in Chang'an that should take measures about it was at a loss. People of the Four Seas were looking at Chang'an, but it could find no way out. Soon after that, both Emperor Xuanzong and the Crown Prince escaped out of Chang'an and fled westwards in great panic. In this situation, Prince Yong Li Lin, Emperor Xuanzong's 16th son, led the troops eastwards, vowing to recover the lost land in the North afterwards. Therefore, Li Bai joined the army of Prince Yong as a matter of course.

---

82 "On the Way of Fleeing".
83 "A Persuasion of Making Jinling the Capital, Written for Mid-Inspector Song".

Li Bai's expectation of Prince Yong is entirely based on patriotism. He has 11 pieces of "Prince Yong Lin's Eastern Patrol", No. 5 of which sighs:

Two kings to the East didn't return.
The Wuling pines made people sad.
Dukes and princes wouldn't save Henan,
Thus, I like the noble prince from afar.
What about Li Bai himself? He wants to:
Borrow the noble prince's jade whip
To lead northwest soldiers in feasts;
The south wind will sweep the Hu dust,
And march west to Chang'an near the sun.

He also says:

Northern soldiers in Sanchuan forced men of
Four Oceans to go south as in Yongjia.
I'll be the stone-like Xie An of Dongshan
To clean the Hu tribes in talking and laughing.[84]

At this time, with infinite excitement, he wants to save the people of the country. His poem "Presented to the Officials of the Pavilion Administration at the Water Army Banquet":

Who knows a hermit living in grass
With the Dragon Spring sword at waist?
It can split clouds into pieces;

---

84 Some people wonder if Li Bai really knows the art of war, and his "talking and laughing" seems to have underestimated the complexity of wars. I think the traditional meaning of "talking and laughing" here should be understood as "he is fully composed because he has a well-thought plan". *Three Kingdoms: Biography of Sun Jian* records that Jian marched to suppress Dong Zhuo, and Zhuo ordered tens of thousands of soldiers and cavalries to fight against him. When Jian heard the news, he was drinking wine. Talking and laughing, Jian ordered his troops to practise battle formations rather than fight without order. Sun Jian is undoubtedly a famous general. After that, Yue Fei's "The River All Red" says that "We want to devour Hu captives in hunger and / Suck Xiongnu's blood in thirst, laughing and talking". Yue Fei is undoubtedly a more famous general. Another example is Du Fu's "Watching the Passing Anxi Troops", which reads: "Unexpected soldiers, though few, will win; / Ten thousand riders save the Central Plain. / Talking and laughing, they'll capture Hebei / With their hearts devoted to the supreme king". Talking and laughing, common words used by the ancients in military affairs do not suggest imprudence. Some people doubt whether Li Bai really knows governance strategies. I think Li Bai himself is at least quite confident. In "Ridiculing Confucians in Shandong", he laughed at a group of unrealistic bookworms: "Old Shandong men moot on five classics' / Words and phrases till white-haired. / Asked about governance policies, / They are lost in smoke and fogs". Regarding governance policies, Li Bai should be clear and logical.

78 *The poet Li Bai*

> I vow to sweep Youyan in the North.
> I'll befriend all the officials
> To discuss the *Book of Gold Casket*.
> We value the prince's kindness,
> Willing to devote all our lives.
> We wish to suppress the rebellion
> And equal Lu Zhonglian in feats.

But unfortunately, the Crown Prince feared that his throne would be usurped once Prince Yong succeeded, so he fought and defeated the prince at Jinling. Li Bai became really wrathful at that time. His "Feelings on Rushing to the South" cries out:

> I swore to the autumn river
> I'd recapture the Central Plain.
> Thrusting my sword at a front post,
> I won't repeat it but sing sadly.

His patriotic conscience had such a miserable experience. That is why "I won't resay it but sing sadly". At that time, Li Bai was 57 years old. Right away, he was condemned as a rebel and finally exiled to Yelang because of Prince Yong's treason. When he was 59, Li Bai was released by amnesty. At that time, the An Shi Rebellion had not been suppressed, and he was still caring about his country's future, saying that "I sighed at midnight many times, / Worrying about our great nation".[85] Undoubtedly, Li Bai is a true patriotic poet.

At the age of nearly 60, Li Bai evidently had deteriorating health after the exile to Yelang; in his poems, we can see diseases he had never mentioned before. When he was 61, Li Bai still volunteered himself when Li Guangbi assembled a great army to fight against Shi Chaoyi. However, he was not able to run about and returned halfway after getting sick. He has a poem "Hearing General Li Would Send a Million Qin Soldiers to Attack the Southeast, I, Though Weak, Asked to Follow Him, but Returned Halfway for Sickness", which was written a year before his death. Is Li Bai a poet in the clouds? Is Li Bai aloof from the world? Facts are the most eloquent illustration of Li Bai's central idea. Before the Tianbao Rebellion, Li Bai insisted on peace for the love of the country and the people; after it, Li Bai constantly strived to join the army to recover the lost lands, which is also for the love of the country and the people. This is the embodiment of his most realistic patriotic spirit.

Thus, Li Bai's advocacy of peace is essentially related to struggles. His poetry reflects people's hatred against the ruling class, their desire for peace,

---

85 "To Jiangxia Governor Wei Liangzai".

their misery and suffering brought about by wars, and their wish to restore the Divine Land (a poetic name for China) from the iron hoofs of the Hu tribes. These patriotic songs reflect the voice in the depth of Li Bai's mind.

Li Bai's political life

1 Li Bai's entry into Hanlin as a commoner

In his three years in Chang'an, Li Bai "had a position in the Gold Throne Palace, and was a member of *Hanlin*, the Imperial Academy", as recorded in the "Foreword to the *Cottage Collection*". At that time, he was actually a distinguished guest or an alien advisor, rather than a formal official. Wang Qi quotes clearly from *Collected Notes of Li Taibai's Poetry*:

> *Encyclopedia of Classics, Reports and Remarks* note: *Hanlin* Scholars were entitled in the 26th year of Kaiyuan by Emperor Xuanzong. At first, the Imperial Secretariat was busy; thus, literary scholars were chosen and named as *Hanlin* on Summons. With Virtue Scholars, they were respectively responsible for drafting royal orders and documents; then, the *Hanlin* on Summons were honoured as Scholars, and the Scholars Academy was established, specially assigned to draft royal orders, with Zhang Ji and Liu Keqian as leaders. The Virtue Scholars then stopped drafting royal orders but focused on compiling classics. Later, Supervisor Zhang Shu, and Sectaries of Imperial Decree such as Zhang Jian and Dou Hua entered the Academy, among others. Afterwards, Han Xiong, Yan Bojun, Meng Kuangchao, Chen Jian, Jiang Zhen, Li Bai and so on were all in the *Hanlin* Academy, but they had no official position but a title. *Chorography of Antiquity* records: Before the Kaiyuan era, those summoned into the royal palace from the North Gate had no title of Scholar or position. For example, Li Bai and his peers were specially called into *Hanlin* for their literary talents, not summoned as officials. That's why people say "Commoners in white entered *Hanlin*". It also notes: The Emperor tried several times to offer Li Bai an official post, but other officials in the court did not agree. It shows that in Tianbao Li Bai had no official post.

Therefore, Wei Wan's "Foreword to *Hanlin Li's Collection*" notes that he was "over 50 years old, but had no salaried position". Even in the *Hanlin* Academy, Li Bai was always in an alien status. Before that, Li Bai had been very generous to help his friends from time to time, while sometimes he had been very poor and needed to "borrow money from others like a beggar". When he was living an extravagant life, it was unknown whether he brought some money from home, whether his rich friends supported him, or whether he married the granddaughter of former Prime Minister Xu Yushi. However, Li Bai's situation at that time is clearly illustrated in his poem "To My

Younger Brother Nanping Governor Zhiyao": "Those used to laugh at my humble birth / Came to pay respect and befriend me". It can be seen that Li Bai was basically seen as "humble" for his identity as a commoner at that time.

It is extremely interesting that Li Bai spent his whole life wandering, which is very common in the Tang Dynasty. For example, even Du Fu had a difficult life with heavy family burdens, and he was not famous, he still spent his whole life wandering around. Du Fu's career as an official only added up to about three years. Moreover, he refused to be a low-rank officer in the River West or a Capital Councillor. How could he spend his life only with poetry writing without taking an official position? At that time, Li Bai had more prestigious reputation than Du Fu, and he certainly had more ways to make a living. However, sometimes he says, "Exiled in Liang without hot food, / I'm like Confucius in the Chen State", and "But what on earth can I achieve? / Just cold and hardship stay with me; / The long wind into my short sleeves, / My hands are cold as holding ice".[86] However, both Li Bai and Du Fu insisted on wandering around. Li Bai called himself "a commoner", and Du Fu also called himself "a commoner" or "a wild old man" in his poems. They could undoubtedly wander around when their living conditions were good. Li Bai left Sichuan at the age of 25, and in "To the Adjutant Li of Anzhou", he complains:

> O, for whom is my lonely sword?
> With sad songs, I pity myself.
> In great anxiety, I have
> No time to warm my small mattress.
> How to be in a unique state?
> I'm helpless like a floating cloud.
> I will not follow the way south,
> But get lost when travelling north.

Li Bai's wandering life was like this from the beginning, trying to find political ways in a state of anxiety. However, he spent most of his life in the heyday of Kaiyuan. As for Emperor Xuanzong, he was not fatuous until Han Xiu was the Prime Minister in the late Kaiyuan era. However, at that time, Li Bai was busy creating his status as a commoner. The status of an opposition politician is not easily attained overnight, nor is the reputation of a poet. Thus, by the time the conditions were met, Li Bai was in his 40s, and the heyday of Kaiyuan had passed. At that time, the sinister Li Linfu became the Prime Minister, and Emperor Xuanzong was infatuated with Yang Taizhen (also Concubine Yang). However, when Li Bai had the opportunity to live in Chang'an, he would naturally realise his ambition. Therefore, political

---

86 "To Hou the 11th" and "To a Xinping Youth".

struggles were inevitable, which gradually attracted slander and libel. Li Yangbing's "Foreword to the *Cottage Collection*" records:

> Li Bai served in the *Hanlin* Academy, providing his ideas about state affairs. Anonymously he wrote imperial edicts and was unknown to common people. If evil officials and good ones are in the same rank, libel against the good ones will arise. If good advice cannot reach the emperor, he will alienate the good ones.

Wei Wan's "Foreword to *Hanlin Li's Collection*" says:

> The 'Proclamation of Sending Out Troops' was written without a draft; though promised to be an Imperial Secretary, he was exiled for Zhang Ji's slander.

Liu Quanbai notes in "Late Tang *Hanlin* Scholar Monsieur Li's Stone Tablet Inscription":

> Because of "Befriending the Tibetans" and "A Grand Plan Magnifying Tang," the Emperor appreciated him and would appoint him to be Drafter of Edicts. Slandered by his peers, he was not promoted; thus began to wander around the world.

These are the most reliable historical records of Li Bai. From these records, we can at least trace his political activities and efforts, and will not feel difficult to understand his being slandered. He has "A Poem on Redressing Slanders for my Friends":

> Rumours in four states may spread in eight directions.
> Dusted rice and busy bees made saints suspected.
> Sadly, no one can understand my constancy!
> That wild woman was less faithful than coupled birds;
> That woman was lusty, less constant than paired quails.
> Lofty men shouldn't be bewildered with flattery.
> That woman's great sins are as numerous as hairs.
> It's useless even if we poured seas to wash her sins.
> Life is so hard that I have been plagued by such scourge.
> As multiple slanders break gold, I chant with sorrow.
> When Heaven is not mad, what can people do to me?
> Daji ruined King Zhou; Sister Bao muddled King You of Zhou.
> Emperors lost their kingdoms mainly for women.
> Queen Lü of the Han fornicated with Shiqi;
> The First Emperor's mum committed adultery.
> Rainbow colours can hide the bright light of the sun.
> Emperors were betrayed, let alone common men!

I've uttered all words with my heart and honesty.
Were there any false word, I'd be punished by Heaven.

How profound and sincere is his bitter indignation and worrying about the country! He also says:

> Cockfighting inside the golden palace
> And playing soccer by the fairyland,
> They are shaking the White Sun with motions
> And commanding the blue sky with fingers.
> How fast they were promoted in power
> While the outsiders were long forsaken![87]

These are similar to what is stated in "Encountering Sorrow": "Those partisans enjoying themselves in secret / Are walking on a shady and steep road. / Do I fear of disasters falling down on me? / I'm afraid my country falls in the end".

After leaving Chang'an, Li Bai has been missing Chang'an without giving up his political ambitions. His poem "Seeing off Brother Shen to Qin" says:

> High above the Ninth Heaven are Chang'an palaces,
> Where I have been working at the Emperor's side.
> Time goes on day by day whereas
> My loyalty has never changed.
> I'm like the haggard Qu Yuan drown in the river
> Or Tingbo exiled to the seaside of Liaodong.

Li Bai's missing of political success is also seen in his early poems such as "The Roads are Hard":

> The mellow wine in gold cups worth ten thousand coins;
> The dishes in jade plates cost ten thousand and more.
> Putting down the cups and chopsticks, I would not eat.
> Pulling out my sword and looking around, I'm lost.
> I would cross the Yellow River, but ice blocked it;
> I would ascend Mt. Taihang, but snow covered it.
> In leisure, I'd fish on a green stream like Jiang Shang.
> Sometimes, I dream of boating by the sun like Yi Yin.
> The roads are hard,
> The roads are hard,
> Facing crossroads,
> Which way to go?

---

[87] "Ancient Style" No. 46.

> Riding the long wind to break the waves one day,
> We hang up cloud sails to march to the vast sea!

Although he used to "fish on a green stream" on the surface, his heart still would "dream of boating by the sun". "Ancient Style" No. 37 also says:

> Their sincerity so touching,
> Nature feels deeply grieved for them.
> What sin did I commit on earth
> To be far from the Golden Hall!

Li Bai's ambitions were still in his mind even after his exile at old age. He says,

> Sword playing only makes me smile. / What's the purpose of my writing? / A single sword can't defeat thousands; / My works are famed in the Four Seas. / These are all trifles worth little; / Sighing, I'll leave the West Capital! / But when I am about to leave, / I shed bitter tears on my tassel.

However, Li Bai never showed his weakness before the ruling class, but expressed his strength in poems on the wandering immortals as shown in "They only know the Gold Horse Gate, / But never the fairy Mount Penglai",[88] which are traditionally "expressing emotions in straitened circumstances". In this way, Li Bai became a *Hanlin* from a commoner and returned from a *Hanlin* to a commoner, which is his stronghold.

II Li Bai's chivalry and Taoist visits in officialdom

Li Bai was in Sichuan before he turned 25. At that time, he said of himself that "Considerate and prudent in my youth, I knew regulations and rules; I would go into a dark room without deception, and would not change even when told to do bad deeds". He adds, "At 15, I was fond of swordplay and visited many local governors. At 30, I made literary achievements and visited high officials".[89] At that time, Li Bai and a hermit Zhao Rui might have reclused in Mount Min; thus, Li Bai called himself "the Hermit Li Bai" when he left Sichuan. According to Yang Tianhui's *Zhangming Anecdotes*, Zhao Rui opines: "He is chivalrous and bold, good at diplomacy. I wrote a book entitled *A Classic of Strength and Weakness* and Taibai had learned from me for over a year before he left for Chengdu". Therefore, Li Bai was actually a chivalrous swordsman keen on diplomacy before he went out of Sichuan. Wei Wan says of him that he was "chivalrous in his youth

---

88 "Ancient Style" No. 30.
89 "To the Adjutant Li of Anzhou" and "A Letter to the Vice Governor Han of Jingzhou".

and killed several villains with his sword".[90] Moreover, all his life Li Bai often praised himself as Lu Zhonglian, a typical wandering swordsman. Han Feizi (280–33 BCE) believes that "Confucians cause turmoil with literature, and swordsmen break laws with martial arts". Li Bai has both characters at the same time. The custom of chivalry is common among young people in the Tang Dynasty. However, Li Bai is determined to embody that in his political activities. His "Song of Meeting Youngsters on the Ground" boasts:

> Befriending the swordsman Ju Meng,
> I often get drunk at New Home.
> Laughing, we cheer with cups of wine
> And kill villains in the city.
> "Song of a Swordsman" describes:
> He left with a flick of his sleeves,
> Deeply hiding his arms and fame.
> At leisure, he drank in Xinling,
> Putting his sword across his knees.
> He ate roasted meat with Zhu Hai,
> And drank wine to counsel Hou Ying.

These chivalrous swordsmen such as Ju Meng and Hou Ying are typical historical figures in political whirlpools. Li Bai was eager to befriend these heroes for political purposes one day. Therefore, "A Letter to the Vice Governor Han of Jingzhou" says:

> If I'm useful in crises,
> I will sacrifice myself.

At this time, his character resembling that of the heroic hermit Zhu Hai would stand out. "To the Adjutant Pei of Anzhou" says:

> At former times I travelled eastward to Weiyang (also Yangzhou) and spent more than 300,000 gold coins in less than a year. Wherever there were declasse intellectuals, I gave them financial help. That's proof of my benevolence. In the past, I travelled in Chu with Wu Zhinan, my friend from Middle Sichuan, but he died in the Dongting Lake. Wearing mourning clothes, I cried bitterly as if my brother were dead. In the hot summer, I fell on his body and cried tears and blood. Hearing my crying, all passers were heart-broken. Even when a fierce tiger came near, I steadfastly protected his corpse until I buried him temporarily by the lakeside. Then I came to Jinling (also Nanjing). After several years, I came back to find that his flesh and muscles still remained; I wiped off

---

90 "Foreword to *Hanlin Li's Collection*".

my tears and used my sword to cut his bones myself with sincere respect after washing his remains. Then I wrapped them up and began travelling with them on my back. When I walked during the day and slept at night, I was always with his remains. Finally, I had a funeral for him in the east of Echeng City after begging for money. His hometown is far away, and his spirit and soul have no owner, so I buried him with the funeral etiquette of migration, showing the deep friendship between us. This is another example of my valuing friendliness and brotherhood.

We know from his "begging for money" that he did not have much money, but he valued "benevolence". Such chivalry is Li Bai's character and also the way of socialising Li Bai adopted. In his later years, his preface to "A Poem for Wu E the 17th" says: "The disciple Wu E deeply valued brotherhood. Unsophisticated, resolute, and brave, he admired the quality of the famous assassin Yao Li". As Yao Li is of the same class as Zhu Hai, it shows that Li Bai has never completely given up his life as a wandering swordsman. However, the wandering swordsmen in the Tang could not play political roles as much as those in the Spring and Autumn and Warring States periods. When Li Bai used up his money because of his "benevolence", he had no friends any more. Then, he says with great regret:

When my gold was scattered, all friends left me.
The white-haired Confucian was despised.[91]

The regret of "the white-haired Confucian" with no way to succeed in politics is repeatedly seen in Li Bai's poems. Li Bai wanted to be a chivalrous swordsman to make friends in finding a way in politics, but this approach did not work. He seemed less interested in it after middle age. His life as a chivalrous swordsman was mainly active in his early years, although it still affected his lifetime character. After he had ostensibly ended his early life as a wandering swordsman, Li Bai became a domineering and arrogant man fond of singing loudly and drinking excessively. *New Tang Book: Biography of Du Fu* notes:

Du Fu once passed by Bianzhou (also Kaifeng) with Li Bai and Gao Shi. Feeling tipsy, they climbed up the ancient Instrument-Playing Terrace and lamented over the past with strong emotions. Nobody understood their profound talks. Zimei (the courtesy name of Du Fu) wrote "Expressing my Feelings": "In the past, I went to a tavern / With my friends Gao Shi and Li Bai. / Their strong emotions and brave thoughts / Made me feel happy in my heart".

---

91 "Thoughts on a Cold Night while Drinking Alone: An Answer to Wang the 12th".

It shows that his character as a brave swordsman is just the same as before. After that, when the An Shi Rebellion broke out, the situation was somewhat similar to that of the Warring States period, and Li Bai seemed to be eager to be a wandering swordsman again. His "Song of the Heroes in Fufeng" states:

> With the four patrons Yuan, Chang, Chun, and Ling,
> How glad they were in the Six Kingdoms period.
> Each vassal had three thousand swordsmen in his halls,
> But no one knew who'd pay a debt of gratitude.
> Holding my long sword and raising my eyebrows,
> I show my heart like clear water and white stones.
> Taking off my hat and smiling at you,
> Drinking your mellow wine and singing for you,
> I wish Zhang Liang hadn't gone with the Hermit Red Pine
> And Master Yellow Stone by the bridge knew my heart.

Li Bai's mind is truly alive on paper. Later, at 60 after being amnestied from a long exile at Yelang, his "To Adjutant Dou on the River" asks and promises:

> Why do you promise a date for such a long time?
> We can boat and sing, looking for joy in the moon.
> I know three thousand fellows of resources, but
> I'd rather make good friends with you with all my heart.

His sentiment as a wandering swordsman is still alive even when he is old. Of course, Li Bai's association with chivalrous men is not totally fruitless. "The Tombstone of *Hanli* Scholar Li" by Pei Jing of the Tang states:

> Li Bai was once good at distinguishing people. When he was visiting Bingzhou (also Taiyuan), he came across Guo Ziyi (later appointed the Governor of Fenyang) in the army. When Guo committed a crime, he not only exempted him from punishment, but rewarded him with prizes. When Li Bai committed treason later, the Governor of Fenyang begged the Emperor to redeem him with his rank and awards. With the Emperor's consent, Li Bai was not killed. This is the so-called requiting.

As Pei Jing and Li Bai almost live in the same period, the anecdote might be credible. However, Li Bai's main political activities are based not on chivalry, but on the commoners' traditional way.

Secluding themselves in Mount Culai, Li Bai, Kong Chaofu, and others were known as "the Six Hermits at the Bamboo Stream". On the one hand, they made a great reputation; on the other, they had to show contempt to the royal court. This is the commoner's traditional way vying for political power. Nevertheless, Li Bai had another set of strategy, that is, the way of travelling around different states as in the Warring States period. He says,

> Zhongni formed his theory at seventy, / But no king invited him to govern. / Lu Zhonglian refused a thousand gold coins, / How can an official rank reward him? / If the time is against my ideals, / I would rather live with the grass and trees.

His political way is modelled on Confucius (alias Zhongni) and Lu Zhonglian. Moreover, Li Bai's passionate and romantic personality disabled him from hiding in the same place for a long time. After he was accustomed to the life as a wandering swordsman, the only similar way of life for him is travelling around the states. He had already started travelling to different places when he was in Sichuan. After leaving there, he says, "With a sword, I left my homeland / And my relatives for a long trip", "In great anxiety, I have / No time to warm my small mattress", and "I will not follow the way south, / But get lost when travelling north". He often compared himself to Confucius who travelled around all the states. He says: "At 15, I was fond of swordplay and visited many local governors. At 30, I made literary achievements and visited high officials". Here he gradually substituted "literary achievements" for "swordplay". Furthermore, he "visited many local governors" after leaving his homeland with a sword. However, the High Tang was a unified empire, and at that time, there were not many local governors to lobby. Besides, a commoner needs to show his pride. In his own words, he should "not stoop oneself, or beg others", "five prefectures wanted to employ me, but I did not want to be appointed".[92] If a commoner visits officials everywhere, he will lose his identity. Li Bai wanted to travel around the states while maintaining the demeanour as a commoner, which is unified in "Not far to find immortals in the Five Summits, / I love visiting famed mountains all my lifetime". Wei Wan's "Foreword to *Hanlin Li's Collection*" says:

> Sometimes he played with singing girls in Zhaoyang, and travelled extensively like Xie Kangle (also Xie Lingyun), earning the nickname of Monsieur Li in Mount East. Besides multiple steeds and beautiful girls, he was greeted with over 12 tons of grain at the outskirts.

This is the way Li Bai travelled around the states in the Tang Dynasty; of course, he was able to meet many political figures. Li Bai's participation in Prince Yong Li Lin's expedition was another version of travelling around the states. That he was rescued later by Cui Huan and Song Ruosi was also the result of his networking. However, Li Bai couldn't always wander around without a reason. Fortunately, Taoism prevailing in the Tang Dynasty

---

92 "A Self-Written Recommendation on Behalf of Mid-Inspector Song".

justified his tours. On the one hand, it reinforces his identity as a "hermit" as in "When hermits are promoted, all people will follow him"; on the other, it provides an opportunity of being "greeted with over 12 tons of grain at the outskirts". He wrote in the preface to "Seeing off Huang Zhong": "As Monsieur Huang was visiting historic sites and following the nobles, I disguised myself and designed the itinerary of climbing mountains faraway from our state". In Li Bai's opinion, "visiting historic sites" and "following the nobles" are unitary. Even though he could not help recommending himself in his life as a wandering swordsman before looking for immortals and visiting Taoists, he knew better that it is not very useful to recommend himself with growing reputation after that. Thus he took the way of wandering around.

The prevalence of Taoism in the Tang Dynasty is not accidental. Before the Tang Dynasty, it was the Southern and Northern Dynasties that witnessed the most prosperous period of Buddhism, though the Taoist origin of "taking medicine to be immortals" was earlier. Buddhism is about the afterlife while Taoism focuses on the current life; Buddhism is about nothingness and nirvana while Taoism worships immortals with crane-white hair and a child's face. The Tang Dynasty is a liberated young era. Religiously, the native and romantic immortals that become youthful at old age naturally replaced the foreign and self-possessed Buddha insisting that all the four elements (earth, water, fire, and air, of which the world is made) are void. Since the Mid-Tang, Buddhism became extremely popular, which shows that the prevalence of Taoism in the High-Tang represented a certain tendency of the time. Thus, it became the reason for Li Bai's wandering.

Was Li Bai really looking for immortals and visiting Taoists? He says, "How come between heaven and earth / I have to be a poor hermit! / I never gave up the world, but / People in the world forsook me!"[93] This is Li Bai's heartfelt remark, which can be seen from his specific actions. First of all, let's see at what kind of place Li Bai stayed the longest. In principle, the areas of Tiantai and Shanxi in Yuezhong (current Zhejiang) with the most beautiful mountains and rivers often praised in his poems were the best places to look for immortals and visit Taoists, but Li Bai didn't spend much time there. On the contrary, he stayed for the longest time in his early years in Anlu probably because his first wife's family was located there. After he came out from Chang'an, he stayed the longest in Daliang (also Kaifeng) as described in "One morning I left the capital, / And stayed in Garden Liang for ten years". Wei Wan also says that "The Banished Immortal at Garden Liang / Misses his loved children in East Lu".[94] However, Daliang is not the most suitable place looking for immortals and visiting Taoists. On the contrary, it is a busy and prosperous city where businessmen, travellers, and

---

93 "Seeing off Monsieur Cen, a Scholar to be Appointed", "Seeing off Mountainman Cai".
94 Li Bai. "Expressing Feeling to Imperial Secretary Cai Xiong"; Wei Wan. "For *Hanli* Li the Banished Immortal at Jinling".

wandering swordsmen came in great numbers, as described in Du Fu's "Expressing my Feelings":

> Ninety thousand homes in the county / Have tall buildings facing big roads. / Around half a world in boats and carts / I travelled in joy to meet friends. / White blades were used to kill villains; / Gold was used up and earned again. / I killed scoundrels in red dust, and / Paid my gratitude right away.

However, Li Bai stayed here for the longest time until he took refuge in Xunyang before the An Shi Rebellion. Soon he participated in the fighting of Prince Yong. It's evident that Li Bai's real interest was not looking for immortals and visiting Taoists. Second, when we read his responding poems, the most striking are the various official ranks such as Privy Treasurer, County Head, Adjutant, Chamberlain, Mid-Inspector, Governor, and Minister. Nine out of ten officials were neither poets nor hermits. However, Li Bai's life was centred around these characters. What on earth is Li Bai looking for in believing that it's "Not far to find immortals in the Five Summits"? If we know that Li Bai still wanted to join Li Guangbi's army when he was 61 years old, one year before his death, we would no longer wonder whether his life has been engaging in politics or looking for immortals.

Li Bai's artistic achievements

1 Typical characters in Li Bai's poetry

Li Bai's outstanding achievement in poetry precisely lies in that he represented the most distinctive feature at the peak of the High Tang poetry, and his typical style made him the most unusual poet in history. All of his rich imagination, liberated personality, popular and lively singing, and youthful and romantic temperament belong to the spirit of that era. His image as shining as the sun affected countless people, showing his brilliant achievements.

If we think that in the feudal era people only have painful groans, then we cannot understand Li Bai, nor can we understand the origin of the magnificent and vivid murals, sculptures, etc. However, isn't it because they are so rich, so vibrant, so magnificent, and so vivid that we love our cultural heritage today? Here we hear the ancient people's victorious voice. People are constantly victorious in the development of society; otherwise, society will not progress day by day. "Beauty" is born in people's victory, of which we are always proud. The lively singing of the common people emancipated from the aristocratic literature, and the free and unique singing emancipated from the feudal ethics are embodied in Li Bai's poetry. His romantic and bold character is exactly the typical character in the typical era of the High Tang.

90　*The poet Li Bai*

Li Bai travelled along the Yangtze River and the Yellow River, the two biggest rivers in China, and visited countless famous mountains and rivers. In the past feudal times, many people staying at home were able to appreciate the magnificence and beauty of his home country through his poems. "Looking at the Sky-Gate Mount" shows:

> Mt. Sky Gate is split open by the Yangtze River.
> The blue billows surging east begin to north run.
> Green mountains on both sides are facing each other.
> A lonely sail comes into sight from near the sun.

What a vast horizon it shows in the embrace of his home country. "Sailing down to Jiangling" (also "Leaving the White Emperor City Early") describes:

> At dawn, from the White Emperor in the coloured cloud,
> We'll rush a thousand *li* to Jiangling in a day.
> While the apes in the gorges are still crying loud,
> Our boat has passed ten thousand mountains on our way.

What a fresh force of life is galloping in the rivers and mountains, and there should be free breathing. This is Li Bai's praise of the landscape of the country. "Farewell at Baling" sighs:

> You left at Pavilion Baling;
> The Bashui water was surging.
> Above the river, ancient trees grow without flowers,
> While the sad spring grass below has a broken heart.
> I asked someone from the Qin State at a crossroad;
> He said it's an ancient way Wang Can used to climb to the South.
> The ancient road goes on and on to the West Capital;
> The Purple Hall at sunset is below floating clouds.
> At twilight, it's high time for our hearts to stay strong,
> As we bear not to hear the orioles' sad song!

The region around Chang'an, the birthplace of the historical Chinese culture, was the capital of the Tang Dynasty at that time. How many historical feelings and patriotic thoughts there are! How distant are the ancient trees growing without flowers, and how cordial is "the orioles' sad song" we bear not to hear! The heart-broken spring grass, like all the good hearts in fairy tales, seems shedding tears of sympathy; the surging water of the Bashui River is running from ancient times till today, and the long ancient way is still extending from east to west; time and space are interwoven with reality and imagination into a rich historical picture, unfolding before the West Capital; the "Purple Hall", "sunset", and "floating clouds" all inspire patriotic feelings. Li Bai's singing provokes endless thoughts. The symphonic majesty of his "Hard are the Trails of Shu", the crystal-carving clarity of "Ballad of Mount Lu", and the dramatic development of "A Parting Song on Travelling in Dream in the Tianmu Mountain" are shown on the thrilling and magnificent summits, along the galloping and shining rivers, and in the inherited legends from ancient times. Together with the free breath and national blood, they are integrated into Li Bai's lively and grand singing that represents the liberated and enlightening style of the High Tang.

For his love of Nature, Li Bai sings about the magnificent rivers and mountains of his home country and demands a great space because he cannot endure any confinement like a cage. He says: "The monastery clouds are full of monk spirit. / How can such a scenery satisfy people's hearts?" He is not satisfied with such a low spirit. What he asks for is:

> Mount Lushan stands up to the South Dipper above,
> Like a vast screen of nine folds with beautiful clouds.
> ...
> Let's climb high and look at the grand heaven and earth.
> The long river flows eastward and never returns.
> The boundless yellow clouds change colours in the wind.
> Nine rivers are running down from snowy mountains.
> The Yellow River falls from the sky to the East Sea;
> In ten thousand *li*, it goes straight into our hearts.[95]

The open and vast world lays the foundation for the emancipation of Li Bai's thoughts and feelings. As a commoner out of office, Li Bai has more chances to be close to Nature. In his lifetime activities, Nature is his origin as well as his background. Natural sceneries are accompaniments to his life, often appearing as different settings. "Thoughts on a Cold Night while Drinking Alone: An Answer to Wang the 12th":

> Floating clouds of ten thousand *li* surround green hills.
> The lonely moon is swimming in the bluish sky.
> The moon is alone and cold, the River of Stars clear,
> The Big Dipper scattered with the bright Hesperus.
> You miss me for the wine drinking on a frosty night
> By the golden well with ice on the jade balustrade.

This is the poem that opposes Ge Shuhan's "blood washing Stonefort to be a purple-robed hero". However, the "floating clouds", "green hills", "bluish sky", "lonely moon", "the River of Stars", "Big Dipper", "Hesperus",

---

95 "At Jiangxia to Wei Bing, the County Head of Nanling", "Ballad of Mount Lu", and "To Pei the 14th".

"night frost", and "golden well" have all become the accompaniments of the protagonist Li Bai, and have all taken on his character. "The sunny spring fascinates me with misty scenes; / Nature provides me food of thought on my writing".[96] Nature, through these accompaniments, makes his character more distinct and vivid.

Li Bai's poetry is the most heavenly, which makes his style astonishingly simple. His famous "Quiet Night Thoughts" says:[97]

> By the well parapets I see the moonlight,
> And I doubt it's frost covering the ground.
> Raising my head to gaze at the mount moon,
> Bending, I begin to miss my hometown.

It's such a plain writing of a common theme with simple images instead of ornament or explanation. Comparatively speaking, many famous poems on home thoughts were written with more efforts. However, this poem begins with looking down to see the moonlight, looking up to see the moon, and then missing home when looking down again. This dialectical process, similar to a pantomime, is so simple but so rich, so clear and so natural. "A seamless heavenly robe" is the best metaphor for Li Bai's artistic genius in poetry. "Dredging Alone" says:

> The curtain's rolled up,
> Opened by any one?
> The bright moonlight shines
> On my pure heart.

The curtain and bright moonlight become living things through Li Bai's heavenly and plain imagination. Or in:

---

96 "Words of Farewell after Treating my Younger Cousin at the Peach Blossom Garden at a Spring Night".
97 The title of the poem in Chinese is "静夜思[jìng yè sī] (Quite Night Thought)" or "夜思 [yè sī] (Night Thought)". In Xiao Shiyun's version, the third Chinese character is "看[kàn] (look)" rather than "明[míng] (bright; next; clear; understand; etc.)", while the 14th character is "山[shān] (mountain)" instead of "明", which might not be right. Hong Mai's *Ten Thousand Quatrains by Tang People* also has this poem, in which the 14th character is "明". As Hong is about 100 years earlier than Xiao, Xiao's version cannot be totally trusted. It is estimated that a few meddling people thought that it is not appropriate to use the Chinese character "明" twice in the four lines of the original poem. Some changed one of the two into "看" as in Hong's version, while others replaced one with "山" as in Wang Shizhen's *Selected Ten Thousand Tang Quatrains*. However, both of the two Chinese character "明" were changed in Xiao's version, or kept as they were in Li Panlong's *Selected Tang Poems* and *A Thousand Poets' Poems*, which is the most popular version for private education in the Ming Dynasty. The last is most probably the closest to the original.

I trample the mud alone.
Deep water shows no moon.
No moon is not bad;
The deep water kills passersby!

What a noble resonance it is that the "heartless" moon in the water evokes readers' sympathy for the passersby suffering in real life. Is this the language that can be imagined by the frivolous people only singing of the wind and playing with the moon? Here we really see Li Bai's patriotic heart with a heavenly and broad mind; here we also know what is profundity out of simplicity. He says:

The days that went away
Were yesterday that would not always stay!
What's disturbing my heart
Is today full of sorrow and trouble![98]

Li Bai shows us his whole heart in the plainest language. Reading such poems, no one will not feel the enlightening style, which is the reason why his poetry is both elegant and popular, and worth reading 100 times. It is also a characteristic of the High Tang poetry, fully embodied through Li Bai.

Li Bai's poetic language is sometimes quite colloquial, as in "Li Bai is ready to go in a boat" ("To Wang Lun"). It is as vernacular as "I'm Zhang Yide, a Yan person", and only Li Bai can master it and write good poems for everyone to recite. In this way, he truly achieved the unity of taste and popularity. It is the natural singing from the bosom of his heart that unleashed the language hidden in people's hearts, which makes him people's favourite poet. People welcome him everywhere, so he has legends everywhere; even his sister Li Yueyuan is memorised with a historic spot called "the Tomb of Yueyuan". Among all the poets in history, only Qu Yuan's sister Nüxu has such a glory. It shows that people sing highly of his excellent poetic genius.

Li Bai's poetry is simple but not shallow, popular but not coarse. Its enlightening style is not due to transparency but due to endless prospects, not simplicity but richness. Its strong appeal lies in its ultimate beauty. A comment at that time goes, "Ordinary people's writings are like mountains without mist and clouds, or spring without trees and grass; Li Bai's writings are enlightening, powerful and unrestrained, with famous stanzas and outstanding expressions intertwined to form a bright, transparent and affecting effect".[99] Although it's about the general "writings", his "poetry" is more worthy of it. "Farewell at a Jinling Tavern" says:

Willows in the breeze, the tavern smells really sweet.
The Wu maid pressed mellow wine to invite the guests.

---

98 "Farewell to My Uncle Collator Yun at Pavilion Xie Tiao in Xuancheng".
99 "To the Adjutant Pei of Anzhou".

> The juniors of Jinling came to bid me farewell;
> All of them, leaving or staying, drank up their wine.
> Tell me, than the endless water flowing eastward,
> Is the sad feeling of our disunion shorter?

Such pretty and distinct images are represented in such a plain and simple language. Naturally, it's attributed to Li Bai's originality and rich imagination. He says:

> White hair of thirty thousand feet. [100]

No poet has had such an extraordinary expression, but who can say that this line is hard to understand? The outstanding effect makes it one of the best examples of poetic language. This explains Li Bai's originality and liberated personality. Also in:

> I send my heart of sorrow to the bright moon,
> Following the wind till the west of Yelang.[101]

Li Bai definitely imagines that his innocent heart could fly out of his body without any difficulty. "The strong wind blows my heart west till, / It hangs on a tree in Xianyang" mentioned earlier can also explain such an unprecedented imagination; however, for Li Bai, it's so natural. His rich and heavenly imagination seems to give life to everything in the world. He says:

> Who are never bored with each other?
> Only the Jingting mountain and I.[102]

Only people look at hills, but Li Bai imagines that hills are also looking at people. Another two examples are:

> The Yellow River falls from the sky to the East Sea.[103]
> The ancient path continued to the West Capital.[104]

The Yellow River and the ancient path are personified and begin walking. Also in:

> The mountain moon returns with people.[105]

---

100 "Songs on the Autumn Ford".
101 "To Wang Changling's Relegation to Longbiao County as an Officer from Afar".
102 "Sitting alone in the Jingting Mountain".
103 "To Pei the 14th".
104 "Farewell at Baling".
105 "Lodging and Drinking Wine when Going Down the Zhongnan Mountains and Dropping by Mountainman Husi".

Such a moon is also peculiar to Li Bai. Tao Yuanming uses it to "Take the moon and the hoe back home", which is similar to "put on the stars and moon", but to Li Bai, the moon follows a person. This heavenly and rich imagination is due to his creative liberation. The more powerful the liberation is, the more profound as well as simple his poetry is. If we say that in poetry, as in stories, there are works equivalent to fairy tales and myths, Li Bai's many poems seem to have combined them with poetry, as if they are fairy tales and myths in poetry. If fairy tales and myths are sources of stories, then "A hundred poems for a barrel of wine" can be explained. All these have endowed him with the most distinct style; therefore, he has the most unique personality, which is a typical illustration of the High Tang as a liberated, creative, and brilliant era. It makes people love him not only for his "poetry" but for his "personality", and Li Bai completely merits the title of "a poet of personality".

II Li Bai and national forms

The development of classical Chinese poetry reached the most mature stage in the Tang Dynasty. Regarding the form, four-, five-, and seven-character poetry appeared one after another; ancient poems, regulated poems, and quatrains were in innovation. Li Bai inherited the fine tradition of previous literature, and was influenced by the mainstream of contemporary literary circle. His spirit of learning was emphasised in many scholars' studies.[106] In these developments, five- and seven-character quatrains and seven-character ancient poems are the most progressive in form. This progress truly represents the peak of the High Tang because it is brand-new on the one hand; on the other, it criticises and changes the decorative style with antithetical parallelism prevalent in the Six Dynasties; in fact, the five- and seven-character quatrains and seven-character ancient poems do not completely reject antithetical couplets, but its dominant spirit is to meet the popular and liberated singing. The most prominent poets in the High Tang such as Wang Changling, Li Qi, Gao Shi, Cen Shen, and Wang Wei are also good at quatrains and seven-character ancient poems in their early writings; among quatrains, seven-character ones are more prominent and active, because they are newer than five-character ones in the Tang Dynasty. This is the innovation of national forms. These poetic forms standing in the forefront of the time are dominant in the High Tang.

Regarding poetic forms, Li Bai is undoubtedly the most outstanding in seven-character ancient poems and seven-character quatrains, demonstrating his unrestrained singing, and heavenly and liberated sentiments, which are recorded in *Anthology of Selected Tang Poetry* that

---

106 See chapter 3 of Li Shouzhang. *Li Bai Studies*, and chapter 7 of Li Changzhi. *Li Bai*.

Taibai's seven-character ancient poems have an imagination beyond the sky, and tend to be vivid by themselves. A great river rolls its waves without wind while white clouds in the sky keep changing until gradually disappear with the wind, which is mostly determined by Heaven beyond human control.

Hu Yinglin's *On Poetry* says: "In Taibai's five- and seven-character quatrains, every word shows a miraculous scene and every poem shows a miracle. To my understanding, even Taibai does not know how he has achieved it". He also says,

> Taibai's five-character poems such as 'Silent Night Thoughts' and 'Jade Steps Complaint' are unparalleled wonders in both ancient and modern times, but they are characterised by the style in the Qi and Liang Dynasties; compared with his seven-character quatrains, other poems have less charm because the lines are too short to express his transcendent spirit.

Generally speaking, these are fair judgements in history. However, it does not mean that Li Bai did not write in other forms. On the contrary, Li Bai wrote many five-character masterpieces and very excellent four-character poems. However, we might as well say that seven-character ancient poems and seven-character quatrains are his most outstanding and typical achievements, which also illustrate his personality. His poems in other forms are also centred around the two main forms. It's precisely because of the powerful effect of the dominant forms that Li Bai is able to write with facility four-character poetry other poets fail to.

When the forms of seven-character ancient poems and quatrains are unified, there appears a tradition of "singing" (commonly known as *yuefu*). Seven-character ancient poems were new songs popular since the Sui and Tang Dynasties, and quatrains were sung everywhere among the Tang people. Although classical Chinese poetry has been continuously developing, it is always on the path of "singing" and closely associated with singing, which is an outstanding feature of Chinese poetry; regarding the forms of classical Chinese poetry, regulated poetry, which Li Bai rarely wrote all his life, is relatively dissociated with "singing", the path of which shows that poetry was really liberated from the aristocratic parallelism of the Six Dynasties and returned to the simple and natural language. Such development helped the Tang poetry to reach the peak in the poetic country, which is Li Bai's progressive path in developing national forms.

Broadly speaking, national forms establish national styles. For example, as China has been a feudal society for a long time, the vast countryside makes people familiar with Nature. Thus, from "Airs of the States" on, Chinese poetry has created lines such as "Three or five little stars are / Shimmering in the East" and "Tall and straight pines grow on the hill, / Tufts of dragon grass in the pool". Based on the tradition of "foreshadowing" in folk songs, they inspired rich metaphors and associations of poetic language, and thus enriched poetic expressions; then people can write about themselves with things rather than human beings, which is a characteristic of the national styles of Chinese poetry. For example,

> Cut water with a sword, it faster flows.
> Drink wine to ease sorrow, it deeper grows![107]
> Tell me, than the endless water flowing eastward,
> Is the sad feeling of our disunion shorter? [108]

"Water" is such an amiable word for Chinese nationalities. Before that, Confucius sighs that "Time flies like the flowing water / In days and at nights!" Jing Ke sings, "The wind rustling, cold is the Yishui shore. / The hero goes away, never coming back no more". "A Young Girl at Green Stream" narrates: "Facing white water and near a footbridge, / The young girl lives alone, without a sweetheart". Lu Sidao "Joining the Army" complains: "Running water, as always, can break people's heart, / Horses often hurt in bones by ice, cold and hard!" It is such "water" familiar to people that inspired the rich poetic sentiments of Chinese nationalities. Among such traditions, the moon in Li Bai's poetry always merits the most attention.

Familiar with the lunar calendar, Chinese nationalities have a special sentiment about the "moon". It tells peasants when to labour, comforts wanderers far away from home, and signifies family union in the Lantern Festival and Mid-Autumn Festival. The legends of Wu Gang chopping the laurel tree, of Chang'e flying to the moon, and of the jade rabbit grinding for an elixir are related to the moon, making it a confluence of all beautiful imaginations. "Songs of Wu" sings: "The crescent moon shining over the Nine States. / Some families are happy while others are sad!" How familiar the Chinese people are with the moon. Shining above people's joys and sorrows, it has become a part of their lives. It is used as a calendar, a living card of months, as in "On the fifteenth day the bright moon is full, / On the twentieth, no toad and rabbit" and "You say you would visit me at the West Mansion; / But you did not though the moon turned round a few times". People love this image of the moon because it is associated with Chinese people's feelings and enriched by Chinese national traditions. Generally speaking, as a national form with broad significance, it has a much broader sense than the "moon" in Western poetry. With such forms favoured by people, Li Bai wrote many masterpieces popular for more than 1,000 years. He says:

> Under a slim moon in Chang'an,
> The sound of pounding clothes is heard.

---

107 "Farewell to My Uncle Collator Yun at Pavilion Xie Tiao in Xuancheng".
108 "Farewell at a Jinling Tavern".

> Autumn wind cannot blow away
> Soldiers' missing at Yumen.
> When will the Hu tribes be chased back
> And good men return from the frontier?[109]

This new moon hanging over the Chang'an City rose with the sound of pounding and washing clothes like the neighing of thousands of horses. No matter how the autumn wind blows, the sentiments are endless. This is the moon commonly seen in Li Bai's poetry. When he says,

> Meditating, lingering under the moon for long,
> I know bosom friends are rare from ancient times on.[110]
> The traveller looks afar at this time but in vain.
> To whom the lone moon above the Long Islet shines? [111]

The "moon" symbolises the emancipation of Li Bai's thoughts and feelings in all aspects of life. "Song of the Moon at Mount Emei" describes:

> The half moon shining at Mount Emei in autumn
> Casts its waving shadow in the Qiangjiang River.
> At night I started from Green Stream to Three Gorges
> To meet you in Yuzhou because I miss you much.

We feel as if the "moon" were always shining by his side. Also in: "I only wish when I'm drinking wine while singing, / The moonlight is always shining in my golden cup".[112] With the "moon", his intimacy is shown in "The mountain moon returns with me" and his enthusiasm in "Almost near the sky to touch the bright moon". It is through these scenes that his poems are more understandable, and his poetic language is so popular with national styles and rich sentiments. It can also explain his writings of other natural sceneries. These are what people love to see and hear, thus enabling him to obtain extensive and typical achievements in national forms.

Does Li Bai have any shortcomings in art? Of course he does. His genius-like "A hundred poems for a barrel of wine" is not rigorous enough, inevitably. Other scholars pointed out that he often used many repetitions in vocabulary and syntax. These are undeniable. However, if we mainly look at his successful breakthroughs rather than his carelessness, his overall achievements rather than his trivialities, then his high degree of unity, typicality, originality, and great progress in arts make him one of

---

109 "Wu Songs at Midnight".
110 "Under the Moon in the West of Jinling City".
111 "The Parrot Sandbar".
112 "Asking the Moon with Wine".

the greatest poets in the world with the most outstanding performance and model achievement at the peak of Chinese poetry.

Li Bai and Du Fu

I The rapport between Li Bai and Du Fu

It's universally known that Li Bai is Du Fu's favourite poet. Du Fu's affection for Li Bai can be attributed to two aspects: politically speaking, he compares Li Bai to Jia Yi, or even Confucius as shown in "Facing owl-like birds in the past few years, / I cried alone at the lucky unicorn". This evaluation has deep respect, so he says: "Crowned nobles fill the capital, / But you look so wan and sallow. / Who says the Heaven Net is just? / In old age, you'll be in troubles"! Artistically speaking, he has the greatest esteem for Li Bai as shown in "His brush pen shocks the wind and rain, / His poems make ghosts and gods shed tears". He also says: "All people think that he should be killed, / But I especially like his talents / Of writing a thousand poems fast / While wandering with a glass of wine". These are from the bottom of Du Fu's heart. Li Bai, on the one hand, is Du Fu's most admired poet among the predecessors. On the other, he is Du Fu's good friend despite great difference in age as described in "Drunk, we shared a quilt in autumn; / In the day we travelled hand in hand".[113] Then, how much is the understanding and rapport between the two great stars of poetry?

Li Bai and Du Fu met only once in their lives, but the meeting lasted about half a year during the third and fourth years of Tianbao when Li Bai was slandered to leave Chang'an for Luoyang. At that time, Li Bai was full of complaints. With his bold and unrestrained character, how could he not confide in such a cordial friend like Du Fu? In the six months of close relationship, Du Fu must have known Li Bai's understanding of the political outlook of Chang'an, his political struggles, and his advocacy of peace. In other words, before Du Fu's stay in Chang'an during the fourth and fifth years of Tianbao, Li Bai's holistic view on politics at that time at least provided an important reference for Du Fu. Did it have a reference? It depends on whether they have any common views on politics in the following period.

In the ten years from their parting in the fourth and fifth years of Tianbao to the An Shi Rebellion in the 14th year of Tianbao, there are five important points on the political situations:

1   In the fourth year of Tianbao, Yang Taizhen was conferred the title of Concubine, her three sisters were awarded residence in the capital, and the Yangs were increasingly arrogant.

---

113 "Twenty Lines to Li Bai the 12th", "Dreaming of Li Bai", "Not Seen", "Visiting the Residence of the Hermit Fan the Tenth with Li Bai the 12th".

2   In the eighth year of Tianbao, Geshu Han attacked the Stonefort City, and tens of thousands of soldiers were killed.
3   In the tenth year of Tianbao, the army led by Xianyu Zhongtong was defeated in Lu'nan County when conquering Yunnan. When Yang Guozhong ordered to force able-bodied men to be conscripted, their parents and wives cried loudly when seeing them off. In the 13th year, Li Mi was ordered to conquer Yunnan again, but the army collapsed without fighting, and Li Mi died in the Xi'er River. In the battles of Yunnan, about 200,000–300,000 people were killed.
4   In the 12th and 13th years of Tianbao, most people lacked food because the rice became extremely expensive.
5   In the 14th year of Tianbao, Luoyang soldiers were deployed to Yuyang. In the third month, An Lushan defeated the Xi and Khitan tribes in Huangshui and intended to rebel because of his increasing power.

Here the first and fourth points are about the political and economic situation; the second, third, and fifth points are about the military situation. The relationship between the two situations is recorded in Li Bai's lines "Three hundred and sixty thousand men / Are shedding tears like falling rain. / They are sad for the recruitment, / Having no time to farm their land!" Which poets wrote on these critical situations? Only Li Bai and Du Fu did. Both of them criticised the Yangs' administration, opposed the policy of frontier expansion, complained of the forceful enrolment of able-bodied men, and predicted the An Shi Rebellion. These are the concrete manifestations of the mutual understanding and rapport between the two great poets.

It is hard to tell who influenced whom here. However, as a matter of course, Li Bai might have more influence upon Du Fu. Moreover, Li Bai's reactions were directed against specific facts such as the Battles in Yunnan and the Battles at Stonefort. However, Du Fu did not explicitly point out those facts.[114] Thus, Li Bai was certainly not influenced by Du Fu. As for the

---

114   I presume that Du Fu's "Song of Soldiers and Chariots" and "Out of the Fortress: Former" were written in response to the conscription for conquering Yunnan, the same as "Three hundred and sixty thousand men / Are shedding tears like falling rain" in Li Bai's "Ancient Style" No. 14. However, they aimed at criticising the general frontier expansion by using such traditional terms as "Qinghai", "the Cross River", "Hu Passes", and "tribe chief". In the High Tang, teenagers were eager to become wandering swordsmen and to serve in the frontier fortress with a heroic mood of making contributions and earning fame. Even in "Out of the Frontier: Latter" written in the 14th year of Tianbao, they were elated in

> A thousand gold coins for a saddle, / A hundred for a broadsword's head. / All my neighbours bid me farewell; / My relatives stood along the road. / The white-haired were seated at top; / After drinking, dishes were served. / Young men who received special gifts / Smiled at their precious swords of Wu.

This is totally different from the sadness described in "Dragging clothes, stamping feet, they cried on the road. / The sound of their crying roared to the sky high above" in "Song

opposition against the Yang's administration, Du Fu's "Song of Beauties" was written in the 12th year of Tianbao at the earliest,[115] but Li Bai had written "A Poem on Redressing Slanders for my Friends" and other works before that. Regarding the successive famines in the 12th and 13th years of Tianbao, Du Fu says in "Autumn Rain Sigh": "A decalitre of grain is worth a silk quilt. / Isn't it worth a debate if they are tradable?" It is the same reflection as Li Bai's "Decaliters of jade at home / Are not worth a plate of millet". In the 14th year of Tianbao, soldiers were deployed to Yuyang, and An Lushan was plotting rebellion, which was reflected earlier in Du Fu's "Out of the Fortress: Latter", while Li Bai's "To Jiangxia Governor Wei Liangzai" was written during his exile at Yelang. It's unknown when Li Bai wrote "Ancient Style" No. 53 in saying: "Faithless officials would seize the throne; / Thus, banded for their interests. / Tian Chengzi, once a fugitive, / Murdered the King of the Qi State". In short, they influenced each other, and it seems that Li Bai had more influence than Du Fu; if the writings were done in coincidence, then these common reflections are more efficient in showing that they are indeed like-minded friends. Their vigilance to politics and sensitivity to reality are the most authentic mirror of the time.

II Li Bai's influence on Du Fu in art

Does Li Bai also have a certain influence on Du Fu's artistic style? When the two poets met, Li Bai was already a world-famous poet. His popular "Song of Xiangyang", "Hard are the Trails of Shu", "Song of Resting Crows",[116] and so on have been known to every family. However, Du Fu was young and inexperienced, fresh new in the poetry circle. It's recorded that Du Fu had only about ten extant works written before meeting Li Bai. Thus, the true maturity and development of Du Fu's poetry were actually after their meeting, even though he started writing early, as shown in:

---

of Soldiers and Chariots". In fact, only the conscription for the battles in Yunnan was similar to the above situation before the An Shi Rebellion. Former research seems incredible that "Song of Soldiers and Chariots" and "Out of the Frontier: Former" were written about the battle of Stonefort led by Geshu Han. Du Fu probably did not reflect on it, which can be proved from his "To General Geshu".

115 It should be noted that Yang Guozhong became the prime minister in the 11th month of the 11th year of Tianbao, whereas Du Fu's "Song of Beauties" says that "The weather on the third day of the third month is new", the date of which must be in the following year or even later years. Qiu Zhao'ao notes that it was in the 12th year.

116 "Hard are the Trails of Shu" was written before Li Bai went to Chang'an, as found in *Stories in Poems* by Meng Qi and *Selected Words* by Wang Dingbao. Only *Fraternal Remarks at Cloud Stream* believes that it was written after the Tianbao Rebellion. Thus, there have been different opinions since the Song Dynasty. My colleague Chen Yixin checked the collection time of the *Anthology of Poems: Spirit of Mountains and Rivers*, and confirmed that the viewpoint in *Stories in Poems* is still the most credible.

When I was a little teenager, / I had been a national guest. / Reading ten thousand scrolls of books, / I wrote poems as if helped by gods. / I composed *fu* to rival Yang Xiong; / My poems resembled those of Zijian.

He also says: "At seven I had a strong thought, singing of phoenix; / At nine I learned handwriting and had a bag of works".[117] However, Du Fu had not fully developed his poetry and earned his name until he met Li Bai. Then, in the face of such a world-famous poet that "His poems make ghosts and gods shed tears", would he be affected? It is beyond doubt because Du Fu has been known as a master of a hundred schools of writing; but to be exact and specific, we would better point out the facts about his writing of seven-character ancient poems.

Before meeting Li Bai, Du Fu wrote a few poems, of which ten extant are five-character regulated poems, forming the majority of his early works. The five-character regulated form was Du Fu's family heritage because his grandfather Du Shenyan was a famous scholar in this form. Du Fu also attached great importance to this family heritage, as shown in "A Prose on the Vulture": "My grandfather Shenyan served in the House of Writing in Emperor Zhongzong's court… With my grandfather's legacy, I started writing poems from seven, and have been writing for about 40 years". He adds, "Poetry is my family affairs" and "With Confucian rules of writing, / I knew their demerits in youth".[118] Zhang Yuan notes: "His grandfather Shenyan was famous for poetry writing, thus he says his Confucian family knew the rules of writing, or "Poetry is my family affairs". It can be seen that Du Fu in his early years inherited from Du Shenyan the family rules, that is, the tradition of five-character regulated poetry, which is the most popular achievement in the Early Tang, through which the Early Tang poetry was liberated from longer regulated poetry in the Six Dynasties. On this basis, it was further liberated in the High Tang. Yang Tianhui's *Zhangming Anecdotes* states:

> At that time Taibai was still young with high heroic spirit. He wrote many poems and proses, slightly similar to the entertaining lyrics in the palace. The county residents collected about a hundred poems, most of which are metrical. Although a little weak, they are like young phoenixes with short feathers.

According to *Stories in Poems*, "He was ordered to write ten five-character regulated poems for entertainment in the palace". Obviously, it's from five-character regulated poetry that the Tang people began their writing.

---

117 "Twenty-Two Lines Respectfully Presented to the Left Deputy Minister Wei" and "Grand Tour".
118 "Zongwu's Birthday" and "An Occasional Composition".

Nevertheless, by the time Du Fu met Li Bai, the latter had already developed into a famous expert in seven-character regulated poetry with a bold, unstrained, and unique style. Du Fu says in "A Simplified Song of the Tipsy Xue Hua at the Banquet of Su Duan and Xue Fu":

In writing modern long poems nationwide.
You and Li Bai at Shandong are the best!

The "long poems" refer to seven-character ancient poems. At that time Li Bai was the nationwide banner. However, Du Fu was still in the stage of writing five-character regulated poems in his early age. Did he obviously make further development for Li Bai's influence? Yes, that's exactly the fact.

The peak of Du Fu's seven-character ancient poetry is achieved in a set of famous poems such as "A Song of Eight Immortals of Drinking", "Seeing off Kong Chaofu back to the River East with an Excuse of Disease, and Presented to Li Bai", "On Viceroy Gao's Steed", "Song of Meibei", "On a Drawing of a Royal Steed", "Song of a Steed", "Song of Beauties", "Song of Soldiers and Chariots", "Sorrow for the Emperor's Grandson", "Sorrow by the Riverhead", "Anguish at Chentao", "Anguish at Qingban", and "Washing Weapons and Horses". Later, though Du Fu still wrote seven-character ancient poems, his peak was embodied in another set of five-character ancient poems such as "Out of the Fortress: Former", "Out of the Fortress: Latter", "The Song of Feelings on Leaving for Fengxian County from the Capital", "Song of Pengya", "Northern Expedition", "Qiang Village", "To Counselors Wei the Eighth", "Three Officers", "Three Separations", "Keeping the Uyghur from the Flower Gate", "A Beauty", and "Dreaming of Li Bai". There is an intersection between the two sets, showing that Du Fu broke through the traditional form of five-character ancient poems from the brand-new liberation of seven-character ancient poems, and created a large number of celebrated works known through the ages. However, the magnificent works that Du Fu emancipated from five-character regulated poems were not written in the 30 years before he met Li Bai, but shortly after their meeting. Is it only accidental? Du Fu's "Seeing off Kong Chaofu back to Jiangdong with an Excuse of Disease, and Presented to Li Bai" is one of his earliest seven-character ancient poems in existence, and its style is also similar to that of Li Bai. However, does "and Presented to Li Bai" imply his intention of showing his skill and soliciting comments from his predecessor?

Although Li Bai and Du Fu have mutual understanding, rapport, and reciprocal influence upon each other, they all have their own original features and deepest reflections on different aspects of life, which enable people to find their difference more easily. However, are the difference and originality rational enough to explain their great foresight and their status at the peak of the poetry circle? Li Bai and Du Fu lived at the peak of the High Tang for the first half of their lives, but Li Bai's life was less complicated. At the end of the Kaiyuan era, Li Bai was 40 years old, and his poems were popular all over the world. We should say that Li Bai's style had already been mature and finalised. Nobody can ever forget his emblematic singing in the High Tang with optimistic and high-spirited quality, enlightening prospects, unquenchable thirst for liberation, rich and distinct imagination, plain and heavenly expressions, and profound thoughts in simple language.

Appendix: Abstract of the book published in 1954

This book is the author's scientific research report delivered at a seminar held in the Classical Literature Department of Peking University in June this year. In this report, the author corrected past misunderstandings about Li Bai with old concepts such as "Poetry Immortal" and "a poet in the cloud" divorced from politics, and restored his original image as a true poet. Combining the development of the spiritual outlook, political struggles, and class conflicts in the High Tang, this text presented Li Bai as the most emblematic poet in this typical era, alive and vivid in the circle of classical Chinese poetry.

The text consists of five chapters divided into 12 sections, including 96 selected poems by Li Bai and five important biographies about him.

3 On exaggeration in Li Bai's poetry

Li Bai has a poem "Always in Yearning":

...
But you're far away at the end of the blue sky!
My watery eyes of yearning
Have become teardrops' spring.
Don't trust my heart's broken?
Return! The bright mirror will reveal my feeling.

It is about a lady in the boudoir missing her husband in expedition. The missing is so bitter that "My watery eyes of yearning, / Have become teardrops' spring". It is undoubtedly an exaggeration that her beautiful eyes have become two springs, but it is still reasonable and could be considered an appropriate exaggeration. However, it is partly unreasonable in that she has to prove that her watery eyes have really become two springs while requiring the mirror to testify for her because her look would be very different when her husband comes back: she would either languish, or be happy with tears. To prove that her heart is truly broken, only the mirror knows best. However, unless the mirror were magical, how could it reproduce her past appearance? Probably this can be done today with a camera. However, if a wife does record it and wait until her husband comes back to prove it, probably he would rather doubt about it; let alone there was no such advanced technology as video recording in ancient times. Assuming that it is possible to record it, it may seem reasonable, but it is almost absurd. Assuming that the mirror can prove the past, it seems unreasonable, but it is closer to the truth. Is the magic of art really able to turn an ordinary mirror into a magic one? In any case, when we read this poem, we have already forgotten the irrationality but feel that it is unusually intimate and touching. It is unreasonable in everyday terms, but reasonable from the artistic perspective. Then, how to understand reasonable exaggerations?

"White hair of thirty thousand feet" is the most famous quotation when people talk about exaggerations in Li Bai's poetry. In "Songs on the Autumn Ford", it is Li Bai's turn to face a mirror: "I don't know in the mirror / Where

I have got autumn frost". "Thirty thousand feet" is simply against common sense on a daily scale; even on an exaggerated scale, it still seems too boundless. If such an exaggeration is reasonable, then to what extent will one become unreasonable? Li Bai has a popular poem called "Looking at the Falls at Mount Lu", which says: "The falls flying straight down three thousand feet are like, / The huge galaxy falling from the Ninth Heaven!" The waterfalls seem to be the galaxy surging down from the sky, but they are only exaggerated to 3,000 feet, whereas the white hair is exaggerated to 10,000 feet from the head; the magic of art seems to become reasonable by overcoming the irrationality on the daily scale, which is absolutely amazing!

Some people think that exaggeration seems to be the main feature of romanticism. However, it may or may not be true. Exaggeration can occur in almost all types of works. In many cases, it is most likely to produce a laughing effect, which has nothing to do with the somewhat tragic or heroic characteristics of romantic works. Wang Zhihuan's "Ascending the Stork Tower" describes: "The white sun hides behind high hills; / The Yellow River flows into the sea. / To catch a sight of thousands of *li* / Needs climbing up another storey". What else can be called exaggeration except for the common phrase "thousands of *li*"? However, this poem is undoubtedly a masterpiece of romanticism. In fact, exaggeration is neither necessary nor unique in romanticism; it is only a general expression. If there are particular affinities between exaggeration and romanticism, it can only be said that exaggeration is likely to reach the utmost unreasonable degree in romantic writings. This is not because exaggeration is unique, but because romanticism is essentially a "macroscopic" approach of writing, just as realism is a "microscopic" approach of writing, thus forming different scenes. In *A Doll's House* (Bokmål: Et dukkehjem), Nora's leaving her family was absolutely unnecessary on a daily scale, but she left resolutely. The white hair in "Songs on the Autumn Ford" is just reflected in the foot-round mirror on a daily scale, but it can reach 3,000 feet. It is often out of expectation to measure everything in the micro- or macro-world on a daily scale. For example, people travelling at close to the speed of light will keep their youth; isn't it simply mythical and incredible? The comparison and contrast between the standards on a daily scale and the infinite charm of art make people feel like facing a magic mirror, and cannot help but think in reverie!

Written in Peking University in September 1980, originally published in *Appreciations of the Tang Poetry*, People's Literature Publishing House, November 1981

4 Starting with the characteristics of the Tang poetry

Readers of all dynasties love the Tang poetry. Why? As quoted in Zhu Yizun's *Poetic Remarks in Quiet Ideal Residence*, "Tang poems are fresh and bright, as if they were just born out of writing brushes and inkstones the other day, but contemporary poems are already old-fashioned when they are created". The "contemporary poems" refer to the Ming poetry. In the Ming Dynasty, the poetry circle represented by the Seven *Jinshi* Scholars only focused on imitating the Tang poetry, but imitation merely follows a set routine and has no vitality. Thus, they are "already old-fashioned when they are created". As for the Tang poetry, it is still so "fresh and bright as if they were just born out of writing brushes and inkstones the other day". How far apart are the two!

Today, rather than imitate it, we learn the Tang poetry to feel the fresh vitality of being "fresh and bright as if they were just born". It is this fresh vitality with a vigorous spirit that is transformed into "the High Tang Voice", showing a magnificent and vast world so that we feel complete artistic enjoyment; this is why the Tang poetry is worth reading a hundred times.

Karl Marx says that "[m]an is therefore affirmed in the objective world not only in thought but with all the senses", and that "in a word, the human sense, the humanity of the senses—all these come into being only through the existence of their objects, through humanised nature. The cultivation of the five senses is the work of all previous history".[1] As a result, excellent poems are always stimulating and awakening people's fresh feelings to promote the development of poetry writing. This is a dialectical historical process, in which the Tang poetry emerged, and constantly inspired people with new writings. The beauty of the infinite is the most interesting pursuit in our learning from the Tang poetry. On the one hand, we are enjoying the famous poems or poetic lines full of life; on the other, we are exploring the emerging

---

1 Karl Marx. Translated by Martin Milligan. *Economic and Philosophic Manuscripts of 1844*, Progress Publishers, 1959. The Chinese translation is quoted from *The Complete Works of Marx and Engels*, People's Publishing House, September 1979, 42, 125, 126.

processes and rules; thus the Tang poetry has become the best model for our learning because of its most distinctive artistic appeal.

The language of the Tang poetry is easy to understand, which we all feel. It is easier than that in any other poetry circle before or after the Tang Dynasty. Taking the poetries of the Ming and Qing Dynasties as examples, they are much closer to our times than the Tang poetry. However, why are they not as easy and understandable as the Tang poetry? Is that not enough to arouse our contemplation? It is not difficult to be easy and understandable, but difficult to achieve such exquisite artistic merit with such a simple and plain language; the poetic achievement of profundity out of simplicity is also a reason for people to appreciate the Tang poetry. Being easy and understandable is not being seen through. If so, how could it be worth reading a hundred times? However, the Tang poetry is worth reading many times, mainly because it is easy and understandable. There are unity and contradiction between them. Some famous and popular Tang poems are not necessarily written in an easy and understandable poetic language. Take Du Fu for example, he has excellent poems that are never easy to understand, as in "Fragrant rice peck at several parrots grains / A green tong-tree perches on a phoenix twig". It should be analysed specifically. Poetic language is allowed to have a certain discontinuity. However, sometimes a relatively abrupt discontinuity will make readers feel uneasy; but if it has achieved a powerful artistic effect, people will love it. The above two lines may be the case. However, such lines are occasional in Du Fu's "Eight Poems of Autumn Expression". Being easy and understandable is a virtue of language. Although poetry is a special language art, it cannot but be rooted in daily life language, away from which the flowers and fruits of poetry will easily wither. Making poetry easy and understandable is a universal way of poetry writing. In the Tang poetry, a large number of masterpieces are easy and understandable, but a few are not. Unity and contradiction can be the best bridge for us to explore the mystery of poetic language art. The value of the Tang poetry lies in the language art unifying profundity and simplicity, which is its highest achievement and the most distinctive feature. This is one of the reasons why the Tang poetry can be so prosperous and flourishing. Because of this distinctive feature, poets of the Tang Dynasty sprung out successively with excellent poems at their fingertips, as if they were endowed with unique talents.

Studying the reasons for its prosperity is also an aspect of our study of the Tang poetry. We seldom see people equally interested in studying the reasons of poetic prosperity in other times. First, the Tang poetry is a universally recognised peak of poetry. This peak is traditionally divided into four undulating periods—the Early, the High, the Middle, and the Late—while we seldom see such a complete epochal division in the poetry circles of other times. Because this is a magnificent and gigantic peak, we can distinguish its front, end, peak, and turning points. Moreover, the four periods coincide with the ups and downs of the whole society in the Tang Dynasty, which is universally recognised as the peak of the rising development of the whole Chinese feudal society. These two peaks are interlinked, adding to the distinctiveness of the four periods. The problem worth our exploration here is not limited to poetry itself, but to the relationship between poetry and time. As a special language art, poetry has its internal laws of development, and how it can be fully mature depends on the objective conditions of its time. It contains a comprehensive political, economic, and cultural life, forming a broad field for our study of the Tang poetry. The clearer the sense of the time, the stronger its breath of life. This characteristic is a high generalisation of the Tang poetry per se.

These distinctive characteristics mentioned above are not conclusions, but my most cordial feelings. It would be better to have more thoughts from different perspectives. When we study any subject, we always need first-hand information to grasp its particularity. These objective and distinctive features are precisely the first-hand information of the Tang poetry. We can study the Tang poetry from any point of view, but the aim is always to approach the essence shown in these distinctive features, without which we cannot find out why the Tang poetry is lovely, nor can we recognise its special achievements or feel its dancing pulses. In our learning from the Tang poetry, these distinctive features will always be the most iconic landmarks guiding our studies.

Originally published in *Knowledge of Literature and History*, 1982 (10)

5   A note on the Tang poetry

"The sunny spring fascinates me with misty scenes; / Nature provides me food of thought on my writing" shows Li Bai's pride, which conveys the sense of the time in the Tang poetry. The youthful poetic lines of "The sea sun rises at the fading night. / The river spring lingers in the past year"[1] fully represent its true essence. The poetry circle of the Jian'an era is characterised by the desolate and high-pitched singing with "the bleak autumn wind" and "the sad wind on the high terrace", while the Tang poetry dominates the poetry circle with its vital freshness like the spring breeze. As for "By a path out of the lush mount / Our boat sails in the green water. / The flat tide makes the banks look wide. / In the straight wind, a sail hangs high",[2] how much vitality of the lush mount and green water is revealed in the poet's pen. Without such vitality, it is impossible to create famous lines about the "sea sun" and "river spring". In "Red beans in the southern land / Grow several twigs in spring. / I ask you to gather a few more, / As they are symbols of missing",[3] the small red beans bring us such a fresh feeling when they "grow several twigs in spring". Without the significant growth, this poem is just to show that red beans are also named as the beans of missing. The reason why it is so popular is due to the burgeoning vitality. Wang Wei's fame for his poetry in his early years affected people with such flourishing vitality. Again in:

> Few passengers wait at the ferry by willows
> For the boatman paddling to the Linyi town.
> My missing is like the spring colour, seeing you
> Off along the south and the north of the river.
>   — "Seeing off Shen Zifu Returning to the River East with an
>   Excuse of Disease, and Presented to Li Bai"

---

1 Wang Wan. "Mooring by Mount Beigu".
2 Ibid.
3 Wang Wei. "Missing".

Here it is not so much about the missing, but about the unlimited spring colours. Du Fu's "An Evening Banquet at Zuo's Manor" describes:

> The fine moon falls into the windy woods.
> Dew on his clothes, he plays the pure zither.
> In the dark, water flowing by the flower path,
> Spring stars are shining on the thatched hut.

In the dark night, the very breath of spring is quietly and unconsciously brought to people. Such superb artistic attainment is rare in Chinese poetry, however seen in his poem "Happy at the Spring Night Rain":

> The good rain knows the time of the year.
> In the best of spring, it would appear.
> With the wind, it falls into the night,
> Moistening things, silent and slight.

This subtle underlying feeling, inaudible and invisible, reveals how much thriving vitality! Its strength finally brings the fresh and replete feeling shown in "At dawn, in the places wet and red, / The Brocade City blooms are widespread". In the An Shi Rebellion, the anxiety-ridden Du Fu wrote numerous famous poems about the hard time, but as soon as the situation changed for better, the flame of rejuvenation was ignited in his heart. His "Washing Weapons and Horses" is literally a long symphonic poem with the melody of spring, bursting out the feelings that were suppressed deep inside. From "When generals recovered the East of the Mount, / The news of victory was heard from day till night. / The force crossed the Yellow River on reed-like boats; / Hu rebels are breakable as splitting bamboos" until

> Hermits stopped singing the song of 'Purple Fungi'; / Lyricists explained and wrote odes of 'River Clear'. / Yet peasants wished for the rain but often in vain. / Cuckoos were urging the spring planting far and near. / The soldiers back from Mount Qi cannot be slothful / As the ladies at City South have dreams of sorrow. / How can strong men make the Heaven River down flow / To wash weapons and horses and lock them for long,

it smoothly formed a triumphant and everlasting masterpiece of rejuvenation! Though the Tang regime suffered setbacks again; however, four years later (763) when the An Shi Rebellion was finally subdued, Du Fu wrote an unstrained poem "On the Army's Recapturing of Henan and Hebei" full of heroic feelings, singing the effusive lines of "In broad day we drink hard and loudly sing. / We'll return to our native land in spring. / From Gorge Ba to Gorge Wu, our boat will go / Through Xiangyang to Luoyang with no stop". The last flowing water couplet fully demonstrated the poet's jovial mood and the return of the spring melody to the poet's heart. These rekindled memories of rejuvenation were temporarily suppressed in the An Shi Rebellion but never extinguished. It was not until 766 after the complete end of the An Shi Rebellion that the poet concentrated on mourning the passing of the heyday with a large number of seven-character regulated poems such as "Eight Poems of Autumn Expression" and "Feelings on Ancient Monuments". There was no news of spring, but a sad song of the depressing autumn. These seven-character achievements unique in the Tang poetry became Du Fu's most representative poems in his later years precisely because the hope of rejuvenation had been so strong in his heart that once he saw clearly that it would finally be gone, he would definitely write down such mournful feelings.

After Du Fu, the Mid-Tang brought about some hope of rejuvenation, and then we heard Bai Juyi's resounding song of "Green is the grass on the plain, / Growing, dying year after year. / A wild fire burns it but in vain / As spring breeze helps it grow again" ("A Farewell Poem on the Old Plain Grass"). "A wild fire burns it but in vain / As spring breeze helps it grow again" can be compared with "The sea sun rises at the fading night. / The river spring lingers in the past year". How far-reaching is the spring melody in the Tang poets' mind! Bai Juyi had so much courage in writing so many satirical poems to assist the world. Isn't it out of this desire of rejuvenation like the return of spring? This is not to say that no other seasons are described in the Tang poetry, but that this kind of melody is rare before. However, in the Tang poetry it has become the major theme with heart-moving affection. Even in the Late Tang, although "The east wind powerless, a hundred flowers are withered", there are painstaking efforts in "A spring silkworm won't stop producing silk till death; / A candle's tears dry only when it's burned to ashes". Of course, the spring melody since the Mid-Tang and Late Tang has been shrouded in a weak tenderness and dreamlike pursuit. What will we feel when we turn back and listen to the powerful and unstrained song as in:

> Away like dragons in deep mountains and great water,
> In the shady wild with spring cold after sunset.
> —Du Fu: "Seeing off Kong Chaofu back to the River East with an Excuse of Disease, and Presented to Li Bai"

What feelings will we have? Spring does not always have the good weather as described in "At the Blue Field under warm sun, jade raises haze". It also has cloudy days and spring cold, which make it the real spring, and evoke the far-reaching call of the spring melody, which I hope will always live in our hearts.

One day after the winter solstice, December 1982; originally published in
An Annal of the Tang Literature Studies, 1983

6 A note on frontier fortress poetry

In recent years, I have been compiling reference materials for the literary history of the Wei, Jin, Southern and Northern Dynasties, and Sui and Tang Dynasties. A large part of my effort was to annotate many selected works, and there arose some problems with frontier fortress poetry. For example, Gao Shi's "Song of the Yan" describes:

> The beacon-fire and smoke of the Han rose in the northeast;
> The Han generals left home to defeat cruel robbers.
> Army men were invincible on the battlefield as
> The Emperor gave them power and generous rewards.
> Beating gongs and drums, they went down to the Yuguan Pass
> With army banners winding their ways amid Mount Jieshi.
> The Commandant's pressing feathered letter flew to Hanhai,
> When the Chief Chanyu's hunting fire was lightening Langshan.
> ...

What is the relationship between "The beacon-fire and smoke of the Han rose in the northeast" and "When the Chief Chanyu's hunting fire was lightening Langshan"? Mount Langshan (also Mount Wolf), located in the north of Wuyuan County, Hetao Region, Inner Mongolia, is about a thousand *li* from the Yuguan Pass (also the Shanhai Pass) in Northeast China. Does "When the Chief Chanyu's hunting fire was lightening Langshan" suggest that they will attack the Shanhai Pass? It does not seem so. Or does "Beating gongs and drums, they went down to the Yuguan Pass" suggest going out of the Shanhai Pass to attack Langshan? It seems not feasible either. So what is the real story? It needs to be clearly explained. Moreover, it happens that there is a similar case in Xu Ling's "Out from the North Gate of the Jizhou City":

> Looking at the north of Jizhou,
> I feel sad and lonely at sunset.
> Yanshan facing ancient temples,
> Daijun is hidden behind towers.
> ...

"Out from the North Gate of the Jizhou City" and "Song of the Yan" have similar themes in that the latter states that "The soldiers at the north of Jizhou looked back in vain". The themes are similar, so is the problem. In the line "Daijun is hidden behind towers", the word "hidden", suggesting "invisible", is easy to understand; "Looking at the north of Jizhou", of course, shows that the poet cannot see "Daijun" faraway, which is also understandable; the third line "Yanshan facing ancient temples" is about what can be seen, whereas the next line "Daijun is hidden behind towers" is about what cannot be seen. The two lines form a good comparison, but the problem is why the poet wrote about what is not seen at all. To describe a hidden city with airs of importance certainly shows good artistry. But, how should we understand the thoughts here? This also needs to be explained. In fact, the problems in the two poems are almost identical, only that one is at the Yanshan Mountains in the east while the other is at the Yinshan Mountains in the west. If we can solve one problem, the other will be readily solved.

First of all, Daijun County in "Out from the North Gate of the Jizhou City" is located in the south of the Yanmen Pass. There are two great walls in the region, also called the Ancient Great Wall of Zhao. One great wall along the Taihang Mountains has the "eight paths of Taihang". Its eighth path is named as Jundu, called the Jimen Pass in the Tang Dynasty, and the Juyong Pass at present. Another wall, the outer great wall, runs along the Yinshan Mountains from the Juyong Pass to Gaoque to the west of Mount Langshan. According to the *Records of the Grand Historian: Records of the Huns*, "the great wall was built from Daijun County along the Yinshan Mountains until the Gaoque Pass, and established three counties of Yunzhong, Yanmen, and Daijun". Daijun is lying between the two great walls. Strategically situated and difficult to access, it became an important frontier town in the northern defence, and often appeared in frontier fortress poems. Yu Xin's "Song of the Yan" begins with:

> The shady clouds of Daibei county dim the day,
> Flying fleabanes drifting a thousand *li* rootless.
> Cold wild geese are crossing Liaoshui, crying loud;
> Mulberry leaves are falling all over Jimen.

Are Dabei, Liaoshui, and Jimen irrelevant places? Daibei in the west, Liaoshui in the east, and Jimen in the centre seem like a trinity often present in frontier fortress poems. In fact, to the east of Jibei are the Yanshan Mountains, and to the west are the Taihang Mountains and Yinshan Mountains. The Great Wall of Yan and the Great Wall of Zhao join here end to end, serving as protective barriers for the North and Northeast China to resist the invasion of nomads having crossed the Yinshan or Yanshan Mountains. Jibei is located at the junction of the two great mountains and the two great walls. Therefore, "Song of the Yan" and "Out from the North Gate of the Jizhou City" have become popular titles in frontier fortress poems, in which the eastern and western sides are bound to be mentioned. Jieshi, Yuguan, and Liaoshui belong to the Yanshan Mountains and the Great Wall of Yan, while Daijun, Daibei, and Langshan belong to the Yinshan Mountains and the Great Wall of Zhao. Because it is in the poet's mind rather than in front of him, it makes sense to say "Daijun is hidden behind towers". It seems as if it should be there, but hidden far away. This was the poet's thought and feeling at that time. Naturally, it can be further developed from here. Therefore, "Sort out ropes to tie up Liangzhou" about the northwest frontier defence is mentioned in the following lines of "Out from the North Gate of the Jizhou City". Nevertheless, Gao Shi's "Song of the Yan" is more specific about the fights along the two great walls. *Tang Decrees and Regulations* volume 73 records:

> The Chanyu and Hanhai Viceregal Administrations were established. The former leads three captaincies of Langshan, Yunzhong, and Sangqian, and 14 prefectures including Su'nong. The latter leads seven captaincies of Jinwei, Xinli, etc., and eight prefectures including Xian'e and Helan.

"The Commandant's pressing letter with feather flew to Hanhai, / When the Chief Chanyu's hunting fire was lightening Langshan" is about this war zone, while Langshan, Yunzhong, and Sangqian are the frontier areas facing Daibei. However, the "Song of the Yan" is a summary of the flames of war in the northeast and the threat from the north. The flames of war in the northeast only refer to "cruel robbers", whereas the North is the real threat, and the battles are even more bitter. Thus, the poem describes in great length with "In late autumn, grass withered in the wild desert. / At sunset, soldiers in the lone city are scarce. / Favoured by the Emperor, they take foes lightly. / Exhausted, they fail to rescue the Guanshan siege". Soldiers fighting in different places are also portrayed in Xue Daoheng's "Singing Songs Every Night":

> Two years before fighting at Daibei,
> This year we leave for Liaoxi.
> No news once soldiers go away.
> Why should we cherish horses' hooves?

Here it says that soldiers fought at Daibei and then in Liaoxi, while the "Song of the Yan" says that soldiers passed by Daibei after fighting in Liaoxi. In short, the soldiers were not able to "cherish horses' hooves". This further explains why it is so easy to think that "Daijun is hidden behind towers" under the line "Yanshan facing ancient temples". Xu Ling's poem was written in the Northern and Southern Dynasties, so his feeling was more complicated. The Yanshan Mountains are only quietly facing ancient temples, and Daijun is hidden behind towers—the mountainous cities in the north are never the same as before. That is just a matter of fact.

From the reunification in the Qin and Han Dynasties to that in the Sui and Tang Dynasties, the Great Wall changed a little (for example, the northeastern walls only reached the Yuguan Pass, but the original outer line of the Great Wall of Yan crossed Liaodong in the north), but basically in the original line of defence. After the reunification in the Qin Dynasty, the three parts of the Great Wall of Yan, Zhao, and Qin were connected from Liaodong in the east to Lintao in Gansu Province. When another great wall along the Yumen Pass in Dunhuang was built in the Western Han Dynasty, the world-famous Ancient Great Wall of Ten Thousand *Li* came into being. The frontier fortress poems of the Sui and Early Tang are still centred around Yanshan and Yinshan, and examples can be found in Chen Zi'ang's "Thirty-Eight Poems on Feelings" beginning with "At dawn I went to Yunzhong County" and "The northern wind blows the sea trees", "I heard of battles at Huanglong" in Shen Quanqi's "Miscellaneous Poems" and his "Ancient Thoughts" beginning with "A young lady of the Lus", etc. In the High Tang, frontier fortress poetry was the most prosperous, but the centre moved to the northwest. One battle line is from the Great Wall of Qin to Lintao, and the other is from the Great Wall of Han to the Yumen Pass. Between the two great walls is Liangzhou, which thus replaced Daijun and became the most common place sung in frontier fortress poems. As shown in such lines as "In the vast desert at sunset / Lintao is gloomy in darkness", "The long clouds above Qinghai darken snow mountains. / The lone fortress is away from the Yumen Pass", and "Front army fought north of the Tao River at night, / Declaring they captured Tuyu Hun the Chief alive", Liangzhou has become the centre. Of course, there are poems about the North and the Northeast China, as in Gao Shi's "Song of the Yan". Another example is Wang Changling's "Army March":

> In the fortress of Han under the moon from Qin,
> No men back from a ten-thousand *li* march are seen.
> With the Dragon City's Flying Chief, we would win;
> No steeds of the Hu invaders could pass Mount Yin.

Therefore, basically frontier songs along the Great Wall, the frontier fortress poems of the Tang poets enriched the singing of a generation with the patriotic enthusiasm and high-spirited tone of frontier defence.

Recently, I read in *People's Daily* a poetic and cinematic essay "Visiting Historic Sites in Inner Mongolia" about this problem written by Prof. Jian Bozan. As a historian, he vividly revealed the regularities of the nomadic activities in the ancient frontier fortress from another perspective, represented the historical background of frontier fortress poems as if reproduced fully herein, and provided an excellent explanation for understanding the nature of frontier fortress poetry. The article states:

> The fertile fields south of Yinshan are not only the garden of the nomadic people, but the springboards for their entry into China. As long

as they occupy the fertile lands, they can cross the Yellow River by force and enter the valleys of the Fenhe River or the Yellow River ... If the Han people want to eliminate the threat of the nomads from the northwest, they must guard the valley of Yinshan. Otherwise, these horseback riders will cross the Ordos Desert and enter the heart of the Han people's residential areas.

Thus, the historical significance of "No steeds of the Hu invaders could pass Mount Yin" will be fully understood, and it is easy to know the emergency state of "The Commandant's pressing letter with feather flew to Hanhai, / When the Chief Chanyu's hunting fire was lightening Langshan". The article also argues:

These herdsmen, riders or soldiers always wanted to break through the Great Wall and enter the Yellow River valley. They either took the plains of the Liaohe River valley or the Xilingol Grassland as their strongholds. Most importantly, the Ulanchabu Plain was taken as their stronghold to knock at the gates of the Great Wall ... If these nomads could not hold their ground in the Yinshan Mountains, they would have to go westward and try to open a way from Juyan to the Taohe River valley or the Qinghai Grassland; if this attempt failed, they could only flee to the plateau by the Junggar Basin, and attack the southern Xinjiang from the eastern foot of the Tianshan Mountains. If resisted here, they would have to go faraway to Central Asia, and put their hopes in the valley of the Oxus River.

The historical images of ancient nomadic people are vividly described. However, knocking at the gate of the Great Wall from the Liaohe River valley, they would confront the Yanshan frontier; if from the Ulan Chabu Plain, they would stand over against the Yinshan frontier; if from Juyan to the Taohe River valley or Qinghai Grassland, they would challenge the Liangzhou frontier. In these main areas, ancient frontier fortress poetry was produced. From the Mid- and Late Tang on, the balance of the frontier forces gradually changed and the defence almost collapsed after the Five Dynasties. The prosperous frontier fortress poetry thus disappeared. These facts are thought-provoking in understanding frontier fortress poetry. As stated in the article, the contradiction between nationalities in history is the ancient people's misfortune. Thus, the frontier fortress poems in ancient times are solemn, heroic, and complicated. "About the fierce battle of the Great Wall, / All border guards talk with a high spirit. / Since ancient till now, in the yellow dust / Lots of white bones are cluttered with wild weeds". Understanding the complicated sentiment is a prerequisite to fully comprehend frontier fortress poetry.

Originally published in the *Wenhui Daily* (also *Wenhui Bao*) on 3 February 1962

7 Wang Zhihuan's "Song of Liangzhou"

The Yellow River rises far above white clouds.
A lone city stands before ten thousand mountains.
Why should the Qiang flute complain of green willows?
The spring breeze does never break through the Yumen Pass.

This is a famous quatrain, with which and a few other extant poems Wang Zhihuan in the Tang Dynasty became an unforgettable poet, especially for its important influence. Some people may doubt that the word "rises" in the first line of the poem is somewhat confusing, because the river water only flows downstream, not upwards. The doubt is certainly based on the principles of physics; however, the poet may only look at the river from a distance, not necessarily noticing the flow of water, similar to what is described in "The flute drowns the lone rover in sorrow; / The green waves are light as if they don't flow".[1] Then, it is not mainly a matter of physics but of cartography. When we paint a landscape painting, the water in the distance is always painted higher. Besides, the drop height of the Yellow River is relatively large. We say either that "The Yellow River falls from the Heaven" or that "The Yellow River rises far above white clouds". One is from far to near, while the other is from near to far. However, they are different in the static or dynamic ways of description. The former is dynamic in consideration of the water flow, whereas the latter is written as a static picture. Therefore, "The Yellow River falls from the Heaven" has a strong and unstrained feeling, while "The Yellow River rises far above white clouds" is close to a bright and clean sketch.

Perhaps because of the same doubt, the first line has another version "The yellow sand rises straight up to white clouds". "The yellow sand" can certainly "rises straight up", but it is "The Yellow River rises straight up to white clouds" in the *Collection of National Elegance* of the Song Dynasty block-printed edition reprinted in the Ming Dynasty. Thus, "the Yellow River" not only dramatically "rises", but rises "straight up". Of course, there

---

1 Liu Changqing. "Listening to the Flute".

are edition problems here regarding the three different poetic lines. However, in this research, the edition research will not be conducted. It seems that those in favour of "the Yellow River" are more than those who support "the yellow sand". Readers are discerning in that most of them prefer "The Yellow River rises far above white clouds". What is the reason? In terms of images, it is not ideal to say that "The yellow sand rises straight up to white clouds" because the white clouds will become yellow clouds if "the yellow sand" rises "straight up to white clouds". "Yellow clouds break the colours of spring, / Painted horns evoke frontier blues"[2] describes a typical scene of the frontier fortress, but the yellow sand is not massive enough to cover the sky. If "The wind and dust in the desert darkened the sun",[3] how can there be any association of white clouds? The image of "the yellow sand" is disunited and incompatible with that of "white clouds". As for "The Yellow River rises straight up to white clouds", it is not good either. Simply speaking, it is more of a waterfall than of a river. But, is "The Yellow River rises far above white clouds" the best? This text aims to answer this question.

To explain why this poem or this poetic line is good, we must first clarify the last two lines. But what on earth do they say? Are they saying that the Yumen Pass area is very desolate, or that it is a nice place? It seems to be a bit unclear.

The poem alludes from "Song of Plucking Willows" in the Northern Dynasties: "You mount the steed not for the whip, / But for plucking willow branches; / You dismount to play the Qiang flute; /The sadness softly kills passers". It is originally a song expressing traveller's parting feelings, and the music is played with the Hu flute, thus naturally with a strong alien flavour. Tang poets often write about how touching the tune is. Li Bai's "Hearing the Flute in Luoyang at a Spring Night" asks:

> Who is playing the jade flute with a beautiful tune? / With the breeze in spring, it spreads all over Luoyang. / Hearing in the songs tonight the 'Plucking Willows,' / Who will not begin to miss their homeland soon?

Liu Changqing's "Listening to the Flute" says:

> Ah, with the flute sound of 'Willows' of complex tones, / The spring colours of thousands of *li* hurt our hearts. / Where will the melodious sound fall with the wind? / Only the deep lake is seen when the song is over. / When we bid farewell to each other tomorrow, / A cry on horseback will make us almost white-haired.

---

2 Wang Wei. "Seeing off Judge Ping Danran".
3 Wang Changling. "Army March".

In the two poems, both "Plucking Willows" and "Willows" refer to this song. What is more noteworthy is that this song is always closely related to the spring breeze, as in the poems of Li Bai and Liu Changqing. Wang Zhihuan has another poem "Farewell": "Willows, as trees of the east wind, / Grow green along the royal river. / It's hard to pluck one recently / Because of lots of separations". "Willows", also called "trees of the east wind", are surely inseparable from the spring breeze. Youth is joyful, separations are bitter, while willows are both joyful and bitter, thus intertwined with a complex mood. Wang Wei's famous "Song of Weicheng" says: "A morning rain has washed Weicheng so clean; / The inn looks thriving in fresh willows green". On the one hand, the "inn" signifies "separation"; on the other, the "fresh willows" are "green". This contradiction is used to express a wealth of thought and feeling. Moreover, the song "Plucking Willows" has a story in history. Another version of this song says, "Along the Mengjin River afar, / Willows are green and luxuriant. / Born in a Hu family, / I know not Han people's songs". The Mengjin River flows in the current Henan province, where the Central Plain was located in ancient times. Of course, there were numerous willows in the native place; thus, the song appeared. However, even though the willows are common, the song is from the Hu tribes. The willows with strong national feelings appear in "Of yore I went away, / Willows would not say bye",[4] "Verdant grass grows along the river banks; / Green willows in the garden are flourishing", and "Lush orchids grow under the window; / Plenteous willows are before the hall". It now appears in a typical touching song of the Hu tribes stating that "I know not Han people's songs", which adds a more complex sentiment. As the history develops itself, the boundary between the Hu and the Han was no longer in the Central Plain, but far away in the Yumen Pass area after the end of the Northern and Southern Dynasties. Are there still many common willows? Since spring is short there, the willows, "as the trees of the east wind", are believed to be rare. Then why do the songs of the Hu flute also have sadness related to willows? This is a natural question from the poet. The poem is about Liangzhou nearer than the Yumen Pass, but the Hu and the Han peoples are living there in mixture, as recorded in "Herding steeds, a little Hu girl in fur coat / Sings two or three exotic songs at dusk".[5] In fact, the sentiment about the frontier fortress has been very strong in Liangzhou. Imagining the Yumen Pass, the soldiers will feel farther away and become more nostalgic for their home. This is a feeling that more cherished if it is rarer. When there is no willow, the sound of "Willows" in the flute then becomes a beautiful nostalgia. Thus, the poet's question shows that he really wants to listen to this song, though he seems to blame it. We may as well

---

4 "Minor Court Hymns: Picking Vetches"; "Nineteen Ancient Poems" No. 2; Tao Yuanming. "Imitating Ancient Poems".
5 Geng Wei. "Song of Liangzhou".

think about the logic of the two lines reversely, that is, since it is an objective fact that the Qiang flute is still heard complaining about the willows, the spring breeze must have come to the Yumen Pass. This has led to a linguistic miracle. It says that "The spring breeze does not break through the Yumen Pass", but quietly the pass has revealed the news of spring. However, what the poem actually says restricts the breakthrough, as if the spring breeze is on the brink of breaking through "the pass". This is about the spring in a frontier fortress. The less the spring, the more longing for the spring. Similarly, after the bitter winter, the icy river begins to break up in the bright wild, and the scenery appearing at the turning point of early spring is especially fresh and charming. In such a scenario, which is better? "The Yellow River rises far above white clouds" or "The yellow sand rises straight up to white clouds"? Isn't it very clear? It is this fresh and distinct feeling and the long-distance longing in the poem that constitute the spring picture at the frontier fortress, and give a reverse verdict to "The spring breeze does not break through the Yumen Pass". Then, the Yumen Pass (also the Jade Gate Pass) is no longer desolate but beautiful, just like the graceful impression of "jade" to people in line with its name.

Originally published in *Journal of Poetry* 1961 (4)

Appendix: Answers to a Reader's Questions

Dear Editor:

After reading Mr Wang Rubi's "Re-deliberation of Wang Zhihuan's 'Song of Liangzhou" published in the 421st issue in your journal, I find it difficult to agree with his arguments. My reasons are briefly summarised as follows:

1   It is inappropriate to assert in his article that the lonely city in Wang Zhihuan's poem must be the Yumen Pass, which was once called a lonely city in one of his poems. A "lonely city" is a very common phrase. In "Kuizhou is a lonely city in the sunset", the lonely city is not necessarily a frontier fortress, let alone the Yumen Pass. In "The paths of Longxi lead to the barren city", this "barren city" can also be called a "lonely city". When the Yumen Pass and the "lonely city" appear in the same poem, they can be one thing or two things. Thus, such a poem is not enough to be convincing proof.
2   According to the explanatory note of "Song of Liangzhou" in the *Collection of Yuefu Ballads*, the research holds that Liangzhou in the poem ""must not refer to Liangzhou in general, but to the specific Western Liangzhou in the current Dunhuang and Jiuquan areas in Gansu Province". However, the "Song of Liangzhou" in the *Collection of Yuefu Ballads* generally rather than specifically wrote about the Dunhuang and Jiuquan areas as in "Cold wind blowing the leaves at Yanmen in autumn, / Ten thousand *li* of smoke and dust dim watch towers. /The horses on the march long miss northern Qinghai; / At night Mount

Longshan is listening to Hu flutes". They specifically show that these "New *Yuefu* Ballads" are general descriptions.

3   Mr Wang thinks that it is "absolutely unacceptable" that the poet wrote about the whole Liangzhou in general when he first crossed the Yellow River and entered the Liangzhou area. Actually, it is not surprising. For example, Wang Bao's poem "Crossing the Northern Yellow River" has "Changshan is bordering Daijun; / Forts surround the Yellow River". Daijun is far from the Yellow River, but when he first crossed the northern bank of the Yellow River, the poet wrote about Daijun, together with the Yellow River. Is that also "absolutely unacceptable"? Entering Liangzhou at first, the poet felt a foreign sentiment of the frontier fortress. Spring had almost no traces here, so he felt as if spring would disappear in Liangzhou, and there would be no spring at the Yumen Pass. Thus, he says, why does the Qiang flute complain so much about such a few willows that represent spring? This is not only justifiable, but quite good in my humble opinion.

These are the main arguments in the research, and I have simply expressed my immature opinions. As for other arguments that some tribes "living" in Liangzhou are tantamount to "occupying" that part of Liangzhou, and that "the nine turns of the Yellow River" makes it impossible to rise "straight up", all counter-arguments should be self-evident without many words. In fact, a "straight" part of the nine-turn Yellow River of about 9,000 *li* might as well be as long as 1,000 *li*. I will not answer them one by one here.

Sincerely,
Lin Geng
Originally published in *Guangming Daily* on 15 July 1962

8   On Liangzhou

Wang Zhihuan wrote about "the Yellow River" and "a lone city" in his "Song of Liangzhou", which has aroused doubts about their co-existence in the same poem because the Liangzhou City (currently the county town of Wuwei) is far from the Yellow River. I remember Mr Pu Dong published an article on this issue in *Literature Research* a few years ago, and thought that the problem had been solved. Recently, I received from readers the same enquiry, and they wondered whether Liangzhou's dependent territory at that time included a city near the Yellow River. It seems that the problem needs to be explained with more details.

Liangzhou was originally a broad area, not only referring to the Liangzhou City, which can certainly be abbreviated as Liangzhou. Besides, the earliest Liangzhou City was not in Wuwei County. From the two Han Dynasties on, Liangzhou referred to the Longyou (also Longxi, or Western Longshan) area. The *Book of the Later Han* (also *Hou Hanshu*): Volume 33 records that under the administration of the Liangzhou governor, there were Longxi County, Wudu County, Jincheng County, Beidi County (now Ningxia County), Wuwei County, Zhangye County, Dunhuang County, etc. At that time, the Liangzhou governor also administered Longcheng, now the Northeast Qin'an County of Gansu Province, which was to the east of the Yellow River. Thus, Liangzhou was originally across the Yellow River. According to the *Book of the Later Han*, Longxi County had 11 towns, Wudu County seven, Jincheng County ten, Beidi County six, Wuwei County 14, Zhangye County eight, and Dunhuang County six. The total towns in Liangzhou were as many as about 80. After the Three Kingdoms, Liangzhou became the county town of Wuwei. In the Tang Dynasty, the strategically important Hexi (River West) Pavilion Administration consisted of two regions of "Hexi" and "Longyou", and the Hexi region established the Liangzhou Captaincy to govern Wuwei. Under the entries of Liangzhou Captaincy and Guzang (i.e., Wuwei) in the *Tang Book*, it is recorded that eight counties such as Gaolan and Helan were established. However, under the entry of Lanzhou, it reads that in the sixth year of Zhenguan, it began to supervise the Western Yanzhou, and in the 12th year, Liangzhou was supervised again. Lanzhou (i.e., Jincheng County) is a strategic place along the Yellow River, and the passage between Longxi and Hexi; thus, it is closely related to Liangzhou. The Commander of Liangzhou set up "Gaolan County", indicating that the southeastern part of Liangzhou is directly bordering the Yellow River. And in its northeast, "Helan County" was also set up, directly facing the North with the western bank of the Yellow River, which belongs to Liangzhou. Is it not very obvious? This is the so-called Hexi area. Undoubtedly, there were big and small fortresses because the county town was located here.

Generally, Liangzhou refers to the Hexi area, and the "Song of Liangzhou" is also a general description of the frontier fortress life in this area. It is not specifically written about the Liangzhou City, which can be proven by many Tang poems entitled "Song of Liangzhou". Even though the Liangzhou City was the centre of Liangzhou, and the location of the Hexi Pavilion Administration. The area described in Tang frontier fortress poems was usually a little more to the East. First of all, "Longxi" and "Hexi" were often poorly differentiated, because the ancient Liangzhou centred around the Longxi area was originally across the Yellow River. They have long appeared in frontier fortress poetry and formed a traditional concept. For example, Wang Wei's "Song of Longxi" depicts:

> For ten *li*, the steed kept running.
> It ran five *li* with each whipping!
> The chief's army letter arrived:
> The Huns are attacking Jiuquan.
> The flying snow on Mount Guanshan
> Has blocked the beacon fire and smoke.

With "Longxi" in the title, the poem mentioned the faraway "Jiuquan County" of Liangzhou. Geng Wei's "Song of Liangzhou" describes:

> National envoys follow the banners.
> Paths of Longxi lead to the barren city.
> Herding steeds, a little Hu girl in fur coat
> Sings two or three exotic songs at dusk.

Singing of "Liangzhou", it actually describes the "Longxi" area. In fact, there were two geographical regions of "Longyou" and "Hexi" in the Tang Dynasty, but Longxi to the east of the Yellow River and Liangzhou to the west were traditionally similar in people's mind. Thus, Liangzhou in the poet's pen is not far from the Yellow River. That is why Xue Feng says in "Song of Liangzhou" that "The nine-turn Yellow River belongs to the Han, / After blood of fights was shed out of the fortress". Liangzhou and the nine-turn Yellow River are of the same fate, rather than loosely related to each other. Some fortresses at that time may no longer exist today. Wang Zhihuan's poem was written probably when he first crossed the border of Liangzhou.

He could not help thinking of the whole Liangzhou and mentioned the Yumen Pass. However, it was still a general description of Liangzhou. According to the use of "a lone city" in the poem, probably the city is not big, and it is not necessarily recorded in history, nor is it easy to preserve. It is difficult to do specific textual research on which city it is, but undoubtedly the "Song of Liangzhou" can be concerned with the landscape and fortresses along the Yellow River.

Originally published in *Guangming Daily* on 19 November 1961

9 "Ancient Style: compassion for peasants"
An integration of realism and romanticism

In the realist poetry in the Mid-Tang, I particularly like this "Ancient Style" by Li Shen. Generally speaking, realistic poetry is mostly narrative; however, this is a lyrical poem. Though existent from ancient times, narrative poetry does not represent the most prominent tradition in ancient Chinese poetry. Chinese poetry is brilliant and unique in the world of poetry because of the astonishing collection of countless lyrical poems. If Chinese narrative poetry has a unique charm, it is because it also combines the characteristics of lyrical poetry, most prominently represented by Bai Juyi's "Song of Everlasting Regret". Lyrical poetry has made glorious achievements and the most mature development in classical poetry circles; however, it seems unsuitable for the realistic writing approach. Nevertheless, this "Ancient Style" has both realism and romanticism in revealing the exploitation:

> When a millet is sown in spring,
> Ten thousand grains grow in autumn.
> No field unfarmed in the Four Seas,
> But peasants are still starved to death!

The problem is raised sharply with concrete facts. The realistic writing approach, starting from the reflection of reality, requires a high degree of specificity. Therefore, it can observe in depth the complex relationship between people and their living conditions, and its authenticity and specificity need detailed descriptions. However, romanticism, aiming to reflect wishes and seek ideals, requires strong intensity and rich imagination, which are more macroscopic rather than specific. Its intensity and imagination bring about a simpler and undisturbed approach, sometimes appearing to be roughly outlined, as in:

> In the fortress of Han under the moon from Qin,
> No men back from a ten-thousand *li* march are seen.
> With the Dragon City's Flying Chief, we would win;
> No steeds of the Hu invaders could pass Mount Yin.

There is hardly anything specific here except a very common theme; however, it is highly generalised, pictorial, vivid, and magnificent. As mentioned earlier, this "Ancient Style" has the best of both realism and romanticism. After a detailed account of labour exploitation through the specific growth of a millet, the poem puts forward the most convincing argument. It also concludes that the hunger was not caused by natural disasters such as droughts and floods beyond human control at that time, but by the evil consequences of ruthless exploitation. The sharp accusation of "No field unfarmed in the Four Seas, / But peasants are still starved to death" depicts in a profound way the peasants' lives throughout the year from farming, harvesting, until being exploited. What an astonishing macroscopic generalisation that the poet describes the complex content in only four lines. This is a high integration of realism and romanticism. What's more valuable about this integration is that it reveals the dark side in a heroic protest without bringing a grey, gloomy, and glum atmosphere. Like a magnificent tragedy, the poem impresses us most with the lofty heroic character. From "When a millet is sown in spring" to "But peasants are still starved to death", the praise of peasants as heroes had reached the peak before it suddenly ended with a tragic turn. This is an intense impact of conflicts with gorgeous and eternal burning flame. Furthermore, in this poem deeply revealing class contradictions, it is precisely the sublime and great heroic images that make the exploiters so small that it does not waste a single word on the ruling class, while letting the labourers' images take full possession. Is this an artistic technique, a writing approach, or the spiritual essence? With such arrangements, the power of labour, the power of conquering the world, is made so brilliant.

In the first three lines, one millet grows to 10,000 grains until "No field" is "unfarmed in the Four Seas". A vast and magnificent situation full of imagination is unfolded in one breath, full of vigour and faith; it is this characteristic that chases away the common gloomy atmosphere in ordinary realist works. This really reflects that working people are always disassociated from pessimism. Is this poem romantic or realistic? To my experience, it is an integration.

There have been many discussions on the integration of realism and romanticism in the past few years. Some scholars think that it is difficult to integrate the two in ancient works, others think that it is a combination or coordination in that a real description of details may be added to a romantic work, or a realistic work may end with a romantic ending. However, this "Ancient Style" provides a different approach, because it is neither coordination of addition, nor a combination of beginning and end, nor a work without obvious characteristics of the two; it is an equally coordinated integration of realism and romanticism, forming a spectacular song with in-depth analysis of contradictions. It is a rare treasure in the poetry circle.

The editor of *Poetry Journal* asked me to write an academic article about poetry, but I found it extremely difficult. However, used to love this poem deeply, I had the above thoughts. Certainly, it is only an example of the integration of realism and romanticism.

24 September 1959
Originally published in *Poetry Journal* in October 1959

10 Spring is late, the green wild graceful[1]

Xie Lingyun's poems are relatively formal and stiff because he emphasises parallelism. However, when it comes to natural scenery, wit and humour are often at his fingertips, as in "In the pond, spring grass grows", and "The bright moon is shining on the snow". Moreover, "Spring is late, the green wild graceful" is especially admirable, similar to "The lotus at sunrise, / natural and lovely" or "Sailing in the East Sea / With mild wind and sunshine". Such praises are not exaggerations when used here.

"Spring is late, the green wild graceful" reflects the changing seasons of Nature. However, the word "late" actually suggests a scene at dusk. The peace and vastness of the dusk, though vague, are turned young with the word "spring". How cheerful and wide-reaching is "At dusk in Han palaces lighted candles are sent, / Light smokes scattered into Five Graceful families", which might be the source of "graceful". The wild and the graceful are absolutely not similar, just as the spring and the dusk represent two different characteristics. However, they are harmoniously integrated and have produced a new force, making the vast wild graceful everywhere. The word "green" further beautifies the scene, as it does in "The spring breeze greens the River South banks again"! The green colour seems caring but ruthless. It is the most harmonious and most lively, signifying Nature's health. We write about departing sorrow with "verdant grass" or "fragrant grass", focusing on the relationship between grass and roads, as in "Blue, blue grass grows at river banks, / Thinking of roads far, far away"; and "Fragrant grass far stirs up old roads". Moreover, the impressions of "blue" and "greenish" are different from that of "green". As for "The autumn grass green has faded" and "The autumn wind drives out the court green", they are not pure green, and not enough to explain the essence of green, which envelops everything but is so fresh that it leaves no trace.

From "Spring is late, the green wild graceful", we only see a green wild with hills and trees. It greens everything in different landscapes and various occasions; thus, it is close to Nature and becomes a vast field. Being in the

1 Xie Lingyun. "Entering the Mouth of the Pengli Lake".

rain for long, I really do not like the misty drizzle. However, those poems about it still arouse my greatest interest, let alone "When cold rain came to River Wu at night" and "Misty rain falls on the neat river grass". Even when I think of people's views of the West Lake that a sunny lake is not so good as a rainy lake, I feel great interest. Usually unworthy of consideration, it is really a question after a second thought. Why is a sunny lake not so good as a rainy one? This is, of course, a one-sided remark because a sunny lake is more common. However, the beauty of a rainy lake is unforgettable because the misty drizzle harmonises everything independent, and moistens everything monotonous, just as the dusk covers up the mess of the world and makes it a whole. In this sense, is there a sunny rain in "Spring is late, the green wild graceful"? It integrates the hills and the wild by blending all the different colours into one colour. Thus, the integral wild coexists with the word "graceful". Here, we sense a rich sentiment and a relaxed beauty, without any worry or the feeling of dusk. Then the universe of spring is accomplished, and we are always delighted as if rejuvenated.

11 On a poem by Xie Tiao

>   Cold sophora trees in clusters,
>   Groups of autumn chrysanthemums,
>   Who can tell me the time of ours?
>   Cold wind missing northern horses.[1]

Xie Tiao's poems have been praised by Li Bai. Indeed, his poems are natural, enlightening, and graceful from beginning to end. The greatness of Nature lies in that it enriches even the smallest things, though it's unknown how many poets fond of exaggeration have written such poetic lines as "The nine gates of Heaven opened in the palace, / All envoys of ten thousand states bowed to the Crown". Here we can truly understand the language needed in arts.

"Cold sophora trees in clusters" describes a scene in late autumn, but with more sentiment. We seem to feel that the branches shrank together because of the cold, which is a tender hint that the "autumn chrysanthemums" will grow in "groups". Then, we add a relationship to this relationship, and more warmth to this warmth. Written about the wandering at the year-end, it has become a deeper nostalgia for the world. The poet, chrysanthemums, and cold sophora trees do not necessarily have relationships, but we relate them by chance. So comes the question "Who can tell me the time of ours?" In "Cold wind missing northern horses", we feel the power of missing and the solemn scene in the wild of Nature, so everything becomes attentive and silent for it. However, where are the horses? It seems to be a groundless feeling and affection. Or is it a broad mind? However, we are not able to make a detailed inquiry into the reasons for the feeling and affection, nor is it necessary. "Falling flowers have no words; / A man is pure as a chrysanthemum", let alone the horses hard to find. As in "Away like dragons in deep mountains and great water, / In the shady wild with spring cold after sunset", we conceal the great sentiment of loftiness in distant imagination like the dragons in great water. "Cold sophora trees", "autumn chrysanthemums", "Cold

---

1 Xie Tiao. "Watching the Sunset in Melancholy".

wind", and "northern horses" listed from near to far have their own merits. However, "Who can tell me the time of ours?" seems to be the most unnecessary line here, since the "cold sophora trees" and "autumn chrysanthemums" have pointed out the time. Why does the poet ask about "the time"? On the contrary, this is the most far-reaching line, because of which the unimaginable melody is played, and the nostalgia of the cold wind becomes universally present. William Wordsworth, a 19th-century British poet, says in "The Solitary Reaper":

> Perhaps the plaintive numbers flow
> For old, unhappy, far-off things,
> And battles long ago:

Great works are manifestations of the most distant sentiments because they are the most untraceable, eternal, and universal.

12 On Yu Xin's poem about Zhaojun

> By the Guanglu Fortress, with knitted brows,
> She looks out at the Madame Fan City.
> Pieces of rouge on her cheeks fade away,
> For the teardrops falling down from her face.
> She leads the horse to cross rivers of ice;
> She walks with saddles on the roads of snow.
> The wind of the Hu is freezing her bones;
> The moon at night is glowing on her heart.
> With the *qin* zither, she plays a Han song,
> But, suddenly cuts in the Hu pipe's sound.

"Zhaojun's complaint" is a traditional theme. However, this poem does not start from the word "complaint", but describes her mood when she crossed the boundary between the Hu and the Han on her way out of the fortress. The poem is about her eternal farewell to her homeland, her uncertain future, and her remembrance of a heroine's story evoked by the Madame Fan City. The original story of the city is recorded in the *Book of Han: Biography of the Hun*, in which Ying Shao notes: "This city was built by a Han general. After his death, his wife led remaining soldiers and their wives and completely secured it; thus, the name". Nevertheless, Zhaojun's peace-making marriage outside the frontier is different from the frontier defence of Madame Fan. Madame Fan leading the remaining soldiers preserved the frontier city of her home country, and her fate was in her own hands; however, what would fall upon Zhaojun when she went outside the frontier for marriage with a foreign chief? In a helpless foreign land and a strange world dominated by others, how much courage was needed for the lonely weak woman to face her unknown fate! What's more, Madame Fan was always inside the country, whereas Zhaojun was doomed to be exiled forever. By contrast, what a complicated contradiction would have arisen here! This poem does not summarise with the word "complaint", nor does it demonstrate the complex contradictions. However, it suddenly condenses thousands of words into a silent beauty, and sublimates Zhaojun's body of flesh and blood to a transparent and glorious image with endless significance.

The poem's most brilliant lines are: "She leads the horse to cross rivers of ice; / She walks with saddles on the roads of snow. / The wind of the Hu is freezing her bones; / The moon at night is glowing on her heart". In the first four lines, expressions such as "knitted brows", "looks out at", "Pieces of rouge on her cheeks fade away", and "teardrops falling down" clearly show her wandering mind. After "She leads the horse to cross rivers of ice", such words all disappear, and she suddenly speeds up her footsteps to continue her journey. "She leads the horse to cross rivers of ice" means that the horse needs to be led to cross rivers, seemingly emphasising the horse; while in "She walks with saddles on the roads of snow", the focus obviously shifts from the horse to Zhaojun though the poem describes the common fate of the human and the horse. In general, these two lines are still describing the outside world of ice and snow. However, when "The wind of the Hu is freezing her bones", the horse is completely ignored, and the description of her image also begins to move from the outside world to her body. The freezing wind in the Hu area is piercing into her body of flesh and blood as if it were an anatomical knife. Finally, Zhaojun's inner world is suddenly illuminated and enlightened when "The moon at night is glowing on her heart".

When the moon is hanging high in the clear and boundless sky above the vast snowy wild, everything is crystal clear; a weak girl, extremely lonely, is moving towards the future of her fate. At this time, only the pure and bright moon is her friend in loneliness to reveal her selfless and pure heart facing everything without shame! This is the reason why "The moon at night is glowing on her heart" is so powerful as the peak of the whole poem. The step-by-step leap to the peak is like the run-up before an excellent jumper leaps over the bar. The necessary run-up is only a process, and the decisive point of time is the breath-taking instant of the leap. The first four lines illustrate Zhaojun's mood, which gradually leaps into a complete state when the four lines to the peak appear. With the leap of the state, the true height of all thoughts and feelings is reached. Without this height, the run-up will not be interesting to many people. Similarly, the poetic language will leave nothing but a refined run-up.

13 On Wang Changling's "Out of the Fortress"

In the fortress of Han under the moon from Qin,
No men back from a ten-thousand *li* march are seen.
With the Dragon City's Flying Chief, we would win;
No steeds of the Hu invaders could pass Mount Yin.

The poem beginning with "In the fortress of Han under the moon from Qin" is probably the best seven-character quatrain in the Tang Dynasty, mainly because the first line is the best in a straight-forward manner. We are surprised at its extraordinary atmosphere, and simply have no time to examine other details. Wei Yingwu posits: "The spring breeze is just for willows. / The night view darkens the mountains". This is about the peaceful beauty of the night, which can be a good contrast to it. The latter says that the continuous mountains are going to disappear, whereas the former reads that the moonlight is drawing a towering pass. The former is graceful while the latter is magnificent. The soft spring breeze makes you feel indulged while the shadow of the moon wakes you up in the darkness. "In the passes of Han under the moon from Qin" is so immovable and historical that everything in space and time has become an indelible impression. It brings to our limited life the understanding of eternal opposites. The softness of the moonlight is usually inappropriate for such an expression on immovability; however, the poet's success just lies in this important opposite. The images in Li Yi's "Frontier frost fell on elm leaves at the pass last night. / The bugle was blown under the lonely city moon" are also impressive for the shadow under the moon. The strong and high-spirited sense of frontier in "Wild geese fly high under the dark moon", and "The seven stars in the North are high" best explain "In the passes of Han under the moon from Qin".

  The immovability of the pass is beyond doubt, and its towering in the shadow of the moon is more imaginable. However, in "The bugle was blown under the lonely city moon", the moon is so solitary, while the moon in "Wild geese fly high under the dark moon" is so dark that it almost does not exist. However, the moon in "In the passes of Han under the moon from Qin" is resplendent and spectacular. It seems that it were shining from the Qin and Han Dynasties to the Tang Dynasty, then "Men never returned from a ten-thousand *li* march" has the vehemence of water rushing down a thousand *li*, and the long march is simply long enough to leap between the Han and Tang Dynasties. This is a picture of history, conveying a feeling of history. The former is standing like a sculpture for thousands of years, while the latter is melodious like the gushing water. The force completely comes from the first straightforward line.

The frontier fortress poetry of the Tang Dynasty is a sound of the prosperous age. After the High Tang, they came to an end, which is why "In the fortress of Han under the moon from Qin" is so representative and so rich in artistic charm. It is a poetic theme brought about by the unification of the Qin and Han Dynasties however, not described until the peak of the Tang poetry. It is not difficult for us to understand the profound and strong power in its vigorous and unrestrained singing.

14 On Meng Haoran's innocent enjoyment

My old friend prepared chicken rice,
And invited me to his farmstead.
Green trees surrounding the village,
Verdant hills lie far from the town.
Out of the window in a garden,
We drink, talking about sesame.
In the Double Ninth Festival,
I'll come back for chrysanthemums.

This is one of Meng Haoran's masterpieces. Especially impressive are the first four lines that have been mistakenly collected in Wang Wei's anthology in the form of a quatrain. It can be seen that this poem is very similar to Wang Wei's works. It has been a long time since Wang and Meng are mentioned in the same breath because later generations lay particular stress on Wang Wei's seclusion poetry. However, even in seclusion poetry, Wang Wei's style is obviously different from that of Meng Haoran. The former is more natural and refreshing, while the latter is more profound and aloof. As for other aspects such as the frontier fortress theme, seven-character ancient long poems, seven-character quatrains, and even in five-character regulated poems such as "Watching Hunting" and "Seeing off Commander Zhao to Daizhou", Wang Wei is quite different from Meng Haoran. Most of Meng's poems concentrate on the seclusion theme and are in the form of five-character regulated poetry with a rigorous and refined style, often giving people a deeper sense of loneliness. Sometimes he is impassioned besides aloofness, as in his masterpiece "Lodging by the Tonglu River and Sending to my Old Friends in Guangling":

In dark mounts, sad apes are crying.
The vast river swiftly flows at night.
The wind blows off the leaves on banks,
The moon shining on a lone boat.
Jiande county isn't my homeland;
How I miss my friends in Yangzhou!
Oh, two lines of my tears will be
Sent to the west end of the sea.

The images here are also rare in Wang Wei's poems. Meng Haoran is characterised by a deep feeling of injustice under the surface of solitude, which is inseparable from his life experience and personality. Of course, Meng also occasionally has some works of innocent enjoyment. "Passing by My Old Friend's Farmstead" is one of the representatives.

To illustrate the innocent enjoyment of this poem, it is better to compare it with his another poem "To Zhang the Fifth after Climbing the Orchid Hill in Autumn", which reads:

> In the North Mountain in white clouds,
> Hermits enjoy their time in peace.
> I climb the mountain to look far;
> My heart flies away with wild geese.
> Sadness triggered by the dim dusk,
> My spirit springs from the clear autumn.
> People returning to the village
> Rest at the ferry by a flat beach.
> Earth-end trees are like shepherd's purse;
> The river islet is like the moon.
> When can I bring wine for a drink
> Until drunken at the Double Ninth day?

This is also a masterpiece. Nevertheless, in this poem, the poet is lonely. Although he saw "People returning to the village", he admired that "Hermits enjoy their time in peace". He saw such a beautiful world on the mountain top, but he could only hide in white clouds, as what "Inviting Recluses" says:

> Osmanthus trees grow in quiet mountains
> ...
> Come back, Emperor's grandson,
> You cannot stay long in the mountains.[1]

Although he feels noble and unsullied in the mountains, the poet cannot help feeling a little desolate. Thus, although this poem and "Passing by My Old Friend's Farmstead" finally conclude with the same hope of drinking with friends on the Double Ninth Day, one sets in the lonely mountains while the other is in a farmstead in the human world; one is looking forward to warmth in an aloof mood whereas the other is enjoying friendship and Nature. Most of Meng Haoran's works actually belong to the former. This poem thus shows the joy a lonely poet can obtain in the human world that is symbolised in such a simple farmstead, only in which our unfortunate poet can be truly accommodated.

---

1 *Literary Selections*, Volume 33.

Tao Yuanming has a well-known poem "On Going Back", showing how happy the poet was when he resigned from his official post and went back to the countryside. It is not difficult for us to understand why Meng Haoran is full of joy in "Passing by My Old Friend's Farmstead". It is this joy that makes him sing about the beauty of a peaceful village life, which only a simple heart can deeply feel. Such an ordinary farmstead has no attractive scenic spot or any particularity but a garden with mulberry trees, sesame plants, and paths for the villagers. Who on earth really loves this little world? However, Meng Haoran did write about this simple little world, which is similar to Tao Yuanming's "Peach Blossom Valley". It is not easy for a poet to create a little world in his writing. The poet has to sing highly of it wholeheartedly with a high degree of unity between his world view and the simple rural life. Thus, a typical peaceful village in an ideal little world is represented through the poet's inner world. Without excessive statements, Meng Haoran authentically demonstrated to us its artistic images.

For further understanding, we need to analyse the poem more concretely. The first two lines seem very simple because of the plain language and the simple hospitality in the farmstead, as shown in:

> My old friend prepared chicken rice,
> And invited me to his farmstead.

Thus, the whole poem begins in the atmosphere of a common life, which is a good start for the whole poem. Through the specific and detailed description of the chicken rice, it builds an image for the whole farmstead. This is harmonious, real, and full of possibilities. Hence appear the famous lines that have been circulated for thousands of years:

> Green trees surrounding the village,
> Verdant hills lie far from the town.

This is the soul of the whole poem, and the peak of integration between the thoughts, feelings, and artistic images. To recognise the real merits of the two lines, we will quote a few lines from Ma Zhiyuan's "A Dual-Tone: Boating at Night":

> The red dust will never fly over to the door,
> While green trees just cover corners of the cottage.
> The verdant mountain happens to mend broken walls.
> A thatched hut with bamboo rails.

This is also a masterpiece in literary songs (or *sanqu*). Individually speaking, Ma Zhiyuan's poetic lines may be more attractive because they are fresh in description. However, when the two are contrasted, we can feel that Meng Haoran's poetic lines are more profound with no unnatural trace while the whole farmstead is vividly exhibited, showing more of the poet's expertise. Of course, this is partly because Ma Zhiyuan wrote it from the corners of a thatched hut, which is a small world of the hermit luckily tied up with Nature. However, Meng Haoran wrote about the whole village, where his poem has more flavour of the human world in a more common world, making it more profound.

"Green trees surrounding the village, / Verdant hills lie far from the town" describes not only the well-arranged close-up and distant view, but the green trees around the village and the verdant hills lying far from the green trees, which are interestingly reflected as a harmonious and unsophisticated beauty. There is no harm in saying that they are closely related to each other, similar to "Who are never bored with each other? / Only the Jingting mountain and I". The green trees, like a gentle mother, are embracing the village, and the verdant hills like sentries watch over it from afar. Their hearts are all in the village, and the town is ignored and left aside. With "Green trees surrounding the village", we know that they are outside the town. But, why did the poet say that "Verdant hills lie far from the town"? In fact, this line is to contrast the unimportance of the town. The verdant hills, green trees, and the village are mixed with each other like water and milk; thus, the town has to stand silently by the side as if non-existent. This is really the most amiable picture. At the same time, through the lingering of the verdant hills and the embrace of the green trees, how intimate we shall feel about this village, as if we should have known it long before. Thus, we feel the green of every grassland, the growth of every crop, and the smell of the earth on every path. These were not written in the poem, but did exist in a glimpse of the verdant hills and the embrace of the green trees. Our unfortunate poet, like a poor child, suddenly arrived at his truly beloved wonderland, and wanted to look around with many questions. Therefore,

> Out of the window in a garden,
> We drink, talking about sesame.

He didn't know how much he would talk about. He really enjoyed himself in the little world unfolded before his eyes. Therefore,

> In the Double Ninth Festival,
> I'll come back for chrysanthemums.

He said he would come back again next time. Of course, he would come back again. Isn't it in the most sincere and touching language? Anyone with a little childlike innocence knows what his innocent heart is going to say when he is about to leave the place he has been playing all day. The world of "Green trees surrounding the village, / Verdant hills lie far from the town" will always live in the poet's heart; thus, this poem will always live in our hearts.

Originally published in *Chinese Learning*, February 1957

15 On Wang Wei's "Song of Weicheng"

"My friend, raise a toast with wine! One more cup! / West of the Sunny Pass no friend cheers you up" in the "Song of Weicheng" were sung as the "Triple Singing of the Sunny Pass". Li Dongyang's *Poetry Talk at the Huailu Hall* says:

> Wang Mojie's (also Wang Wei) 'West of the Sunny Pass no friend cheers you up' is unprecedented before the High Tang. Once written, it was often recited. When reciting was insufficient, it was rewritten in the triple singing. After that, other poems chanting about departure can hardly go beyond its sense even though they have thousands of words.

Excellent lines about the border pass include "In the passes of Han under the moon from Qin" and "The spring breeze does not break through the Yumen Pass". Each of them was said to be the best quatrain. However, the line about "the Sunny Pass" describes a different scene, as in "The sun shines on the Tongguan Pass of four opened gates". This scene can help explain the relationship between "sunny" and "pass".

The loneliness of the wilderness always accompanies the beginning of all civilisations. When this historical significance is recognised, literature and art have a significant value. "Trees at the Hanyang town stand by the shining shore; / The Parrot sandbar has grass in the lush, green state". With bright colours, the texts forcefully show the implicature besides the original meaning. Although the poet might not have noticed this when he used these words, his unconscious choice decided the success or failure of the expressions, and this creation is thus the expression of real spirits. Reading "Your black crossed collars", we would be impressed with the colour word "black". Here we want to discuss another word "Yellow". The suggestiveness of colour is most affective in literature and art. If the yellow crane in the regulated poem on the Yellow Crane Tower were changed into a white crane, the whole mood would have been changed, and the couplet beginning with "The trees in Hanyang town stand by the shining shore" would have lost a base for contrast. Yellow is the colour of the sun and that of the soil. It seems to be the primitive people's bright footprints. Moreover, were they not walking on the "Xianyang ancient path" when they went out of "the west of the Sunny Pass"? However, the freshness shown in "The inn looks thriving-green in fresh willows", and the antiquity shown in "No sound or dust on the Xianyang ancient path" are intertwined in this poem. How can it stop people from having one singing and three sighs?

In "My friend, raise a toast with wine! One more cup! / West of the Sunny Pass no friend cheers you up", the expression "One more cup" naturally means "more than one cup". Moreover, "raise a toast with wine", in fact, suggests "bottomless". Wei Zhuang's *ci* poem says, "Cherish the host's heart as a deep / Drink of wine means deep affection", and then the expression of "no friends" actually means "there are friends". Here, the ideas in contradiction cannot be differentiated; thus, they are not merely ingenious but profound. The feeling of farewell has been described in "The most sadness is the separation alive" by the ancients. However, the purpose of art is to bring people to a higher ideal, rather than to make them dependent on life. The reason why tragedy is often more moving is that it awakens people with fresh inspiration. We know again in this world our own lives, which are more distinct after cultivation. The merit of "Song of Weicheng" lies not in its feeling of farewell, but in the deeper feelings of life blended in it.

16 On Wang Wei's "Farewell in the Mountain"

> The spring grass will be green next year.
> Will the Emperor's grandson return?[1]

Wang Wei's poem reads: "Seeing off my friend in the mountain, / The wood gate is half-closed at dusk. / The spring grass will be green next year. / Will the Emperor's grandson return?" In fact, the third line also reads, "The spring grass will be green each year". As for the difference of one word in the poem, we have no way to check it because it was written a long time ago; thus, the two lines exist simultaneously. Only in this way can we feel the excellency of "The spring grass will be green next year". The short poem has four lines with two completely different scenes. The first half is in the dusk, while the second half suddenly becomes bright. At sunset, the wood gate is half closed, then what else can be said? However, the poet's heart is outside the gate. "Spring is full of energy; / All things suddenly appear". Thus, out of tranquillity there comes excitement, and out of peace there is joy. The dusk suggests the end of all things, while spring is the beginning of all things. What about the gate? It is both the beginning and the end. The double scenes arise in the instant of closing the gate. Tao Yuanming says that "At sunset living beings rest". There is a subtle feeling of gratitude and the beauty of home. It contains everything, so it can nurture everything. The vitality is expressed with the poet's sentiment. Of these four lines, the first half is the background, while the second half is the main body, which is a common allusion recorded in "Inviting Recluses" saying: "The Emperor's grandson won't return. / The spring grass grows luxuriant". So he asks: "The spring grass will be green next year. / Will the Emperor's grandson return?" But "Inviting Recluses" originally notes: "Osmanthus trees are growing in quiet mountains... Climbing up osmanthus twigs, I'll stay for a while". "The Emperor's grandson stays" in the mountains. His "return" is naturally concerned with whether he leaves the mountains or not. "Return" here is rather like saying "come or not", which is really hard to clarify. In

---

1 Wang Wei. "Farewell in the Mountain".

short, mountains make people reluctant to leave, and the feeling of reluctance is all due to a word "明[míng] (bright; next; clear; understand; etc.)" in the original poem.

We are familiar with the expressive power of "明" in Chinese, which can also be interpreted as "bright". If we remove "bright" in "The waning moon is bright by our faces. / The sad tears of farewell drop until dawn", the poem becomes weak. Another example is "The sun shines on the road back with sunset glow bright". Only with the word "bright" can the beauty of the peacock in the following line be fully expressed. Obviously, the Chinese word "明" here is intentionally used while the simplicity and innocence of the Tang poetry are between the intentional and unintentional words. "明年[míngnián] (Next year)" obviously refers to the coming year. However, there is unintentionally a feeling of "brightness" in the eyes because "明" also means "bright", which is what cannot be said in the poem.

We think the Chinese word "明" can be well used by anyone. However, sometimes it means "bright", while other times it does not; still sometimes it becomes "bright" when you do not want it to light up. Here can we have no hesitation in diction? The use of "年年[niánnián] (each year)" in Chinese was originally a feeling of flowing water. Li Shangyin's "Each year by the Silver River in the blue sky, / It's time for the golden wind to meet the jade dew" shows the meeting time of the Cowboy and Weaving Girl in Chinese legends who meet once each year on the seventh day of the seventh lunar month, while the word "明" seems to be counter-time. Years going away are similar to the flowing water, but the word "明" bestows it with a sense of brightness in the eyes. This is the charm of poetic language as if the spring grass will be brightly green. Then, what should the Emperor's grandson do? The brilliance and vitality of spring are the beginning of all beginnings. Moreover, all the news in the world are not willing to be left alone; thus, it is impossible to hide them with a wood gate.

Postscript to the Chinese edition

The Tang poetry is a glorious milestone in the history of ancient Chinese poetry. Its fresh artistic feeling, simple but profound language, vigorous atmosphere, and liberating sentiment all leave an unforgettable impression on people. It's impossible to inquire about the nature of this peak and to explore its mystery in a few words. Therefore, I tried to achieve some general understanding of the poetry in the High Tang from different perspectives. In this way, I wrote articles whenever I had ideas, some of which are relatively direct while others are relatively indirect. The first part is called "The Peak of the Tang Poetry" and the second part "Far Notes of the Tang Poetry", which are combined into the book *A Comprehensive Study of Tang Poetry*. It includes "The Poet Li Bai" published as a book earlier. "Essays on Poems" at the book's end consists of 19 short essays, most of which were written in the early years on poems from the beginning of classical Chinese poetry to the Tang and Song Dynasties. Most of the essays are my understanding of a few poetic lines not worth serious discussion, which are included as the residual sound of the book.

    The compiling of this book cost a long time in finding and reproducing the publications in newspapers and journals because nine out of ten of my manuscripts were lost in the Cultural Revolution (1966–1976). Zhong Yuankai and Shang Wei, postgraduate students at Peking University, have successively helped to complete this work. When the manuscript is published, I would like to express my deep gratitude to them. Hereby I conclude the postscript.

In Yannan Garden on 10 December 1985.

Appendix
Mr Lin Geng's academic chronology[1]

Lin Geng, alias Jingxi, was born in Beijing on 22 February 1910 (the 13th day of the first lunar month) to a family from Minhou County (now in Fuzhou City), Fujian Province. His father is Lin Zhijun (1879–1960), alias Zaiping, a famous scholar and calligrapher who studied in Japan in his early years.

1928

Graduated from the High School Affiliated to Beijing Normal University; enrolled in the Department of Physics, Tsinghua University.

1930

Transferred to the Department of Chinese Language and Literature, Tsinghua University. Joined the "Chinese Literature Society" under Zhu Ziqing's guidance and founded with his poet friends a student magazine, *Literature Monthly*, in the Department of Chinese Language and Literature, Tsinghua University.

1931

Published in *Literature Monthly* 16 *ci* poems such as "To the Tune: Exotic Dancers Called Buddhists". Began to write new poems in free verse after writing ancient poems; wrote a new poem "Prayer at Twilight", which was published later in *Youth Music* in 1942 (Volume 2, No. 4), and made into music by Zhang Dinghe.

1932

Wrote for himself: "A little spark can start a fire that burns the entire prairie / Too much ash is useless / I will explore why a little spark burns a prairie /

---

[1] This chronology is in reference to "The Annalistic Record of Lin Geng's Works" co-authored by Peng Qingsheng and Fang Ming.

And trace the beginning of all beginnings", which became the motto of his constant exploration and transcendence in his studies and career.

1933

Graduated from the Department of Chinese Language and Literature, Tsinghua University; began working at Tsinghua as an assistant of Zhu Ziqing, and assessed students' homework in the course of Chinese for Wen Yiduo. At the invitation of Zheng Zhenduo, became an editor of the *Literary Quarterly*, responsible for soliciting contributions to the column on new poetry.

On 18 September, published his first new poetry collection *Night* at his own expense, for which Wen Yiduo designed the book cover, and Yu Pingbo wrote the foreword. This collection selected 43 new poems in free verse written from 1931 to 1933, including "Through the Mist" and "Night".

1934

At the beginning of the year, resigned from the teaching assistantship of Tsinghua University to prepare for professional writing. In spring, went to Shanghai, Nanjing, Suzhou, and so on, and became acquainted with writers such as Shi Zhecun and Mao Dun.

In summer, returned to Beijing; taught the History of Chinese Literature as a lecturer at the Peping Republic College.

In October, published his second poetry collection, *Spring Wilderness and Windows*, in the Peping Literature Review Press, for which his fiancée Ms Wang Xiqing painted the cover. This collection includes 57 new poems in free verse such as "Spring Wilderness", "Dawn", and "Nature".

Began to write new poems in metric rather than in free verse.

Set out to write *A History of Chinese Literature*.

1936

Continued to teach in the Peping Republic College, while teaching part-time at the Women's College of Arts and Sciences of Peping University, and Peping Normal University.

On 22 February, published *Peiping Love Songs*, his third collection of new poems in the Peiping Wind and Rain Poetry Society, including 58 new metrical poems such as "An Autumn Day", "Dream Talks by the Stove", and "Ancient Feelings".

In November, published *Hibernation Melody and Others*, his fourth collection of new poems in the Peiping Wind and Rain Poetry Society, for which Qiming (Zhou Zuoren) wrote the book title and Feiming wrote the foreword. This collection contains 32 new metrical poems such as "Hibernation Melody", "The First Lunar Month", and "Fine Drizzle", followed by the "Postscript" written on 1 November.

Had 19 new poems translated into English and collected in *Modern Chinese Poetry* (London, 1936), edited by British Professor Harold Acton.

1937

The Lugou Bridge (also the Marco Polo Bridge) Incident broke out, and the War of Resistance against Japan began. At the beginning of September, invited by Zhu Ziqing on behalf of Sa Bendong (also Adam Pen Tung Sah), President of Xiamen University, to teach as a lecturer. Went to Xiamen from Tianjin via Hong Kong on a British ship of the Swire Pacific.

1938–1940

In the summer of 1938, promoted to the associate professorship. Published articles "On the Xiang Legends" and "On the Forms of New Poetry".

1941

Promoted to the professorship.

Published in Xiamen University Press the first three mimeographed editions of *A History of Chinese Literature*: *The Age of Enlightenment*, *The Golden Age*, and *The Silver Age*. First proposed "the Youth Spirit in the Tang poetry" in "The Peak of the Poetic State", the 14th chapter of *The Golden Age*.

1942–1946

Published two new poems "Autumn Colours", and "A Dialogue at Dawn", as well as an article "A Random Talk on Teaching Selected Poems".

1947

Published *A History of Chinese Literature* in Xiamen University Press, for which Mr Zhu Ziqing wrote the foreword.

In summer, resigned from Xiamen University.

In autumn, returned to Peping and served as a professor at Yenching University.

1948

Wrote more than ten poems and articles. Put forward in "The Forms of New Poetry Revisited" for the first time the "half-pause law", insisting that a slight pause in a five-character or seven-character poem always divides the characters into either two-three, or four-three in terms of Chinese characters.

1949

From 2 to 29 July, participated in the First National Congress of Literary and Art Workers in China. Was a representative of each following congress.

In September, completed a long poem "People's Days", which was published in *Popular Poetry* in 1950 (Volume 1, No. 2).

1950

In May, participated in the First Congress of Literary and Art Workers in Beijing. On 31 May, made a speech at the closing ceremony, and was elected as a council member of the Beijing Literature and Art Federation.

1951

Published in *Guangming Daily* (also *Enlightenment Daily*) "Re-discussing Nine-Character Poems", "On the Idea that Content Determines Form—Answering Mr Pu Yang", and an article about Qu Yuan.

1952

Became a professor in the Department of Chinese Language and Literature of Peking University when Yenching University merged into Peking University in the national adjustment of institutions.

In August, published *A Study of Poet Qu Yuan and His Works* in the Bush Cherry (also Tangdi) Press.

1953

In June, attended on behalf of China the 2230th anniversary of the death of Qu Yuan, one of the Four Famous Men of World Culture, and gave a lecture "The Emergence of the Poet Qu Yuan", which was published in *Ta Kung Pao* on 13 June.

1954–1955

From 1 March on, served as an editor of the newly founded *Literary Heritage*, a supplement of *Guangming Daily* until June 1963 when it ceased publication.

In June, finished writing *The Poet Li Bai*, and made an academic report in the Department of Chinese Language and Literature of Peking University.

In September, published *A Brief History of Chinese Literature* (the Upper Volume) in Shanghai Literature and Art United Publishing House. By November, it was reprinted three times totalling 10,000 copies.

In November, published in Shanghai Literature and Art United Publishing House *The Poet Li Bai*, which consists of 12 sections in five chapters and an appendix of 96 poems by Li Bai. In 1955, supplemented and revised the fourth section, and wrote a postscript for the third edition. From November 1954 to February 1958, it was printed seven times for circulation totalling 61,000 copies, which is rare in the research history of the Tang poetry. However, due to the overflow of "ultra-leftist ideological trend", his views have been constantly challenged and criticised.

1956–1957

In 1956, became the Director of the Teaching and Research Office of ancient literature in the Department of Chinese Language and Literature, Peking University. Served as the Director until retirement.

Peking University began to enrol doctorate students for Associate Doctorate Degrees, and Liu Xuekai became his first doctorate student for an Associate Doctorate Degree. In April 1957, gave the Advanced Party School Journalism Class an academic report entitled "A Bird's Eye View of Classical Chinese Literature", which was published in *Journalism and Publication*. In May, gave another academic report entitled "Four Greatest Tang Poets" in Qingdao. In the two years, published more than ten poems and articles.

1958

In summer, specially investigated and underwent "key criticism" when the nationwide "Educational Revolution" focused on criticising "Capitalist academic authorities" and "pulling out Capitalist white flags".

In winter, summoned for collaborative scientific research by the Central Government. Led with Mr You Guo'en some teachers in the Teaching and Research Office of ancient literature, Department of Chinese Language and Literature and the students of Class 4, Grade 56 to conduct studies on Tao Yuanming. In August 1961 and January 1962 respectively, two books, *A Collection of Research Materials on Tao Yuanming* and *Collected Reviews of Tao Yuanming's Poems and Essays*, were compiled and published by Zhonghua Book Company.

1959–1961

Published scores of poems and articles such as "Song in Early Autumn". Among them, "Yanshan and Heishan in the 'Song of Mulan'" published in *Wen Wei Po* on 1 April 1961 made a breakthrough in an unsolved problem.

1962

In January, published *A Collection of Research Materials on Tao Yuanming* in Zhonghua Book Company.

In March, co-edited with Chen Yixin and Yuan Xingpei and published in Zhonghua Book Company the upper and lower volumes of *Literature References of the Wei, Jin, Southern and Northern Dynasties*, which were "selected and noted by the Teaching and Research Office of Chinese Literary History of Peking University".

1963–1965

Published five poems and articles, and edited the first and second books of the upper volume of *Selected Poems of all Dynasties in China*, which were published by the People's Literature Publishing House in January 1964.

1966–1972

Suffered in the "Cultural Revolution". Read *Journey to the West* at night.

1973

In April, published "An Analysis of the Battle of Red Cliff" in the *Journal of Peking University* (1973, No. 2). Later, it was included in *Talks on Journey to the West*.

1974–1982

Wrote nearly 20 poems and articles. In November 1979, co-edited and published the first and second books of the lower volume of *Selected Poems of all Dynasties in China* in the People's Literature Publishing House.

1983

In June, published in the People's Literature Publishing House *Commentaries and Notes on "Questions to Heaven"*, which consists of "Reading 'Questions to Heaven' Three Times" (preface), "Notes on 'Questions to Heaven'", "A Modern Language Version of 'Questions to Heaven'", and four articles related to the work.

Since this year, served as an editor of the *Encyclopaedia of China: Chinese Literature*, an honorary consultant of the *Chinese Education Dictionary*, and a consultant of the Chinese Society of Qu Yuan and the Association of Tang Literature of China.

1984

In June, published in Peking University Press *Asking for Directions*, which includes 109 new poems and 15 articles on new poems written from 1931 to 1981.

1985

In August, published in the People's Literature Publishing House *Lin Geng's Selected Poems*, which includes his 72 new poems from 1931 to 1981.

1986

Retired this year, but was still a doctoral supervisor in the Department of Chinese Language and Literature of Peking University.

1987

In April, published in the People's Literature Publishing House *A Comprehensive Study of Tang Poetry*. Prefaced with "Why Do I Particularly Love the Tang Poetry", it includes 21 articles such as "Chen Zi'ang and the Jian'an Spirit", "The High Tang Atmosphere", "Symbols at the Peak of the Tang Poetry", "Language of the Tang Poetry", "The Four Great Tang Poets", "The Poet Li Bai", "On the Artistic Reference of Classical Chinese Poetry" and "On 'Wooden leaves'"; and 19 articles on Tang poems such as "In the Wild There Died a Deer", "The Song of Yishui", "A Short Ballad", "In the Passes of Han under the Moon from Qin", and "On Meng Haoran's 'Passing by My Old Friend's Farmstead.'"

1988

In September, published a revised edition of *A Brief History of Chinese Literature* (Upper Volume) in Peking University Press.

1990

On 22 February, celebrated his 80th birthday. Wu Zuxiang wrote a scroll reading "Innocent as white snow, / As sunny spring as warm; / In sixty years, we know, / Your actions set the norm".

In August, published in the People's Literature Publishing House *Talks on Journey to the West*, which was noted by Shang Wei based on Lin Geng's oral instruction since 1987.

1991–1997

Published more than ten poems and articles. At the end of 1992, began to compile *A Brief History of Chinese Literature* (Lower Volume), which was published in Peking University Press in July 1995.

In August 1992, published *Tang Poems Recommended by Lin Geng* in Liaoning Children's Publishing House.

1998–1999

Published four articles, of which "From Free Verse to Nine-character Poetry" was published in *Literature, History and Philosophy* (1999, No. 3). It was later used as the preface of the book *Metrics of New Poems and the Poeticisation of Language*. This article reviewed the long history of new poetry creation over half a century from the 1930s to the 1990s, and summarised his creation practice and theoretical propositions on the forms of new poetry.

2000

In January, published the first edition of *The Poet Li Bai* in Shanghai Chinese Classics Publishing House.

In January, published in Peking University Press *Reverie in Space*, including 27 new poems unpublished before. Among them, 12 poems were interpreted with his proses.

In January, published in the Economic Daily Publishing House *Metrics of New Poems and the Poeticisation of Language*, which is one of the *Oriental Cultural Collections* edited by Ji Xianlin. This book includes the preface of *Asking for Directions* and 15 articles on poetry, three articles on new poems in *A Comprehensive Study of Tang Poetry*, "Nature of the Character '兮' in *Chuci*" in *A Study of Poet Qu Yuan and His Works*, and the articles on new poetry since 1995 including "Assumptions on New Poetry: Transplantation and Soil" and "From Free Verse to Nine-character Poetry" (preface), in addition to three interviews. They basically reflected Lin Geng's theoretical research on new poetry and his exploration of creating new poetry forms over the past 60 years.

In December, published "My Research on *Chuci*" in *Ways to Success in Chuci Studies: Reflections of International Chuci Experts* in Chongqing Publishing House. Based on the recordings and notes of Lin Geng's oral instruction, it was compiled by Dr Chang Sen from the Department of Chinese Language and Literature of Peking University, which was revised and finalised by Lin Geng.

2001

In October, published a seven-character regulated poem "On Li Bai" in *Knowledge of Literature and History*.

2002

On 4 April 2002, published a seven-character regulated poem "On Li Bai" in *People's Daily*.

In June, appointed as a consultant and the honorary president of the Chinese Society of Qu Yuan.

2003

Published an interview "The World is Searching for the Traces of Beauty" in *Literature and Art Research* (2003, No. 4).

2004

Appointed as the Director of the Poetry Centre of Peking University.

2005

In February, published nine volumes of *Lin Geng's Poetry and Articles* in Tsinghua University Press. Among them, Volume IX, *A Collection out of Collections* edited by Lin Geng himself, includes 90 individually published or unpublished poems, essays, articles, and interviews from 1931 to 2003. Lin Geng himself wrote the title of the book.

In November, published *A History of Chinese Literature* in Lujiang Publishing House.

2006

In September, invited by Peking University Press to publish *A Brief History of Chinese Literature* (with illustrations), which was finally published in August 2007.

On 4 October, bid farewell to life at the age of 97.

Index

An Shi Rebellion xv, 1, 15–16, 30, 33, 35, 43, 72–73, 75, 78, 86, 89, 99–101, 111–112
Ancient Style v, 19, 29, 35, 45, 52–54, 56, 58–59, 62, 65–66, 68–69, 72–73, 82–83, 100–101, 126–127
antithetical parallelism 95
art xii–xiii, xvi–xvii, xx, 77, 98, 101, 105–106, 108–109, 140–141

Bai Juyi xxix, 1, 28, 30–31, 33, 35–42, 66–67, 69, 74, 112, 126
bamboo xxi, 3, 66, 138
Bao Zhao 29
Book of Songs see Shijing
border 69, 70, 73, 117, 124, 140
bridge xiv, xxi, xxiii, 86, 108

Cao Pi xxiv
Cao Zhi 25
Cen Shen 50, 95
characteristic i, xiv, xxii, 18, 93, 97, 109, 127
chivalry 83–86
Chuci ix, xi, xx–ii, xxix, 3, 152
ci poem xxiii, xxvii, 38–42, 66, 141, 145
ci poetry 39–41
civic literature 33, 36–40, 42, 66
classical Chinese poetry i, vii, x, xviii, xix–xx, xxii–xxiii, xxvi, xxviii, 43, 95–96, 104, 144
commoner 14, 18–19, 46, 49–57, 60–62, 64–65, 68, 79–80, 83, 86–87, 91
Confucius xx, 26, 59–60, 80, 87, 97, 99

Dongfang Shuo 46
Du Fu xiv–xv, xxiv, xxix, 1, 2, 4, 23–33, 39, 43–44, 47, 49–50, 60, 65, 70, 77, 80, 85, 89, 99–103, 108, 111–112

Du Mu 66
Du Shenyan 102

Early Tang 23, 26, 50, 102, 116
East Sea 23, 91, 94, 128
exaggeration v, xvi, 5, 8, 21, 105–106, 130

five-character ancient poems xxvi, 29–31, 103
flute xxiii, 5, 10, 118–120
folk literature 38, 61
form iv, xv, xix–xxii, xxv–vi, 3, 18, 29, 36, 47, 49–50, 59, 62, 64, 93, 95, 97, 102–103, 114, 136
four-character xx–xxi, xxvi, 96
frontier fortress poetry v, xxiv–xxv, xxix, 113–117, 124, 135
fu xxvii, 18, 46, 72, 102

Gao Shi 25, 85, 95, 113, 115–116
Geshu Han 18, 72, 100–101
grass xxiii, 6, 12, 28, 55, 67, 74, 77, 87, 90, 93, 96, 112, 115, 120, 128–129, 140, 142–143
Guo Pu 29

half-pause law xxi–xxii, 147
Han and Wei Spirit 29
Han Yu 31, 35–36, 38
Hanlin 16–17, 37, 49, 60–61, 79, 81, 83–84, 87
Hengjiang vii–viii, xvi, 23
hermit 1, 12, 17, 77, 83–84, 88, 139
High Tang i, xiii–xviii, xxvi, xxviii–xxix, 1–5, 8–9, 11–15, 17–18, 20, 22–27, 29, 31–33, 35, 42, 44, 50, 58, 60, 67, 70, 73, 87, 89, 91, 93, 95, 100, 102–104, 107, 116, 135, 140, 144, 151

Index

High Tang Atmosphere xiii–xiv, xvi–xviii, xxviii–xxix, 23, 151
Hong Mai 92
Hou Ying 84
Huang Tingjian xxiv

image xvi, xxiii–xxv, 20, 26, 30, 32, 89, 97, 104, 119, 132–133, 138

Ji Chong 37
Jia Yi 99
Jiang Kui xvii
Jiangling 38, 40, 90
Jiangxia 61, 75, 78, 91, 101
Jiaoran xvii
Jinling 76, 78, 84, 88, 93–94, 97–98
Jinshi 51, 67, 107

Kaiyuan 4, 44, 48, 63, 69–71, 79–80, 103
Kong Chaofu 27, 86, 103, 112
Kongzi xx

landscape poetry xxiv–xxv, xxix, 13–14
language i, vii, x–xii, xiv, xvi, xviii–xxix, 13, 27, 33, 38–39, 41–42, 48, 65, 93–94, 96–98, 104, 108–109, 130, 133, 138–139, 143–144
Laozi 58–59
Late Tang xiv, 26, 42, 61, 66–67, 81, 112, 117
level xi, xvi, xvii, xxvii, 27
Li Bai v, vii, xiv, xv–xvi, xxix, 1–4, 6, 8, 10, 14–20, 22–27, 29–33, 35, 43–106, 110, 112, 119–120, 130, 144, 148–149, 151–152
Li Bi 16–17
Li He 40
Li Jinfa xxv
Li Panlong 92
Li Qi 4, 22, 70, 95
Li Sao 3–4, 30
Li Shangyin 26, 29, 40, 143
Liangzhou v, 22, 47, 70, 116–125
Lin Geng i–iv, vi, ix–xxx, 122, 145, 151–153
Liu Changqing 118–120
Liu Quanbai 61, 81
Liu Yu 34, 38–41, 50
Liu Yuxi 34, 38–41, 50
Longxi xv, 5, 121, 123–124
Lu Sidao 97
Lu Zhonglian 15–16, 62–63, 76, 78, 84, 87
Luoyang xvi, 75, 99–100, 111, 119

Ma Zhiyuan 138–139
May Fourth New Culture Movement x
Meng Haoran vi–vii, xvi, 2, 31, 136–139, 151
metrical pattern xxix
Mid-Tang xiv, xxvii, 31, 42, 61, 88, 112, 126
Minor Court Hymn xxiii, 120
modern poetry xxiii
moon xxiv, 2, 5, 9–10, 15, 18, 20–21, 26–27, 40, 43, 48, 54, 62, 68, 70, 74, 86, 91–95, 97–98, 111, 116, 126, 128, 132–137, 140, 143

Nine Arguments xxiv
Nine Songs xxi, xxiii–xxiv, 3–4
Nineteen Ancient Poems 120

Ode to the Orange xxi
Old Du 32
Ouyang Xiu 41

palace poetry 39
parallel prose xxvii, 41
patriotism 65–66, 68, 77
peak xiii–xiv, xvi, xviii, xx–xxii, xxvii–xxviii, 2, 8, 11, 13, 15, 17–18, 23, 26, 28, 32–33, 39, 43–46, 89, 95–96, 99, 103, 108–109, 127, 133, 135, 138, 144
Pei Jing 86
pipa 2, 33, 38, 42, 47
poeticisation xix–xxix, 27
Prince Yong 16–17, 76–78, 87, 89
profundity xvii, xxv–xxvii, 9, 25, 28, 31, 33, 39, 93, 108
prosification xix

Qiang flute 22, 118–119, 121–122
Qin Guan 39
qin zither 132
Qinghai 18, 70–72, 100, 116–117, 121
Qiu Zhao'ao 101
Qu Yuan ix, xi, xxiii–xxiv, 25, 30, 54, 57–58, 63–66, 82, 93, 148, 150, 152
quatrain 13, 29, 67, 118, 134, 136, 140

rain vii, xvi, xvii, xxiii, 3, 9, 11–12, 41, 60, 68, 73, 99–100, 111, 120, 129
realism v, 30, 106, 126–127
regulated poem xxvi–xxvii, 4, 26, 29, 31, 95, 102–103, 112, 136, 140, 152
River South 38, 41, 128
romanticism v, xiii, xviii, 46, 67, 106, 126–127

Index

roving immortal poetry 57–58
Ruan Ji 29, 59

semi-regulated poem 29
seven-character ancient poems xxvi–xxvii, 26–27, 29, 95–96, 102–103
seven-character quatrains xxvii, 95–96, 136
Shandong 19, 71, 77, 103
Shen Quanqi 116
Shijing xx–xxi
Sima Qian 49
simplicity xvii–xviii, xxv–xxvii, 9, 25, 31, 33, 39–40, 93, 108, 143
Song Jing 69
Song Yu ix, xxiv, 25
Sunny Pass 7, 140–141
sunset 11, 27, 67, 90, 112–113, 115–116, 121, 130, 142–143
swordsman 5, 17, 61, 83–88
symbol xx, xxii, xxv, 67

Taizong 1, 69
Tang Book 16–17, 51, 60, 71, 73, 85, 123
Tang poetry i, v, vii–ix, xi, xiii–xiv, xvii, xx, xxiii, xxv–xxix, 1, 3–4, 14, 23, 26, 31–32, 39–40, 42, 45–46, 96, 102, 107–112, 135, 143–144, 147, 149
Tao Yuanming 26, 29, 57, 95, 138, 142, 149
tavern 85, 93
Tianbao 4, 16, 48, 60, 65, 69–73, 78, 99–101

Wang Bao 122
Wang Can 90
Wang Changling v, xvi, xxiv, 4, 94–95, 116, 119, 134–135
Wang Ji 38
Wang Jian 38
Wang Wei vi, xiv–xv, xxix, 1–4, 7–14, 18, 22, 32, 47, 49, 95, 110, 119–120, 124, 136–137, 140–143
Wang Zhihuan v, 22, 106, 118–124
water xv, 3, 9, 11–12, 15–18, 21, 27, 40–41, 46, 48, 55, 59, 67–68, 72–73, 86, 88, 90, 93–94, 97, 110–112, 118, 130, 135, 139, 143
Wei Wan 60, 79, 81, 83, 87–88

Wei Yingwu 38, 134
Weicheng vi, 6–7, 9, 120, 140–141
Wen Tingyun 40
West Capital 45, 83, 90, 94
White Emperor 26, 40, 90
white hair xvi, 88, 106
white sun 5, 53, 106
willow xxiii, 119–120
wind vii, xiii, xvi, xxiii–xxiv, 3–4, 6, 8, 10–11, 14, 17–18, 21–23, 25, 40–41, 45, 53, 60, 70, 72, 77, 80, 83, 91, 93–94, 96–99, 110–112, 116, 119–121, 128, 130–133, 136, 143
wine 3, 5, 7–8, 15, 20–22, 25, 39–40, 46–48, 54, 57–58, 67–68, 77, 82, 84, 86, 91, 93–95, 97–99, 137, 140–141
Wu Zetian 35

Xianyang 5, 21, 32, 45, 47, 74–75, 94, 141
Xie Lingyun 87, 128
Xie Tiao v, 15, 25, 43, 46, 93, 97, 130–131
Xuanzong 16–17, 35, 52, 57, 63, 65–66, 69, 71–72, 75–76, 79–80
Xue Daoheng 115

Yan Yu xvii–xviii, 31
Yangtze River xxvii, 23, 90
Yanshan 75, 113–117, 149
Yao Chong 69
Yelang 17, 63, 78, 86, 94, 101
Yellow Crane Tower 140
Yellow River 17, 22–23, 44, 73, 76, 82, 90–91, 94, 106, 111, 117–119, 121–125
Yin Fan xvii, 48
Youth Spirit i, xii, xv, xxix, 5, 147
Youzhou 14, 47, 71
Yu Xin v, 24, 29, 39, 114, 132–133
Yuan Jie 31
Yuan Zhen 35–39, 47, 66–67
Yuanhe 35, 37–39, 66–67
yuefu 30–31, 96
Yumen 22–23, 70, 75, 98, 116, 118–122

Zhang Hu 37
Zhang Jiuling 29
Zhang Zhihe 38
Zhaojun v, 132–133
Zhenguan 50, 123
Zhongnan 3, 8, 12, 20, 50–51, 57